Back on Track

For the people and dogs on my journey who have taught me, given me opportunities and stuck it out through the tough times.

To James & Maeve. Thanks for sharing your dad with so many other kids. You probably won't learn much here that you didn't already know!

A NOTE FROM BERNIE

When I was first approached about writing this book, I had to think about it for a bit. How could anyone capture the real essence, the real heart, of what we do at BackTrack – how it is a team effort and how dedicated the staff, local community and supporters are to help the young people who come to us for assistance. I decided to go ahead with the book with the wish that it will provide hope and inspire others.

Kids from all walks of life, from the North Shore of Sydney to the remote western deserts, are toughing it out. I was lucky growing up. I had a family that loved, cared and supported me. Sadly, the reality is that many young people are not so fortunate. I hope this story can show that no matter what, and no matter how tough we've had it, we can all make a difference in our community and in the lives of others.

Like many success stories, ours had a humble start. A burning idea, an empty shed and seven busted kids who we believed wanted a better life. We turned to the local community and its leaders for help and they responded generously, and still do to this day. We are forever grateful for all the help and support we have received, particularly by those who saw our potential in the early days and have stood by us ever since.

BackTrack was a hard grind at first but we stuck to our core ideas that we will give these young people as long as they need and keep putting opportunities in front of them. They are all different, they have all had tough times, and each takes as long as they need to turn their life around. It's not easy, and requires incredible patience, skill and dedication from all staff – the backbone of the organisation – to help these wild kids through.

We've been around at BackTrack long enough now to know what works, and we've seen it time and time again, not only here in Armidale but also in other communities who are now taking up the challenge to provide similar programs. Our hope is that the BackTrack approach can take seed in many more communities. BackTrack will always be ready to assist in any way we can.

Bernie Shakeshaft, 2019

AUTHOR'S NOTE

This book is the story of Bernie Shakeshaft and the organisation he founded: BackTrack. Both are extraordinary.

The major interviews for *Back on Track* occurred at Bernie's home and in his office. However, such is his affable nature, Bernie rarely gave the impression he was being interviewed. Instead, it seemed he and I were just having a very long chat, the type mates might have at the pub when they haven't caught up for a while. As a result, I hope this comes across in *Back on Track* where at times readers may not only feel they are being told stories, but are part of an ongoing conversation. It must be said that Bernie can slap expletives into his language at a cyclonic rate, and regularly drops consonants off the ends of words. Occasionally I have put some of these in verbatim; for the rest of the time the reader need only use a little imagination. Also, Bernie uses a specific term to describe Indigenous Australian people in the Northern Territory: he calls them 'countrymen'. It is a word he uses with the utmost respect, and, as you will read, the influence of countrymen on his life has been profound.

There are many secondary interviews in this book. Nearly one hundred in fact. Bernie's parents and siblings; his partner; his children and his friends; BackTrack staff, both current and former staff; BackTrack boys, girls and their families; teachers; youth workers; police officers; businesspeople; a horse-breaker; graziers; drovers; an advertising executive; a Test-cricket legend; a school principal; a psychologist; an Aboriginal elder; a dog handler; a dingo tracker; a politician; a filmmaker; a council employee; a former Governor of New South Wales (now the Governor-General of Australia) and his wife; and a former ward of the state (one of the first people Bernie helped in an official capacity). Most of these interviews were conducted face to face at locations across New South Wales and Victoria. The remainder were held over the phone and one by email. Due to the sensitive nature of some material, and the age of some interviewees, some names have been changed or not used at all. Also, some place names aren't included, and at other times, descriptions of people and places have been kept to a minimum.

Also, a quick word about style. Each chapter begins with a small scene setter about day-to-day happenings at BackTrack. Some themes in these pieces then carry through, in both big and small ways, to the body of the chapters. I have done this to provide greater insight into an organisation that is so rich with stories that it is impossible to tell them all within the pages of this book.

There are people who might read *Back on Track* and think: 'Why doesn't Bernie stop those kids from smoking?' or 'Why do the kids swear so much?' In a perfect world, maybe we wouldn't have to ask those questions. But, this isn't a perfect world, is it?

Working with high-risk kids is a game of inches. We are talking about kids who've suffered unbelievable trauma in their lives: domestic abuse, sexual abuse, alcoholism, drugs, crime, broken homes … the list goes on.

As a result, there are many more incredibly complex issues at play. At BackTrack they make choices every day about what battles they choose to fight. Do they work on stopping a kid from smoking? Or should they be more worried about where that kid will sleep that night? And if he doesn't sleep in the right spot, what are the chances he might hit the ice until he lands back in the Accident and Emergency Department? In the work at BackTrack it is rarely ever a case of simply saying: 'Please stop doing that, there's a good boy.' Sadly, *tragically*, with the kids at BackTrack (and others like them), changes in behaviour and attitudes can take years. One step forward, twenty back. All right, let's go again the next day. Two steps forward, ten back. That's an improvement. A game of inches.

Some readers might be offended by some of the things they read in this book, but as Bernie says, these things are happening in the not-so-perfect world. Not only that, but they might be happening on your street, or just around the corner from you. The issues you'll read about are very, very authentic. There's no sanding off the edges. These things are happening in our society, and you can't un-happen what's happening.

Bernie and I thank you for coming into his not-so-perfect world.

Finally, I have to say that the personal journey while working on *Back on Track* has been revealing. I feel so very privileged to have been allowed into so many lives. Everyone willingly shared stories with me, even when some of those stories exposed individual vulnerabilities and raw emotions. My eyes, mind and heart were opened more than I ever could have imagined. Thank you to everyone involved. BackTrack is an amazing organisation. It takes my breath away.

James Knight, 2019

PART ONE

When I was twenty, I was bulletproof and I knew
everything. When I got to forty, I was thinking:
'Oh, there are a couple of things I've still got to
work out.' When I got to sixty, I went: 'Shit, I need
to learn a lot. I know nothing at all.'

Paul Roots, cattleman and former drover

1

Armidale, 2018. The home town of BackTrack.

The nor'wester blows across the hills. It scuffs up dust, bends yellowing grasses and sends a shiver through the lustreless leaves of the eucalypts. A few clouds hurry by; earlier in the morning some had teased the earth but the rain that fell wasn't enough to wet a pebble. It's the middle of a long winter. It has been a much longer drought.

A dark grey Holden Colorado dual-cab heads out of town. Its driver wears a black puffer jacket, a blue woollen jumper, blue shirt, blue thermal vest and dusty, grease-stained blue jeans. His eyes are also blue. So is his language.

'I'll fuckin' sort it out later,' he says to someone over his phone's loudspeaker. His delivery is direct but not brusque. He holds a steaming cup of coffee that has failed to wash away the nicotine gravel in his voice.

Even when sitting he appears lanky: skinny legs, long arms, bony fingers. His skin is scarred and blotchy, and his reddened face is framed by wrinkles across his forehead and a grey-speckled gingery beard on his chin.

He drives further out of town, occasionally easing his work boot off the accelerator to look at a shed, a business, a paddock, a fence. He knows them all. Finally, he heads over a crest on the bitumen and finds what he has been looking for. A small mob of pregnant Angus cows, as black as the morning, are dawdling along the side of the road. Behind them, a teenage boy sits on an idling motorbike. When the boy notices the Colorado pull over, he stop-starts on the throttle until he reaches the vehicle. The driver winds down a window.

'Good to see you got the warnin' signs out, well done.'

The boy nods. His eyebrows are stitched together by the squeeze of a balaclava and tight helmet. Pimples and freckles dot his face. A drop of snot hangs off the tip of his nose.

A short exchange follows:

'Where you pokin' em to?'

'That gully over there.'

'Much traffic?'

'No.'

'You keepin' an eye out in case one of 'em starts droppin' a calf?'

'Yeah.'

The boy's answers can barely be heard above the wind.

'All right, just one more thing,' says the driver. 'What would happen if that helmet fell off?'

'Um, I um, I could hurt my head.'

'Well, then, it might be an idea to tie up the fuckin' chin strap.'

The boy, with his fingers stiffened by the cold, does as he should.

'That's the way,' says the driver. 'Stay safe, all right?'

The Colorado moves off, and for a moment the driver watches the boy in his rear-vision mirror.

Then he does what life has taught him to do. He looks ahead. As Bernie Shakeshaft always has.

Bernie Shakeshaft lives on a sixty-acre 'piece of dirt' near Armidale, in the northern tablelands of New South Wales. The house he shares with his partner, Francesca, is about eighty years old, a weatherboard homestead with a wooden-floored verandah flanked by gauze-covered windows that overlook a garden. An old cart tips its nose into the weeds, and further away is a yard holding a few horses, each with a story. The bits and pieces on the verandah could be sifted through time to many bush homes across Australia: black-and-white wall photos of cattle being sold, an esky, whips and reins, a rusting rabbit trap, a pair of elastic-sided boots left near the outside door, a sideboard holding a magazine whose front cover shows a smiling red kelpie … all and more are statements of life and work under big skies.

If, above all, there are objects on the verandah that define Bernie's life, they are found on a row of hooks: jackets of various makes and sizes, creased and marked by use and abuse but now just hanging around with shoulders slumped, waiting to be filled with purpose. Over the years Bernie has seen too many youngsters whose lives are like the jackets. He knows them well because he too has spent time on the hook.

'I've had my moments,' says Bernie, smiling slightly as he settles into a black cane chair at the end of the verandah. He's wearing a few layers of clothes, all blue, to ward off the morning chill. Shirt, jumpers, jeans and socks. No boots. We've just begun the first interview for this book, and Bernie appears very comfortable.

'Right, where do we start?' he asks.

'At the beginning. And we'll see where that leads us.'

—

Bernie was born in Sydney in 1967. His father, Joe, and mother, Denise, were Catholics. Joe worked for the NSW Child Welfare Department, a government organisation (a predecessor to the current Department of Family and Community Services) whose main duty was the provision and supervision of foster-care services. Denise was a teacher, although she surrendered her job to domestic life after she gave birth to her first child, Maree. Then came Bernie and Anthony. Three children in as many years. It was an abrupt awakening for Denise, who was in her early twenties. Nowadays, she lives with Joe in a small, neat timber home in Sydney's north-western suburbs. They were well prepared when I went to speak with them. There were photo albums and pictures on the kitchen bench, and on the kitchen table sat plates of chocolate biscuits and fruit, waiting to accompany a fresh pot of tea.

'Looking back, I didn't know how to be a mother,' Denise said, while picking a crumb off her pink jumper. 'When Bernie was a baby, I wasn't able to breastfeed. One time when he was very upset, I didn't know how I was going to settle him down. I went to the doctor and he looked at me and said: "Go buy a tin of Carnation milk, take him home and give him a feed. That's all that's wrong with him."'

As was the way of the time, Joe had a less hands-on parenting role. He was the worker, the provider; he reflected his generation – this is what a father did. From orchardist stock near the Hawkesbury River just north of Sydney, he had hoped to become a priest, but after spending five years in a seminary he turned to the public service. Beginning as a clerk with the Child Welfare Department he worked in various offices across Sydney, where he became familiar with the 'Fridge Test', a popular criterion used by senior staff when evaluating the ability of junior employees to identify problems in family homes. Joe learnt it was sound practice to always check the fridge – an empty one was commonly a sign of hardship.

With the need to put food on the Shakeshaft table, Joe accepted a transfer to Orange in central-west New South Wales after he agreed to do a minimum of three years' country service. It was a difficult move for Denise. Although born in the NSW bush town Warialda, she had spent nearly all her life in Sydney, where her father had been the head mechanic at Liverpool Ambulance Station. Her mother died when she was young, and Denise became both a sibling and a surrogate mum to her younger sister. She was also close to her two brothers. So, while a relocation to Orange may well have promised new opportunities for a young family, it also shut some doors to an older one. However, trepidation faded over time and Denise discovered that Orange provided 'too good a life for us to go back to Sydney'.

The Shakeshafts stayed for five years, until Joe was promoted to the head role at the Child Welfare Office in Armidale. The town, population 18 000, was about seven hours' drive north-north-west of Sydney, and only two-or-so hours from the coast. It was the commercial and administrative hub of the New England region, home to the Anaiwan Aboriginal people. It had four distinct seasons, was renowned for wool growing and education – there were three boarding schools, a university and a College of Advanced Education (formerly a teachers' college) – and was a popular tourist location close to spectacular gorges. It was also the preserver of the legend of Captain Thunderbolt, the area's most notorious bushranger of the mid-nineteenth century. But all this meant nothing to Bernie. He was too young and spirited to regard his new home town as anything but a playground, and as he tore through his childhood, his enthusiasm for physical adventures grew. 'Bernie was always fleet of foot, fast to jump fences,' said Maree, speaking to me over the phone. 'We were always chasing each other round. Bernie and Anthony fought a lot, too. They were very competitive with each other.'

By the time Bernie was in early primary school, he had two more brothers, Paul, born in 1972, and Mark, 1975. To Denise, it seemed that she had 'two families of children', the former of whom were well on their way to developing their own distinct traits: Maree was the sensible older sister; Anthony was quiet, organised and studious like his father; and Bernie was the 'one with the most get-up-and-go'. Significantly, he could also talk himself out of any situation. This didn't mean he was a troublemaker, but he could be mischievous, and his penchant for launching into action without thinking of the consequences ensured he was never going to walk a straight-and-narrow childhood. After the family rented a house for a short while, they bought a place in a residential area in north Armidale that was just starting to develop. The lure of nearby paddocks and bush was irresistible for Bernie in an era when many parents were comfortable to impose no greater play rule on their children than: 'Just make sure you're home before dark.'

And the dark was something that Bernie kept his parents in. All these years later, Denise admitted: 'I hate to think what the kids did. There were probably lots of things that we never heard about.'

'We had a cracking old time,' recalls Bernie. 'I kicked round with two, three or four mates, just small crews. Some of it was harmless stuff; you know, go for a bit of a look in a farmer's hay shed. But, crikeys we did some stupid things around town, too.

Some of us would hide in busted old cars in gullies, and the others would roll down big rocks until someone got whacked, and then we'd change teams. We also used to crawl like rats up stormwater drains, for hours. Geez, if I saw someone do that today I'd be letting them know what could go wrong. And when we got a bit older, sorta late primary, we made bombs out of shotgun shells; you know, pipe bombs and that sorta shit. Anything that would go bang. How we've still got all our fingers is beyond me. But I wasn't always that lucky. As more houses were built in our area, we worked out the half-finished places were full of great cubby holes. Of course, you had to pick your mark when the builders weren't there – in other words, weekends. One day I was with this kid who was a bit craftier than me and he was saying: "Walk here, don't walk on that beam," kinda stuff, then all of a sudden he yells out: "Quick the builders are coming!" and I ran over a spot for a chimney, straight through some gyprock and *crash*! Two storeys down, a busted ankle, but we still got out before the builders came.'

Bernie spent much of his childhood nursing various injuries. At Freeman Crescent, where the Shakeshafts lived in a double-storey, double-garage red-brick home, there was a sharp downhill left turn on the bitumen road, perfect for getting the pulse racing in a blue billycart that Joe bought for the kids. With ropes for steering, and cement wheels at the back, it wasn't a well-designed contraption, but, 'Shit it was quick!' Amid spits of gravel and sparks, skin was ripped off, feet were smashed, knees were banged, but heads somehow managed to stay intact. On wet days, when water rushed down the road that was yet to have drains, the billycart was left in the garage, and out came large plastic box-like containers (which had been 'secured' by Bernie and others). Normally they were used for home deliveries, but never mind meat and vegetables, these containers were big enough for 'a lad to sit in', and strong enough to handle the toughest rapids in the neighbourhood.

Yells of fear and delight on the bitumen were matched by the stereotypical summer shouts from backyards. Bernie, wearing thongs, Stubbies shorts, and an Adidas T-shirt with three stripes across the shoulders and running down the sleeves, held the same dreams as many boys of his time: he wanted to play cricket for Australia and be the next Dennis Lillee to terrorise the poms, or Greg Chappell flicking a ball through mid-wicket on his way to another century. Long, hot afternoons with Anthony and all the neighbourhood kids who could be mustered were pierced with *'Howzat!'* on the front lawn or driveway of the Shakeshaft home.

Sport was important to Bernie. Whether he was playing cricket, soccer, rugby league or competing with Maree and Anthony to climb to daring heights and hang upside down by their legs on playground equipment, Bernie never held back. However, his zest was noticeably absent from another integral part of his childhood. 'He wasn't one to sit down and read a book or do a jigsaw puzzle,' said Denise. And that meant that formal education, particularly in the constraints of the classroom, did not dovetail with a boy who was at his happiest when he could walk out the door, scale a few fences and feel free.

Bernie attended St Mary's Catholic Primary School, which was on the same block as the Saints Mary and Joseph Cathedral. Dominated by its spire that towered above Armidale's business district, this dark-bricked bastion of traditional faith was to become a symbol of confusion for Bernie. Among his earliest problem-makers was a nun described by one former pupil as 'having arms like hams'. When children lined up for one thing or another, misbehaviour was frequently dealt with by a smack or tap that could send youngsters 'falling like skittles'. Another ex-student still remembers 'the sting of that nun's hand on my back'. It was inevitable that Bernie's free spirit would collide with conformity, but the most painful moment still came unexpectedly: 'I was drinking at a bubbler at the wrong time, and then I got whacked by that nun. My head snapped forward, and my mouth banged the bloody bubbler hard.

Like many others, Bernie experienced the rap of a ruler everytime he touched something with his left hand while in school. 'I was growing up in a right-handed world. I think that probably messed my head up with maths and spelling and things. Throughout my schooling nuns, brothers and lay teachers either loved or hated me. There wasn't much inbetween. I always felt like I was down the bottom of the class. I learnt the art of being seen as naughty rather than stupid, which helps me make sense of things in my work at BackTrack today.'

In hindsight, Denise believes Bernie had some degree of dyslexia, a condition that only began to gain widespread medical acceptance in the 1970s a decade after the term 'learning disability' was first used. Bernie told his mother that words used to bounce on the page. Slower to read than his classmates, he needed to place a ruler under lines to guide him, but this didn't help him to eradicate such problems as mistaking b's for d's. Nowadays he is a much more competent reader, and his writing is legible, although his style is awkward as he curls his right hand at such an angle around the pen that his fingernails are hidden – the left-handers grip transferred to the right hand.

From very early on in his education Bernie thought: 'This is not a good place for me, this school thing.' His fondest recollections are of playing the fool and pushing the limits by breaking rules, such as mucking around with his mates in out-of-bounds areas, including underneath the nuns' convent where hide-and-seek was a favourite pastime. 'This one teacher used to get angry and come in looking for us with a torch, but there was no way we were coming out, and we knew he was too big to come in all the way and get us. One day he locked us in, you know there was a big padlock on the hatch, but that was all right coz locks are only for keeping out the honest, aren't they?'

The ends of Bernie's mouth curl ever so slightly upwards when he tells that story. Sitting in his verandah chair, he appears content to be unveiling his past. At times during the interview he pauses and utters a crackling 'uuuuum' or 'aaaargh', and at other moments he squints into the distance to check on the horses, or yells, 'Be quiet Gibson!' to a barking dog, one of half a dozen or so tied up out of sight on the other side of the house. Meanwhile his two 'senior citizens', Girl and Lou, black-and-white collie sisters who are partially blind, curl back to back in a patch of morning sun in the garden. As the interview continues, Bernie's words are periodically threaded with blue wisps, statements of an addiction that too was founded in his childhood.

'I probably got into smoking because someone along the way would've told me: "You can't do that." And that was enough for me to say: "Wanna bet?" The old Nelsons; they'd sell them to you in the shops even if you were in primary school. I don't know how many people I taught to smoke, especially down in the gullies where the cars were. I even taught Anthony, but then he dobbed me in. Mum and Dad tried to stop me – a few good belts with the wooden spoon, and grounding me – but that wasn't gonna happen, was it? I think I started to get that "little black sheep" thing going on.'

Anthony, now a university professor, remembers a big brother who 'wasn't out of control, but he was always on the larrikin continuum'. 'He was obviously very adventurous,' said Anthony in a phone interview. 'He'd duck off and do naughty things that I wouldn't have done. He was quick to work things out too. He worked out Santa Claus didn't exist and told me about it!'

To Denise, Bernie was 'lively and different' but he wasn't a black sheep, and nor was he the subject of any complaints from the community or the school. Indeed, Bernie's Year Six report showed no cause for concern:

'Bernard is a friendly and co-operative student. He is well accepted by his peers and has established a good rapport with the teachers. Bernard willingly applies himself to the set task and his improvement academically and socially this year is pleasing. Bernard participates actively in a wide range of school activities including sport, drama, music, singing, art and craft.'

But such a summary was perhaps rendering over small but spreading cracks that no-one other than Bernie really felt. In the eyes of Joe and Denise, 'Bernie was just Bernie', but for the boy himself there was some form of a rebel rumbling close to the surface. Some indications were innocuous. In Year Six he set up the 'Black Mitten Gang' a small group of friends who each wore one mitten on a hand. There were no crazy rituals or reckless dares, but there was a sense of belonging. One member, Justin Flint ('Flinty'), who has been close to Bernie since they met in Kindergarten, recalled the gang as a combination of brawn and brain. 'Bernie was definitely the brains, he was the stability in the group. It was only really a school thing, mostly roaming around in the playground. But you know, we could have thought of something better. Wearing gloves without fingers in an Armidale winter wasn't much chop.'

While frost at the fingertips left no lingering damage, fire at the fingertips was a more troubling by-product of Bernie's developing character. A young bloke who puffed durries when away from adults was also likely to take other risks, especially when he had accomplices in his pockets.

'I was always muckin' round with matches,' says Bernie. 'One afternoon this grass fire got away from us on the edge of town. It wasn't deliberate, but a few fences were burnt down, and the police were called. I wasn't in the hot seat for that one; someone definitely got into trouble, though. We'd actually started out trapping birds – we were always making traps and catching things – but I don't know, the matches came out and next thing you know: "Shit, we've got a problem here!"'

It was not the type of behaviour expected from an altar boy. But … Bernie *was* an altar boy. Having to wear 'white dress things with different coloured belts for new and old players', he and Anthony and some of their mates, including Flinty, participated in weekday and Sunday mass. Sometimes he would leave home before sunrise and hurtle his pushbike down a few steep roads, through the fog, before reaching parkland near Dumaresq Creek from where he could see the Cathedral's spire. Then, it was head down, puff hard uphill for a few minutes to complete the three-kilometre trip. Bernie didn't enjoy being an altar boy, but although he rebelled in other aspects of his life, he wasn't yet ready to completely oppose his parents' religious wishes. 'At least it gave me the chance to swig on the wine,' he jokes. The ultimate delight came at the end of Sunday services when Joe and Denise often bought their children small treats, including Scanlens rugby league footy cards; the memory of opening a pack to be hit with the sweet scent from a stick of pink bubble gum will surely never be forgotten.

Despite adhering to his family's religious conventions, Bernie began questioning 'the whole Catholic thing' when he was in late primary school. His incident at the bubbler, together with other hard knocks – 'You know, bashed on the knuckles by some of the nuns and being told how dumb you are' – did nothing to endear him to the church. As he grew older, his resistance grew too, but never in a way that led to heated dinner-table debates with his parents. Indeed, his statements against Catholicism were wrapped in a naughtiness that befitted the skits of the popular Irish comedian of the time, Dave Allen.

'Yeah, I was very confused by it all. Who was God? I don't know. Prayers before dinner, Rosary on Friday night, don't blaspheme ... bugger that. I think I only ever heard my dad swear once, and that was when he hit his head on something and said, "Shit!". I nearly died.'

Catholicism may have prompted ridicule, but it also worked on Bernie at a deeper level, one that indisputably shaped his attitudes and the type of person he is today. Soon after they were married in 1965, Joe and Denise began taking home and caring for a young boy from St Michael's Children's Home in Sydney's Baulkham Hills. At first it was for a day or two at weekends, and then for the Christmas holidays. They were too busy to do it in Orange, but once they'd settled well into Armidale, they resumed 'doing what we felt we should do'.

The Shakeshaft children became well used to trips to the south side of town in the family's beige Ford Falcon XB station wagon. Up and up they seemed to go, passing a few houses and many vacant blocks, until they turned a corner from O'Connor Road and looked ahead. There it was at the top of the hill. Dark and daunting. Through a child's eyes it was an enormous building: two storeys high with arched windows, a steep roof, verandahs, crosses reaching for the heavens, and a white statue of a bearded man holding a staff and standing high in a curved shelter. St Patrick's Orphanage, run by the Sisters of Mercy, had been operating on the site since 1919. As Joe drove closer, the crunch of gravel underneath the tyres announced entry to a curving driveway. Sometimes there were children playing, reading, sitting and chatting in the expansive gardens. Joe would park near the building and leave his kids in the car as he went inside, then minutes later he would return with one or two other children, often Aboriginal Australians. Colour differences meant nothing to Bernie and his siblings; seeing Aboriginal children in the playgrounds, classrooms and around town was part of everyday life. But Bernie had already learnt that some came from desperately poor families; one tell-tale sign was when they wore to school the only shoes they owned: footy boots.

Armidale, as with every country settlement across Australia, had its own distinct relationship with Indigenous people. It was only in the 1950s and early 60s that about one hundred dispossessed Aboriginal Australians lived next to the municipal garbage dump. They built shelters from corrugated iron, cardboard, hessian – whatever was sturdy enough to provide protection. There was minimal water, no sewerage, no electricity. Some town locals knew it as The Dump, others referred to it as Dark Town, a description open to varied interpretations.

To Joe and Denise, the only difference that mattered was one of circumstances. The need to help the hapless was in their souls. So, they took the orphanage children and gave them what they could: fish and chips, balls to kick and catch, Lego, soft beds, *The Flintstones*, and for one boy a camping trip to the Warrumbungles

National Park 320 kilometres away. It didn't matter that Joe and Denise rarely had money to spare, because personal richness could never be measured in dollars. 'It was just us. We had to help,' said Denise. 'Without us actually telling them much, our kids picked up on what we did,' continued Joe. 'There was never any judgement.'

Nevertheless, the cogs had begun turning in Bernie's mind.

'I can remember going and picking up those kids and thinking: "There's something not right about this system." The poor little bastards, you could see their relief when they came out with us. But a lot of them didn't smile much, either. I didn't form any great friendships with them, but I knew they had to be looked after. And I did look after them, especially at school. I was pretty tidy with the knuckles. With a name like Shakeshaft you learnt to have a smart mouth or fight like someone possessed. I was always in dust-ups, not all because of protecting others, but that was one of the things that got me fired up.'

That behaviour didn't surprise Denise and Joe. While their eldest son may have had a rough-and-tumble persona, they had witnessed enough incidents to know he had an ability, rare for someone so young, to recognise injustices. And then, he acted on them. Bernie may not have been able to correctly spell such words as 'empathy' or 'sensitivity' – and nor would they have been on high rotation in his vocabulary – but he modelled them in a manner that left no doubt of their importance to him. Denise remembered: 'In Bernard's very first year of school, there was a little boy in his class who had cerebral palsy, and Bernard stood up for him. Any kid who pushed this boy or did anything unkind to him, Bern was there: "Don't touch him!" I remember very clearly we had a birthday party for Bernard when he turned six, and he was so protective of him that day. From those initial years, we could see he had something inside that drew him to help others.'

In an efficient and blunt assessment of behaviour, the type for which Bernie is now renowned, Joe said: 'Bernie knew when to put his foot down and say: "I don't want bullshit, this is what we're going to do."'

But there would be one critical exception to this modus operandi. As Bernie approached his adolescence, little did he or his parents know that he was entering a period of destructive paradox. It may have been in his nature to help others, but would he know how to help himself?

2

The sunrise sets the clouds alight. Golden pink, glowing at the edges. Blue smoke loiters low above the streets; with the smell of burnt wood, it's a reminder that at this time of year Armidale spends the evenings stoking and billowing and wakes in the morning to ashes in the fireplace.

Early light spills over the racecourse and stretches along the fences of the straight before it reaches the iron tips of a rotating walker in which two horses, wearing rugs, step with indifference. Elsewhere the light travels across MacDonald Park where leafless trees stand in the cold. Weatherboard houses, brick houses, stone houses all begin to bask in the rising sunshine, and so does the clock tower of the old courthouse that stands in the mall. Magpies sit on power lines along Dangar Street and set melodies adrift, while a semi-trailer laden with hay bales turns a roundabout and grumbles towards Tamworth. On the other side of town, the Wollomombi school bus heads out with seats to be filled on return.

An hour later, gates are unlocked at a compound that was once a council work depot. A red dog, not a kelpie, but a welded statue with a body made from an old compressor, stands on its hind legs, props its front ones against a fence, and watches passing traffic through its eye-bolts. Occasionally a vehicle comes in. Teenage boys get out in ones or twos or threes. Many wear sneakers and either jeans or tracksuit pants. Hoodies are the jumper of choice, an unofficial uniform.

Most boys gather in the car park. Some are sitting on rolled-up swags that have been tossed on the gravel next to a 4x4 dual-cab. A pair of denim legs and boots poke out from under the vehicle. A shifting spanner lies nearby. Elsewhere, four or five collies meander through legs. Hands rub snouts, ears are tugged. A black-faced pup, a long way short of growing into its paws, is cradled by a boy who has sleep-dust in the corners of his eyes.

'His name's Maximus,' the boy says to a visitor.

'He's the runt of the litter, so we had to give him a big name,' adds team leader, Daz.

Another boy comes across. He's the only one who wears a cowboy hat, black and battered. Peach fuzz curls and points off his chin.

'How did you get here?' he asks the visitor.

'My car.'

'Which one?'

'The Hyundai over there.'

The boy scoffs, then scuffs his boots and turns away.

'What's the matter with that?' asks the visitor.

'Oh shit, you know, I'm a LandCruiser man, myself.'

Laughter erupts near the swags. Two boys are wrestling, wriggling in and out of playful headlocks. Others are content to chat and blow smoke rings.

'Big day, today,' says one boy.

'Where are we stayin'?' asks another.

'The Sydney Cricket Ground. The SCG, they call it.'

'Yeah, do they? Must be good.'

'Yeah, I reckon it is.'

Soon enough, the boys hurl the swags into the back of the dual-cab. Doors open and shut, Eminem shouts from the speakers, and the journey begins. Six or so hours ahead. Then get ready for a dog show and a sleep-out with the stars.

Sydney, eh?

What a different world.

The weekends were filled with family activities for the Shakeshafts. Joe and Denise were the regular sports parents, taking their kids to tennis, hockey and football games. They were outdoors people. Dangarsleigh Falls, a short drive south of Armidale, was a popular recreation spot for them. They had barbecues, went bush-walking, and admired the views in bushland dominated by cliffs and plunging gorges that came alive with waterfalls after rain. Maree Shakeshaft celebrated her thirteenth birthday there. While her parents remained in a picnic area at the top, Maree walked with some of her friends and Anthony and Bernie to the natural pool at the bottom of the main falls, where they then did as many a country youngster has done, and it was only once they returned to Joe and Denise that they realised their larking had been seen by others. 'We went skinny dipping,' recalled Maree, 'and apparently some teachers saw us from above and told Mum and Dad. I think they were too far away to realise we didn't have clothes on, but they were worried because we were swimming in an area that could be dangerous.'

As much as it was an incident that told of childhood fun, it was also symbolic of who Bernie had become: when in the bush, he was so very comfortable in his own skin.

But then, life became tougher.

At the end of 1979, Joe and Denise decided to return to Sydney.

It proved a troublesome move. After being granted a transfer with the Child Welfare Department to the northern beach suburb of Dee Why, Joe needed to begin his new job in January 1980. However, the search for Catholic schools in which to enrol the children was a challenge during the holiday period, and when classes finally resumed, only Maree had been successfully placed. The Shakeshafts were suddenly fragmented. Maree stayed with family friends and went to school in Strathfield in Sydney's inner west; Joe lived in a hotel in Manly; and Denise, without a car and facing the added stress of trying to sell the family home, remained with the four boys in Armidale, where Bernie began his high-school education at O'Connor Catholic College.

By about Easter, the family's shifting pieces fell into place and the Shakeshafts were together again. The Child Welfare Department helped them secure accommodation in an old Victorian home on Marrickville Road, Dulwich Hill just a handful of kilometres west of Sydney's CBD. To Bernie, the evolving landscape of flats, shops, cottages, Lebanese, Greeks (some called 'em 'wogs'), concrete, red brick, red rooves, red rattlers, kebabs, graffiti, too many traffic lights, too few trees, screeching tyres and sirens was an enormous culture shock. He attended De La Salle College, a bus ride away to nearby Ashfield. It was an all-boys school that had a considerable population of students with Italian heritage. After his upbringing with Aboriginal Australians, Bernie had never judged a person by skin colour, but as a country boy he'd barely had any exposure to foreign cultures, and after his first few days he returned from school and told his parents: 'These kids have got funny names.' But while that was a new experience for him, there was a worrying theme of sameness as he resumed his altercation with formal education. In Years Five and Six in Armidale he'd been buoyed by working in open-plan classrooms where copying others' work needed no great subterfuge, but at his new school, desks in single file demanded risky sideways glances and forward leans with eyes searching beyond the shoulder of the person in front. On the scale of school misdemeanours such actions were minor, but the fact that Bernie practised them was telling: he was not a model student, nor was this classroom a place in which he felt eager to learn.

Bernie spent a mere few weeks at De La Salle before a moment outside of school led to a premature end to his time at those single-file desks.

'I was doubling a cousin on a bike out the front of our house. It was on a roundabout sort of driveway with space for parking, and I can't quite remember what happened, but I think I might have got too close to a car and hit its mud flap. It's not a flash thing to do when you're in bare feet. I nearly cut off two of my toes on my right foot and ended up having microsurgery in Marrickville Hospital. How lucky is that? Perfect timing. No school Monday.'

By the time Bernie had recovered, he and his family had moved to Eastwood, and Bernie was enrolled at the local Marist Brothers High School. There he discovered that one teacher had three different canes: one called 'touch up' for minor offences; a slightly bigger one to 'shorten you up'; and one the teacher called Big Brother, which was 'the longest piece of bamboo' Bernie had ever seen. The new kid who'd arrived in class with a slight limp soon enough found out that his two injured toes weren't the only appendages to suffer from numbness, albeit temporarily: 'I think I got caned in my first lesson for not shutting up, and that straightaway put me into this state of mind: "It doesn't matter how much you're gonna hit me, I'm not gonna bend."' So, stinging fingers all became regular parts of Bernie's learning outcomes. However, these never deterred Bernie from 'standing up for the fellas who couldn't stand up for themselves', and his clenched fists found their targets more often than they missed. But in his self-appointed role as a protector, Bernie also opened his hands and cradled the vulnerable in ways that were as unexpected as they were incongruous for someone with such a tough exterior. One day, when he was in Year Seven or Eight, he arrived home with a shetland dog. Time has toyed with the memories of those involved – Bernie thinks he asked his parents to mind it because the teacher who owned it was going on holiday, whereas Denise remembers Bernie telling her that the teacher had moved house and didn't have a fence. Either way, the boarding of Brandy was meant to be temporary, but the little sheepdog lived with the Shakeshafts for many years until he died in old age. It was Bernie's first true experience of looking after a pet; the family had had a dog in Orange, but Bernie was too young to recall much about it, and in Armidale he had befriended a stray dog, Scruffy, but it came into his life just before the move to Sydney, and the wiry-haired bitza was 'surrendered to the pound'. 'That was pretty traumatic for me,' says Bernie. 'I knew what was likely to happen to him at the pound, so I gave him a chance before that. I hopped on my pushbike and took him for a run along this dirt road out of town. I picked my mark where I took off, then I rode like a lunatic for ages before I lost him. Job done. But then I got home and the bugger was there waiting for me.'

Bernie bonded easily with most animals – except cats, which he was 'never much good with'. In Sydney, as they moved from Dulwich Hill to Eastwood, and then to the home where they still live today, Joe and Denise became used to Bernie welcoming surprise additions to the family. Among the most memorable were a pregnant guinea pig that was given to Bernie by a friend (a litter was later discovered in the shed out the back) and two chickens, both merely days old, that Bernie brought home for a school project. When he announced the first one's arrival he told his parents: 'We've got to be its mum and dad and see if we can raise it.'

'I was very uncertain about doing it,' said Denise. 'We put it in a box and had to have a light on it all night, but I was worried about doing that in an old house, so we turned the jolly light off and the poor chicken was dead next morning. Oh dear, wasn't I in trouble for that!'

Looking forward and not to be denied, Bernie brought the second chick home that day, and that night the light stayed on. The first few weeks of 'parenthood' were so successfully negotiated that Bernie built a cage in the backyard to house his bird, Winky, which was allowed out during the day to roam. All went well until a few months into the chicken's life the Shakeshafts were woken by 'cock-a-doodle-dos' that grew in decibels and regularity over the following weeks. 'It used to chase everyone round the yard and crow at all hours,' remembered Joe, laughing. The teacher in charge of the project agreed, euphemistically, to take the rooster 'back to the farm'.

Amid the comings and goings of Shakeshaft creatures, Bernie collected his first 'busted thing' in an act that set a precedent for the years ahead. He was in the early days of his first real job, as a pamphlet dropper in the Ryde area, when he found a pigeon with a broken wing in a park. While nursing it back to health, he put it on the handlebars of his pushbike, and rode from letterbox to letterbox in what was a twist on a carrier pigeon's convention.

The bird lived for only a few months, but this was much longer than Bernie held onto his job. After a week or so of working for a pittance – 'I think I only got about fifty cents for a whole round of drops' – he decided 'to do a bit of erosion control'.

'I kept riding past this gully and started thinking: "That's a pretty good place to finish a round pretty quick." So, I dumped all the pamphlets there one afternoon. The problem was, the bosses had these houses that they checked on to see if I'd done the deliveries. Yeah, that didn't end well, for me and pigeon.'

Nevertheless, all his pedalling over many years served him well. Although he continued to smoke, Bernie remained fit enough to excel physically. By the middle of high school, his focus had shifted from cricket – 'it was hard to have a Nelson on the field' – to basketball, a sport that suited his tall, lean frame. But despite his stature and athleticism, it was his leadership that stood out; he read the game well, and from his position as centre, he organised and inspired his teammates. In his senior years he was a logical choice as captain of the school's Firsts.

If only he could have shown the same qualities in the classroom. But that would have taken leaps greater than the ones a rookie named Michael Jordan was soon to make famous in the NBA. There was, however, one exception: in Year Ten he was hand-picked for a TV production course that was run by industry professionals and an American man who was one of the few school teachers Bernie connected with. They produced numerous film clips and stories, including one about an Aboriginal hostel they visited in Kempsey, on the New South Wales mid-north coast. Bernie didn't like editing, but he had a good eye for camerawork and showed promise as a scriptwriter. 'It was fun, and probably the first time I'd ever had a decent experience at school. It was practical. You know, we were doing real things with real skills.' Finally, he'd found a subject that interested him. He was happy to learn. After the course finished he packed away memories that he would only come to truly understand and benefit from many years later.

TV production and basketball were two safeguards for Bernie at a time when he was becoming increasingly reckless. The Venturers (Scouts) was another. After accepting an invitation from neighbours to go on an outing he found himself relishing expeditions in Sydney's national parks and further afield. But no number of bush tracks was ever going to keep him off the path to an uncertain future.

Now, standing on his verandah and holding a lit cigarette in a tunnel made by his fingers, Bernie reflects on that period with suitable bluntness: 'Those middle to late years of high school were the start of me really not giving a fuck about myself.' We will never know the definitive reasons – Bernie is not one to deeply analyse his past – but it's reasonable to suggest that his dislike for school, the reaction of some teachers towards him, and his move from the bush to the city were all contributing factors.

Unsurprisingly, wild streaks of adolescence clashed with baby-boomer conservatism in the Shakeshaft home. In particular, Bernie argued heatedly with his mother. 'Yep, we had some cracking blues, but I now know Mum was always doing what she thought was right; it's just that I was a rogue and there was no way I was going to listen to her. I gave her a pretty tough time.'

In response, Denise acknowledged: 'I guess I had a chequered relationship with him at times because I was the tough one, whereas Joe was laidback. I have a few regrets, but that's the way it goes. If we could go back, we might do a few things differently, but we are who we are, and we did what we could.'

Back on Track

At times Bernie hung with the wrong crowd, and on other occasions he *was* the wrong crowd. He was 'thickest' with his schoolmate Rob, who was much smaller than Bernie but a feverish example of Mark Twain's timeless quote about the fight in a dog counting more than its size. He was a brilliant scrapper. Fast. Impeccable timing. 'He used to challenge kids just for fun,' says Bernie. 'He'd say: "I'll give you the first three hits for nothing." If you'd been smart enough you'd have picked up a baseball bat and dropped it right across the bridge of his nose and hoped that knocked him out. I never saw him go down from a punch. Kids would lay their best ones on him, and then he'd carve 'em up. He taught me a lot about fighting, especially that it's not about how good you can throw a punch, it's how good you can take one. And you know what else? I always made sure I was on his side!'

Rob also put his hands to another valuable use: he was a very good forger of signatures. Even Denise's complex twists were no match for him, which meant Bernie had the luxury of his very own get-out-of-school-free cards, and wagging became one subject in which he and Rob were proficient.

While cursives may have helped bring the two errant mates closer together, it was their need for greater and faster independence that most bonded them. Getting a driver licence and having a vehicle for cruising has long been a rite of passage for teenagers, and Bernie was no different. He began his passage under Joe's direction in the family's XB, which was subjected to the traditional kangaroo hopping of a learner searching for symmetry; work the feet between the clutch, brake and accelerator, steer with one hand, and how the hell do you get that bloody stick into position? Clunk, clunk, the good old 'three-on-the-tree' (three-gear stick on the steering column). Joe may have provided the 'proper school instruction' but Bernie also learnt from individual trial and error, and from Rob. However, for these latter two teachers, something essential was needed.

'We were only in the two-hundred-dollar-club when we bought out first car,' laughs Bernie. 'My parents didn't want it to happen, but it happened! A two-door, four-on-the-column Cortina. She was a ripper. We kept it at Rob's place. I think he might have just got his P's; I dunno if I had my licence yet or not, but that's a minor detail. We used to sneak out in the middle of the night and drive up to Gosford and back. About a hundred and twenty k's. On other nights we'd go into school and do doughnuts, stupid shit, on a grass bank. We got bogged there once.'

Apart from his disregard for his own wellbeing, Bernie was confident he would not get caught; he was one of those youngsters who had the knack of avoiding trouble without really meaning to. This wasn't to say that he slipped the net on every occasion. However, when he stood toe to toe with authority, usually at school, he often found he had someone of regard who was willing to defend him. His TV production teacher was one such ally, although on one occasion Bernie tested his loyalty to, if not beyond, the limit.

'Holy shit, we were lucky,' recalls Bernie. 'Rob and me, we'd been wagging class, but we weren't far away from it. I was driving. No seatbelts. Didn't give a fuck. I wheeled around this corner and rolled the Cortina. Upside-downed her. We jumped out, full of adrenalin. No-one was hurt. "One, two, three!" – we flipped this thing back on its wheels. The roof had caved in, windows smashed. Then our teacher drives around the corner and sees us. I'm already thinking: "How do we get out of here before the cops turn up?" But this teacher walks over to us, looks at the mess, then he looks at me and in this deep American accent he says: "Shakeshaaaaft, what are those Tally-Hos doing in your top pocket?"'

Bernie grins and his eyes glint with mischief. Before continuing, he shifts in his verandah chair as though he has just completed a bumpy ride. 'Yeah, cars, we had a few of them.' He then talks of pulling apart motors, fiddling with suspensions, and 'wheeling and dealing' in sales. Even the Cortina was found a new, unsuspecting owner who was ignorant of the car's accident history and the concrete and silicone cosmetics that two young bush-cum-burb mechanics used to fix it. 'We sold her for the same price as we bought her. We must have put a bag of concrete into that thing's roof.'

In terms of dollars and time spent on repairs, Bernie didn't break even on the Cortina, but he did profit in a way that will forever be impossible to measure. When he rolled the car, he also, unknowingly, raced headlong towards a poignant turning point in his life, but to reach it, he needed someone much older and wiser than Rob in the passenger seat.

Father Liam Horsfall had chosen a life in the clergy after being inspired by two chaplains he'd met during his senior school years; both had been prisoners of war at a Japanese concentration camp in New Guinea. In devoting himself to God, Father Liam studied and worked in the United States before accepting a posting in India, an intoxicating yet infuriating and heart-breaking country that would influence him for the rest of his life. Eventually he returned to Australia, and on a journey of many career-based twists and turns, he found his way to Marist Brothers High School where he became chaplain. He was in his mid-fifties, bald and short, and nuggetty like an old-fashioned rugby-league hooker, with a handshake that could surely crush ice. To Bernie, he was 'as tough as all get up', but crucially, he looked, listened and absorbed;

just as the TV production teacher had, Father Liam recognised that the oldest Shakeshaft boy needed help. So, he stepped in. He monitored Bernie's progress at school, and in a service that went well beyond standard procedure and curriculum, he became another to teach Bernie how to drive. In a Cortina. A yellow one. A station wagon. And best of all, it was an automatic.

'He'd pick me up early, about six o'clock, from home. Then he'd let me drive to the gym I went to in St Leonards, or we'd go somewhere else not too far away. He had a lot of tricks, which I still use with kids today. Like, we'd be driving along and he'd say: "Hey, look at that over there." Then, as soon as I took my eyes off the road, I'd get a good clip under the ear. That's a life lesson that stays with you.'

But the content of other lessons raced in and out of those ears. No matter what help Father Liam gave him for the classroom, Bernie continued to struggle, and towards the end of Year Eleven he wanted to leave school. It was 1984, a time of mesh ties, tight jeans and canvas shoes. Bob Hawke was Australia's Prime Minister, Medicare was new, and so was the shiny, gold one-dollar coin. INXS had its first national hit, 'Original Sin'; tuna fisherman Dean Lukin became an Olympic weightlifting champion; a robot named Dexter churned out compatibility scores on *Perfect Match*; and Milperra, a little-known suburb in Sydney, shuddered in the world's spotlight after six bikies and a fourteen-year-old female bystander were killed in a car-park shoot-out on Father's Day.

Life. And death.

Bernie hadn't given much thought to either. He just didn't care. But others did. And they weren't giving up.

3

The three tables, topped with wood-grain laminate, are pushed together to form one long island in the middle of the room. It is rarely an island of tranquillity. Controlled chaos comes more readily to mind. This morning it is deserted. Its usual inhabitants are spread in groups of three and four on chairs around the room. Behind them, on one side, tall tan metal lockers stand as a reminder of the cut lunches, Thermoses and form guides they once stored. Elsewhere, a yellow hard hat sits atop some folders; it tips at a slight angle as though deep in thought. On a wall is a picture of former prime minister Julia Gillard holding a collie; the redhead is smiling, the black-and-white dog looks nonplussed. There are many framed awards, and a didgeridoo lies on mounts made from two upturned horseshoes. Above it, a dozen or so dull white beanies are stuck in a permanent hover.

'Right,' says Warnie, 'I want each group to pick an article from the newspapers, and talk about it among yourselves. Then we'll get together and chat about them all.'

Warnie is the teacher. In his forties. Carted a mean crash-ball on the rugby field in his day.

The groups do as they're asked. Most of the time. The only girl in the room seems entranced by a fresh cut just above her ankle, and two boys have a rally with their rulers, using each other's head as a ball. In between these distractions – and others – the groups glance at and sometimes read articles. One draws special interest: 'COPS APPLY HEAT ON ICE'. Some of these kids know. They just know.

Another story also attracts attention: 'SERENA FINGERS SEXISM FOR LOSS'. It's about tennis star Serena Williams. Two days ago, in the final of the US Open, she called the male chair umpire a thief. She was penalised a game. She later lost the match.

'She fucked up,' says one boy. 'Yer gotta own yer own shit.'

'Doesn't help she's a famous black woman, but,' says another.

Within earshot, a globe of the world stands still. It is covered in a fine layer of dust.

Joe and Denise didn't know what to do. They didn't say no straightaway, but how could they say yes? Two thousand dollars was a lot of money. Money they didn't have. It took them a while to digest what Bernie had told them: Father Liam was taking a group of boys to India for about a month-long trip to do charity work, and he wanted Bernie to go.

'We ummed and aahed,' said Denise, sitting opposite Joe at the kitchen table in their home. 'I wasn't working much because Mark, Bernie's little brother, was still young. Then, Father Liam came and saw us and said the parish priest in Eastwood, Jack [John] Haseler, wanted to give a thousand dollars towards taking the boy who Father Liam thought would most benefit from the trip. And Father Liam said to us: "Bernard is the one I want to give it to." You know, Bernard has had a magic life in many ways.'

Between sips of tea, Denise talked of other acts of kindness. In Armidale, when Bernie dabbled with playing the trumpet, the city band provided free tuition, and in Year Eleven, he was tutored in chemistry for free by the mother of one of his mates. 'This is what I mean. People just picked him up wherever he was,' said Denise.

Bernie, though, could also do the lifting. The trip to India was planned for the holidays at the end of Year Eleven. He was still to decide if he would return to school in Year Twelve, but there was one certainty: he was going with Father Liam's group. So, he packed shelves at night at a Franklins supermarket. It was a progression from being a trolley boy, a job he'd had for a while. With the lure of the subcontinent motivating him, he improved his work behaviour; there was no more tying fishing lines between trolleys and cars in the car park. 'Shit, it used to be funny. These customers with these big, shiny bull bars on their vehicles. They'd drive away and see a trolley coming with them, so they'd go faster and the trolley would go faster too.'

Bernie knew little about India. A few geography lessons might have taught him about overpopulation, poverty and religions, but that was it. India was just a country that was so very different from Australia, in part of the world that seemed so very far away. How many hours on a plane to get there? Nearly a day, with a stop-over somewhere or other. Yeah, that's a few decent trips between Sydney and Armidale in the old XB.

At the time, India was politically fragile. Prime Minister Rajiv Gandhi was new to his position after he replaced his mother, Indira, who had been assassinated by two of her Sikh bodyguards in October 1984. Thousands were killed in India's north in anti-Sikh riots, for which Rajiv offered no apology: 'When a big tree falls, the earth shakes,' he said.

It was against this backdrop that Father Liam and a group of about twenty senior students and old boys arrived in India. Some of the details are now 'sketchy' to Bernie, but others are seared into his memory.

'We stepped off the plane and I remember walking down this flight of stairs onto the tarmac and being hit by this wave of heat, and seeing all these soldiers with properly serious assault rifles. And then getting into a bus and seeing this mass of population. People everywhere. The next few days were a massive culture shock for a fella who'd grown up in little Armidale. The noise. It was like you'd just smashed a beehive off the wall. All quiet in the morning and then it builds. Cars, motorbikes, pushbikes, bells, horns, metal sheets being hand pulled by cart and scraping along the ground. Then you try crossing the road. What do you do? Do you run? Do you walk? Traffic everywhere. Are there rules? Just a jumble of machines. Take a wrong step and it's all over for you. Then you get the kids tugging at your shirt: "Mister, mister." And the smell. It hits you. Can make you sick in the guts. Pools of shit and stagnant water. One of our lads got his passport pinched. He was using a little bag as a pillow at a train station; a hand comes through a window behind him – quick as you like, the bag's gone. Things just happening everywhere. We visited all these different places, like leper colonies, and I couldn't stop thinking: "Is this for real? Or is it all out of a movie?" Fingers missing, toes, crook eyes …

'Then, we got the bizarre other side of it. We stayed at this bishop's place. It was like a fortress, with two guard-bears that they left out at night. I sat on the roof with a couple of the older guys in our group and smoked hashish; I doubt I'd ever had hashish before. So, here I was living the dream, and looking down on these bears.'

India, the world's greatest mosaic of absurdities and incongruities wedged and crafted in a picture that continually draws the eye back to its central, most resilient, feature: the people and the streets. Beggars on skateboards, prayers at the temple, dahl, incense, chai. Booksellers, rickshaw wallahs, a barber snip-snipping by the roadside next to a man click-clacking on a typewriter. Cover drives in the maidan. The hiccups of tuk-tuks. Sandals slapping. Children crying. A nonchalant cow at the traffic lights … A traveller might leave India, but India, in some way or other, never leaves the traveller.

And that was the way it turned out to be for a teenage boy who had never thought much about looking beyond the moment he was in. Even if he had, he could never have prepared himself for what would happen in Calcutta (present-day Kolkata), an ants' nest of a city in which too many people saw each new day as a battle to survive.

'It was the first real turning point of my life,' says Bernie. 'A huge one. In hindsight, I reckon I'd been on this mission to die. You know, risk-taking behaviour, cars with no seatbelts, how much I hated school. There was a lot of anger inside me, but I don't think I realised how much, back then. I don't know what I hoped to achieve by going to India, but I trusted Father Liam; the big fella knew things I didn't. We visited Mother Teresa's hospice [Kalighat Home for the Dying]. We were in a small group – others, I think had gone to the Taj Mahal – and we were in this little room. It was stinking hot and all the windows were open. It was about sunset. We were just sitting there. Then, in walks this tiny woman in a white-and-blue tunic and a head-scarf type of thing. Mother Teresa. She stood next to a wall, and all this noise was coming up from the street through the windows behind her. Then she started speaking. Spoke to us for a good while. Just us kids from Australia. I was up the back and couldn't hear a word over the street noise. She was so quietly spoken. But oh boy did I learn about presence. She was the most extraordinary person I've ever listened to. She just had this manner, this aura. I didn't know what she was doing there that day, but I've got some ideas now, with my learnings from Aboriginal people. There are things that happen that words can't explain. Is it spirit? Is it energy? I don't know what it is, but there's something there that can be so powerful. You know if you see a magician hypnotising people on stage? It was like that. I was mesmerised. The next day we had the option of working in the hospice or kicking round Calcutta. I'll tell you what, I was busting to get into that hospice.'

Mother Teresa, a winner of the Nobel Peace Prize, was known in Calcutta simply as 'The Mother'. She'd founded the home, formerly an abandoned temple to the god Kali, in 1952. It accepted people of all faiths, for free. Sisters and volunteers saw to its day-to-day running, and although it was heavily criticised by some experts for its medical standards, it went to the heart of The Mother's devotion to serving 'the poorest of the poor'.

It also opened a mind.

'By that part of the trip, there was this developing theme in my head,' says Bernie. 'I was starting to question a lot of things about myself: "Mate, do you know how lucky you are? What happens if you were a leper? Or how would you feel if you got bloody sick in India and had nowhere to go?" So, I went into the hospice with my conscience spinning a bit. The first thing that hit me were all the stretcher beds in this room about the size of a basketball court. Sick people, dying people, all on these small beds in this room. It was hot, and the stink … I don't know why but I was drawn to this one kid. About my age. He didn't speak any English and I didn't speak any Calcuttan [Bengali]. He had a bandage on his leg. I helped another volunteer take it off, and all his flesh … yeah, it was a shock. There was an old woman there – I think she may have been German – and I asked her what had happened to this guy, and from what I could work out he got an infection living on the streets, maybe just from a simple cut, and it had gone all cranky, and the maggots had got into him and eaten all the flesh off his leg right up to the hip. All the way to the bone. And the smell …

'I couldn't walk away from this kid. So, I stayed with him that day, and I went back the next. Part of my job was to wash his bandages and bring them back and put them on him again. I washed them in this skanky, stinky sink in a side room. I don't remember running water.

'This kid, this boy, he reached out and touched my hand, and I was going, "Oh man!" I didn't hold boys' hands. I was a tough boy, you know. No holding hands for me. But I did. And that's how we communicated. By touch and feeling. Here was me thinking I was a hard fucker, but this kid? Not one groan, not one complaint. No Panadol, no clean bandages. And the pain … I could see it. I'd take the bandages off and there'd be hunks of skin on them. And to see the bone. I don't think I really knew that he was dying, but I bet he did. I reckon he was accepting of his fate.

'I held his hand while he passed away. They took him away pretty quick after that, and I don't know what happened to him. The next sick person came in, and that was it.

'That kid taught me what tough is, and he taught me: "Righto, enough of the whingeing. Be grateful for what you've got."'

Bernie lets those words hang as he looks beyond the verandah to the horse paddock. A magpie sings from a tree. Cockatoos screech in flight.

'Yeah, so a pretty powerful little time, that time in Calcutta,' says Bernie, finally. 'It still makes me shiver. It didn't make me feel any differently about the Catholic faith. It was nothing about religion. It was just black and white. You're either alive or you're dead. If you're lucky you have a good life, a full one. If you're unlucky, like that boy, you're born without the chance to have a decent shot. Makes me wonder about gratitude. Some parents might get wound up because a truck has blocked the road and poor Mum or Dad can't drop their kids off to school without backing up and taking a detour. Don't bang the horn and blow up about being late. Think about what you have. I mean, really think about it. You've got a lot. That boy in that hospice had nothing. I knew that at the time, but now as an older fella, I can see more. Probably like to think I know more too. We can all be guilty of thinking we're hard done by. But how many of us really are?'

It wasn't Bernie's first experience of death. A few years earlier, his nan, Nellie (Joe's mother), had died, and although he wasn't especially close to her, Bernie 'struggled with the experience'. Denise remembered her son 'sobbed and sobbed and sobbed' the night she died. It was another revelation of softness beneath the surface.

When he returned to Australia, Bernie told his parents about his experience with the Bengali boy. 'Sitting with someone dying really got to his heart,' said Joe. But it soon became apparent that it was an experience to be stored away in the memory rather than one to dramatically shift immediate behaviour. Despite some initial fire – 'He came back all guns blazing and ready to go and do his HSC,' remembered Denise – the reality of school quickly destroyed the enthusiasm and Bernie resumed his role as a struggling student who had no desire to curb the wildness.

In the final weeks of first term, Joe and Denise felt the tether was close to snapping. They saw a son who 'was going nowhere'. Denise recalled: 'His marks weren't good, he was being really disruptive, and emotionally he couldn't cope with it.' So, they decided to let Bernie leave school, but before they could plan the right moment for the conversation, Bernie came home and said to them: 'Father Liam can get me a job, so I'm going to leave school.' Joe and Denise didn't protest.

Dove Travel Agency, in Sydney's CBD, handled travel arrangements for various Catholic organisations. Through his contacts, Father Liam arranged for his former student to work in the bookings section, but with a sigh and a grin Bernie says it was a bad fit. 'It was all maths, and maths was a "no-go area" for me; the number of tickets I stuffed up!' It didn't take long for Bernie to be moved to deliveries; he walked around the city delivering tickets and packages to clients, and occasionally he was a chauffeur for various members of the clergy. There was only one thing he liked about the job: he wasn't at school.

Bernie persevered until the end of the year. It was 1985 and he was eighteen years old. If he'd stayed at school – and had been a student with further academic ambitions – he would have had a nerve-wracking wait until HSC results were posted out in January; then there would have been more anxiety until university admissions were announced in the newspapers. For many, it was all part of the process of building a career. But what to do, if you didn't know what to do?

Basketball was one of the few positives that came from Bernie's schooling. He'd begun playing for the Parramatta Wildcats at a high level in western Sydney leagues. His dedication was tested by other pursuits, namely 'chasing girls and drinking a few throwdowns'. It was a very predictable juggle for someone of his age, but the pieces he tossed around were buffeted by his rising urge to escape Sydney. Yet he stayed. And ironically, he did because he wanted to return to the classroom. Firstly, there was an invitation from his car-driving mate Rob. It seemed a peculiar suggestion, but it took just a quick stroll along a corridor at Meadowbank TAFE to realise it was a 'cunning plan'. 'Rob wanted me to do a typing course with him. What the hell was he on about? I'd never been to a TAFE college before, but then Rob took me for a look one evening and oh my God we saw this whole room of beautiful young women learning to be secretaries. We signed up that night! Didn't learn to touch type too well but crikey we had some fun. There was a pub just across the road. Heaven. I still can't type for shit, but there are times when I start an e-mail now, and I've gotta smile back at good ol' Meadowbank TAFE. Even though I didn't finish the course.'

The course turned into a stepping stone for further TAFE studies. When a basketball mate said he was going to complete his HSC without the pressure of going to school, Bernie was interested enough to find out more. And with no firmer plans in place, the thought of 'having another crack at the piece of paper' grew on him. Furthermore, doing it without the formalities of school – 'You know, uniforms, attendance records, and boring assemblies.' – was comparatively appealing. Of course, there was also the lure of co-ed learning.

Bernie enrolled in a TAFE college at Gore Hill, not far from the gym that he and Father Liam used to drive to. The college was also within walking distance to, and more than the occasional stagger from, the St Leonards Tavern. Nevertheless, Bernie devoted enough time to his study to score in the low 300s out of a possible

500 in the HSC. Not only did he take away a piece of paper, but it was there he met someone of a similar age, from Sydney's northern beaches. Mel Phillips now lives in central-west New South Wales.

'My early impressions of Bernie were that he was a really nice guy, caring, engaging, easy to get along with. We had a very close friendship right from the beginning,' said Mel. As time passed, Mel realised Bernie was 'an incredibly unique soul'. He was generous with his time and would always 'find a piece of his heart to offer when needed' yet, curiously, he was not always comfortable with himself. 'He was a lost soul; he had a chip on his shoulder is probably how I would best describe it. I didn't know why. We didn't talk about it, but I knew there were things stirring inside him.'

Regardless of his state of mind, Bernie had secured enough marks to gain entry into a Catholic teachers' college at Castle Hill in Sydney's west. What followed was a blur of incidents, many of which could have dramatically changed, or ended, Bernie's life.

4

It's morning, before school and welding start. Some work gangs are already out and about, fencing, gardening, picking up litter. The boys who remain at the depot are, as always, a mixed bunch. They're sitting with staff, making a familiar loose circle in the smoko room. Every seat is filled. The smell of freshly made toast is strong, and mugs of steaming tea sit on a few armrests. On a seat near the door, a boy flicks his cigarette lighter and leads the flame in a dance around his shoes. He's so slumped that his body appears to have been poured onto the vinyl and will soon drip onto the floor. Another boy bites on the string attached to his hoodie, while others respond to spasmodic pings and rings by putting their heads down and skimming their thumbs over tiny keyboards.

Jokes are being told. One about Bob Hawke; another about a bloke at a bar; and then there was this dress-up party and the French maid's outfit.

'Any others?' asks Dawso, one of the staff.

'Yeah, I got one,' says one of the most confident boys in the room. 'So, youse have heard how cigarettes can't light petrol up? Well, that's all a lie. My cousin, he was a heavy smoker, but he's quit now after this incident I'm gonna tell you about. Me and him were drivin' along in a car and he's smokin', smokin', smokin', and throwin' butts out the window and affecting the environment. He lights up another one just as we pull into a servo, and I tell him: "Put that out right now." And he goes: "It's right, it's right." But I keep tellin' him to stop, so he puts it out. Then we fill up the car, and the dickhead, as he's pullin' the nozzle out of the car he spills petrol all up his arm. We jump back in the car and we're drivin' and he lights up again and bang! His arm combusts into flames. So we're drivin' up the highway and he's swingin' his arm out the window screamin' his head off. Long story short: we got pulled over by the cops and charged with havin' firearms.'

The room fills with laughter.

It's a good start to the day.

Joe Shakeshaft is tall, like Bernie, but unlike his eldest son he's a quiet man who confesses to being shy. During the interview for this book, he was content to listen while Denise did most of the talking. When he did speak, he often began by touching the rim of his glasses and leaning back into his chair.

'Cars,' he said, smiling softly. 'Bernard wanted to buy this one in Epping from a lady who used it to run to the shops. I could see there were rust problems and I said: "Don't do it, it's going to be a heap of trouble." Anyway, he goes and buys it. Then he got a puncture and put it up on a jack out in our front yard, and the jack collapsed; the rust wouldn't hold the bloomin' car up. That'd be Bernie.'

Stories about Bernie and his cars abound in the Shakeshaft family. Joe was once driving one of them when the seat gave way; he managed to stay upright for long enough to make safety. And Maree laughed when she remembered her university days, and how

Bernie was generous in letting her borrow whatever car he had at the time: 'You don't know how anxious you become when you're waiting on a hill for the traffic lights to change, and you're driving a souped-up rally car with a roll cage, and you know there's only a tiny gap between first and third gear, and the vehicle behind you is a police car.' By far and away the overarching theme of many stories is described most succinctly by Paul: 'My brother was into all sorts of wild driving.'

During his late school and college years Bernie had so many episodes with cars that his memories are now crammed into a timeline along which colour takes precedence over chronology. He introduces one recollection by shaking his head and inhaling deeply – without a cigarette – in a manner that says: *Listen to this, just listen to this.*

'Nearly got in some deep shit at teachers' college. Those days were just a drinks fest. Anyhow, we went into a twenty-four–hour McDonald's out around Baulkham Hills. It's late. A full load of us. It was my car, but I wasn't driving. We're all pissed and being stupid and we go into the drive-through. We pull up behind this BMW and someone says: "Reckon we can pinch the light globe over the number plate?" Yep, righto. So, someone goes and does it while the guy in this BMW is waiting to get served. But it must have set off some sort of alarm because a lunatic comes out of the car – and it was one of those sobering moments when you think "Shit, this prick is for real" – and he opens his boot and pulls out a handgun. By that stage we're panicking, reversing out at four hundred miles an hour with this bloke walking after us and going off his banana. But we got away and had our laughs.

'The next day I got a phone call at home. It was the police: "Are you the owner of such-and-such a vehicle? Where were you last night?" Blah, blah, blah. It was all the standard stuff, but they didn't tell me what I'd done wrong. I was told I had to go to the cop station at Parramatta, and if I didn't there'd be a warrant out for my arrest. I get there and I find out one or more of us from the night before might be charged with attempted robbery of a payroll, coz the bloke in the BMW had a load of cash in his boot, didn't he? Eventually it all got sorted out, and we didn't get charged. We'd just stepped into the wrong spot with the wrong gag at the wrong time. We were playing way out of our league.'

At that stage, Bernie was working part-time for an importing business near the city. He had to pick up his boss early most mornings and drive him to various meetings. There was a 'lot of driving', but that suited Bernie. He felt free behind the wheel, even when he was constrained by his job. But it was after hours that he really clocked onto the joy, the thrill, of moving. And the reason was a blue Datsun 1100 with a custom-made six-speed gear box and roll cage.

'It was the same car we had at McDonald's,' says Bernie. 'Still the fastest thing I reckon I've ever driven, let alone owned. I was really moving up in the world, really trying to kill myself. That was in my street-racing days. You know, just more of the same, not worrying about what happened to me or anyone else on the road. No fear of death or injury. You know that windy road that goes up into Chatswood? I was racing this idiot at night and we were both going way too quick into this dip; I was behind him, almost touching him, and I'm thinking: "When's he going to brake?" He finally hits the brakes and I clipped the back of him, hit the side rail and went end over end. I got cut out. The car was trashed. The other driver didn't hang around, but the cops and ambos came. Flashing lights everywhere. No charges, though. It happened between a crematorium and a cemetery. I could've gone to either of them but ended up in Royal North Shore Hospital with a hairline fracture in my neck. I remember being shown the X-rays; the specialists said I had no idea how lucky I was. "Could've been in a wheelchair for the rest of your life, champ." I discharged myself from hospital a few days later. Had a neck brace but didn't keep it on for too long. Yeah, whatever. That's the sort of boy I was.'

Reckless, audacious, careless, apathetic ... Bernie being Bernie. But at what cost, to both himself and those around him? The answer came by way of another car: a green two-door Cortina, 'an old piece of shit with souped tyres'. In a twist of coincidence, the Shakeshafts lived in the same street as some cousins of Justin Flint, who'd kept in touch with Bernie long after the black mittens had been tossed away, and a beige XB had moved a good mate south. They caught up every so often, as they did on a wet night somewhere during Bernie's time at teachers' college. Flinty arrived at the Shakeshafts with his cousins, Timmy and Spud. And they left with Bernie, who paid scant regard to his parents' advice: 'Be careful, it's raining.' They got into Bernie's Cortina. Timmy strapped himself into the passenger seat. Flinty and Spuddy were in the back. They had no seatbelts.

'We got to Carlingford,' remembered Flinty. 'Coming up a hill on Pennant Hills Road and going round this bend. Bernie wasn't mucking about, but all of a sudden we were sliding across the road and were pretty much sideways. Then the lights of this other car came over the hill towards us, and we were going for a full side-on hit. Somehow Bernie managed to tweak the Cortina around so that the nose hit the other car. The front of our car, just in front of the dash, was gone and got knocked onto a telegraph pole and we went spinning sixty metres down the hill. Timmy was unconscious, and Bernie had his arm tangled up in his door. Spuddy had hurt his knees but I was okay. Bernie told me to ring his parents. So, I scarpered out the back window – a crowd was already starting to come around us – and I went into a house to make the call. Joe answered, and I just blurted out: "We've had an accident."'

'I had visions of bodies being splattered around,' said Joe. 'These things shake the life out of you. I took Maree with me; Denise stayed to look after Paul and Mark. I didn't know what we'd find at the other end.'

Meanwhile, at the accident scene, Bernie looked over at Timmy. He thought he was dead. An ambulance officer came over. Bernie couldn't work out how the man was standing where the bonnet and engine should have been. He was asked if he could feel his right arm. He couldn't. 'I thought it was still holding onto the steering wheel, but it was up around behind my shoulder somewhere. I can't tell you much more than that. Except that it was floggin' down rain.'

A short while later, Joe and Maree arrived at the scene to find the whole road closed. Maree walked towards a tow-truck driver.

'You better stay back from here,' he said.

'But my brother was in that accident.'

'Oh sorry, the ambulances have just left.'

Maree and Joe hurried to Westmead Hospital, where shock soon mixed with relief. All in the accident had survived. Bernie woke up in bed to find Timmy and his mother sitting near him. 'It took me a little bit of blurry time to realise Timmy wasn't dead. I remember having these nightmares when I was out to it; I was thinking: "It's one thing to kill yourself, but to kill someone else is something very different." As it turned out I was knocked up much worse than anyone: shattered my arm, stitches in my hands, broke a hip. It shook me up. The man in the other vehicle walked away with only a few knocks to the face.'

Bernie wasn't charged with any driving offence. He remained in hospital for eight days before he was discharged. Today, occasional aches and pains in his right arm remind him of the night.

When recalling his memories of the accident, Flinty sat in a cafe in Armidale, where he still lives. His voice was deep and strong. 'Bernie pushed the envelope, I suppose. There was a lot of seat-of-the-pants stuff, but whatever happened, we came through it.'

The same, though, couldn't be said for Bernie at college. Although Denise considered her son a 'born teacher', which was in no small part due to his gregarious nature and ongoing desire to help others, he yet again struggled with learning in a formal setting. Furthermore, he was drawn to question: What is education? A good mark on a piece of paper? Sit up straight, do what you're told, there's a good lad, have a gold star? There had to be more. Much more. It was a conversation Bernie had many times with his closest college friend, Dusty, a strong, athletic country boy from Barraba, in central-north New South Wales.

'We talked about teaching, and we didn't really agree with the way that went,' Dusty said in a phone interview. 'You know, teaching to the middle of the bell curve and there's little or nothing on the fringes. Bernie and I talked about that without really knowing what we were talking about, I guess.'

The two may have been drawn together by education, but it didn't take them long to realise they had much stronger similarities. They both yearned for rural life – something that prompted them to occasionally camp in swags in the bush at the back of the college campus – and they had a love for driving that, little did they know, would defy logic but define mateship in the years ahead.

Bernie and Dusty battled through lectures and tutorials without ever feeling certain they were doing the right thing. Become a teacher? What good would that do anyone? Perhaps Bernie's destiny was summed up by one of his earliest practical sessions in front of a primary-school class. With the teacher and supervisor watching from the back of the room, Bernie launched into a poem about an octopus, and a slip of the tongue turned tentacles into testicles. The students were none the wiser, but, like the poem's subject, the trainee teacher felt all at sea. At other times, however, Bernie, was at ease when instructing. Mark Shakeshaft, who was a promising middle-distance and cross-country runner at school, has fond memories of his eldest brother always showing a 'keen interest', and offering advice as a coach-cum-mentor.

In so much that Bernie did, there was a common denominator: movement. Coaching; driving; shooting hoops; couch-surfing; teaming up with his old Marist and India travel-mate, Dave Webster, in the 111-kilometre Hawkesbury Canoe Classic (it took them sixteen hours). Bernie needed movement. He also needed space, the type that allowed him to walk out the back door, jump a fence and keep walking without the annoyance of hitting his next-door neighbour's clothesline or stopping at a corner for the lights to change. These needs had grown relentlessly ever since Bernie had gone on a fortnight-long horseback trail ride in the Snowy Mountains with some of his TAFE friends. 'I fell in love with that high country,' he says. 'There was a feeling of belonging, and I left there thinking: "I'm comin' back. This is where I wanna be."'

It had to happen.

Bernie pulled out of teachers' college after 'a year or so'. Then, he left Sydney. Late at night. Without fanfare. He had little money, no job to go to, no plan about where he would live or what he would do when he arrived. But he did have an old cream Holden HG ute with a tailgate upon which Dusty had painted the words, 'Irresponsible Freedom'. He also had a swag, and a dog. It was a blue heeler with an undershot jaw that Dusty had 'picked up a good while earlier' at Castle Hill. Dusty had named it HOD, ('He's Our Dog'), as confirmation it was a 'shared pet', but as time passed Bernie had become its sole boss.

Mel Phillips, who'd been one of Bernie's closest friends ever since their TAFE days together, was one of the last to say goodbye. She felt Bernie 'just needed to go and sort his shit out'. 'Whatever that was, I don't know, but he needed to sort it out. I don't remember having any deep conversations with him about what he should do. He just went. When I say he had a chip on his shoulder, maybe there was a bit of arrogance and an ego, I don't know. Maybe it was the cowboy-type thing, putting up a brick wall. Which male at that age, particularly if you're trying to be the tough one, wants to expose vulnerability? It's much easier to be the cowboy. A cool dude and all the rest of it.'

Looking back, from the comfort and safety of his verandah, Bernie admits he was vulnerable. 'In Sydney, I was on this mission of self-destruction. When I left, I dunno if I was searching for who I was, but I was looking for a different life. I'd been burning bridges, and I certainly wasn't going to be a teacher. I was pretty happy to get away from home and stop terrorising everybody.'

So, he headed for the mountains. A young man on the move. A young man heading for wide open space. A young man who was yet to find his purpose.

5

The main shed at the depot is this morning's heartbeat. Five boys are in the welding room. Four of them stand near a partially made dog box. They're inspecting their work with Matt Pilkington, a rangy man with a red bushranger beard and a blue tea-cosy beanie. Earlier, Bernie had joked to the boys their teacher had a 'head like a dropped pie'; Matt had been the first to laugh. The fifth boy is hunched over a glow that zaps. The stench of burnt metal is strong. He stops, straightens, pulls up his visor and looks down at what he has done.

'It's a pretty ugly weld, but it's better than the others. But I'm gonna fix it.'

He starts again.

Behind the shed, in a mix of shade and sunlight, and flanked by coils of fencing wire, two boys are working on two hefty slabs of wood. The whines of the electric sanders ensure there's no conversation. Further away, behind the woodworking shed, a boy with a dead rollie hanging off his lips hammers in a hinge on the door of a dog cage.

It's about ten-thirty. Bernie, who has been on the phone and in meetings for much of the morning, comes out of the smoko room and squints at the day. For a moment, there's a break in the screech of the sanders, and a song on the radio in the welding shed can just be heard. It's one of Cher's biggest hits: 'Strong Enough'.

'I lived on eating rabbits,' says Bernie. It's an unexpected introduction to his recollections of arriving at the Snowy Mountains. 'I also had this mate who was working at a supermarket in Sydney. Before I left, he looked after me. Gave me some tinned stuff and flour to help get me through the first few months. Gave me a "charity sack", let's call it.' Bernie grins; it's impossible to tell if he's more pleased with the memory or his euphemism. Either way, the moment seems to have energised him, and he settles into his verandah chair and focuses his thoughts on 'this beautiful country, trout country' between Adelong and Adaminaby, about 400 kilometres south-west of Sydney.

'When I got there, I had no plan. The dog and me, we camped out near this river. I had a rabbit trap and a slingshot, so it was pretty basic sorta living. Swag, billy, camp oven, canopy over the HG, and no other people. I musta done it for a few weeks, maybe a month. Then, I got a job pulling down fences for this bloke, and I was put up in this homestead that no-one had lived in for a long time. It had a couple of unbroken windows here and there and gravity-fed water that I had to sort out; the joint was full of brown snakes too. It was just busted. Anyway, the work didn't really pan out, and I reckoned I was better back out in the bush, but I needed money to put fuel in the car.

'Then I met this wild fella with a big red beard. He was the overseer on a property, and he saw that I was doing it a bit tough, so he offered me a job just doing bits and pieces. He gave me a dog, a black-and-tan kelpie, Possum, a beautiful thing. Fast. But I gave it back a while later. You know, circumstances weren't right. This fella was also the one who introduced me to riding horses at night – he had station horses we could use – and we also used to ride to campdraft schools about twenty k's away in Tumut. It was all cross-country riding. I hadn't done Pony Club or anything like that at Armidale, but I'd been on a few horses here and there; I hadn't done a whole lot of riding, but I knew I liked it. I wasn't afraid either; didn't get freaked out by ones that bucked. I can't put an accurate time on it, but maybe I was with this bloke for two or three months. Staying in his house, working for keep and getting fuel thrown in.'

It was an existence that, like a strand of fence wire, needed support to keep going. But unlike the wire, Bernie had no set direction. Nor was he going anywhere. He might not have recognised his plight, but those around him did, including a man who was to become one of the most influential people in his life. 'But be careful when you meet him,' says Bernie. 'Coz he can speak in riddles.'

Paul Roots lives on forested cattle country, near Hernani, an hour's drive east of Armidale. He has further land at Adelong. When asked over the phone if he had time to be interviewed for this book, he replied: 'You see, we got a drought going on.' Six weeks later – with the ongoing dryness punctuated by a few scattered inches of rain in the area – he and his wife, Annette, sat at their kitchen table and cheerily gave their time. Paul, grey-haired, short and wiry, wore blue Wrangler jeans, and a red-and-blue-check flannelette work shirt that had pearl stud-buttons; he had left his boots at the door. Annette, with auburn hair in a bob, was dressed in a light blue shirt and jeans. Even after an hour's ceaseless conversation, they shook their heads when asked if they'd had enough of all my questions. 'No-one's hungry at the moment,' said Paul. 'The cattle are fed, we're all good, still at the top of our game.' So, they continued to speak over an extended lunch of corned-beef sandwiches, chocolate cake and cups of tea, about the progression of a 'young fellow we met when he was out of money, out of food and out of petrol'.

The journey to this meeting began long before Bernie arrived in Adelong. Paul grew up in rural Luddenham, at the eastern fringe of the Blue Mountains, close to Sydney's main water supply, Warragamba Dam. The son of a cattle buyer worked hard as a boy, training trotting horses, feeding pigs and milking cows before he went to school; he remembers being only fifteen when his father sent him off driving a truck to pick up loads of stock from the Homebush Saleyards (the site of the 2000 Olympic Games). After finishing Year Ten, Paul 'took off' to Queensland and worked as a station hand at Mount Isa. Meanwhile, his family bought a property near Adelong where Annette, a member of a well-known and respected family in the district, was born and raised. When she was only thirteen, her father was killed in a campdraft accident, and in the way of the bush, locals rallied around. The Roots family was among them, and in the years ahead, when Annette was pursuing her own campdraft career, Paul's father, Sonny, and another cattleman, Jimmy Matthews, regularly drove her to competitions. Amid all this, Annette and Paul 'got together' and soon enough were married and then, with 'no money and a handful of cattle' they bought a property. 'It was foolish, really, and I still really don't know how it happened,' said Annette, laughing. 'Suddenly we were thinking: "How are we going to pay for this?" The bank gave us seven years to pay for a thousand acres.'

Annette and Paul sought the advice of Jimmy Matthews, who had built a stock and station empire in Victoria. The next day, Jimmy rang back: 'I've got jobs for you,' he said. And that's how Annette and Paul began six years of droving, primarily pushing mobs of cattle from sale to sale in Queensland and New South Wales. 'In the first year we had a trailer for the horses, and we slept outside in our swags,' said Paul. 'We cooked by the side of the road, and all that sort of stuff. And then we had a caravan when our son, Dave, was born. I was toughing it out and you were in hospital taking it easy.' Paul looked across at Annette, held back a smile, and buttered some white bread. The palms of his hands were extraordinary: intricately cobwebbed with deep creases. Eye-catching biographies of sixty-odd years in the country.

The droving was fruitful. Paul and Annette not only paid off their property but bought the place next to it, and then, when they knew it was time to leave the long paddock behind, they also opened a saddlery in Adelong. It was here, well away from corrugations and fence lines, that an intersection of lives finally gave one life some sense of direction.

'I got talking with one of my customers one day,' said Paul, 'and I don't know, I was probably in a situation where geez I was a bit busy and I must've said: "I don't know how I'm going to get all this work done on the properties." Well, this customer said: "I've got a young fellow who might just be what you need. He's been out with me, and I don't know what to do with him. I'll send him over."'

Bernie chuckles at the memory. 'Rootsy and his riddles,' he says with affection. 'When we met, he asked me: "Do you know anything about cars?" Shit yeah! At that age there wasn't much I didn't know about anything. "Could you put a diff in a one-tonner?" Oh mate, could I put a diff in a one-tonner! Of course, I could. Or that's what I told him. But, I had no idea. Anyway, I helped him put that diff in, and then he said he desperately had something to do the next day and could I help him out again? So, I did, and before I knew it, I was working for Paul and Annette and living in their drovers' caravan at the back of the saddlery down by a creek.'

It happened thirty years ago, but Paul's and Annette's memories remain clear. When I asked Paul why he gave Bernie a job, he tipped his head to his left and chose understatement over elaboration. 'Was I really looking for someone? Shit no. He [Bernie] only got in the road. But we took him in because I suppose he was in a bit of a fix, a bit of a situation, and I suppose we felt or seen it. He needed some help.'

'And we didn't ask questions,' added Annette. 'We still don't know to this day why he was there. It was none of our business. We weren't judging him on anything that had happened or where he was at in his life. That wasn't part of who we were.'

Paul and Annette lent Bernie a motorbike, which he rode out to the properties each day. After getting to know their randomly acquired farmhand they agreed 'he didn't really know anything, but he'd never bat an eyelid about having a go'. Obviously he needed guidance, and this came embedded in a bush wisdom that would ultimately become one of the most powerful lessons of Bernie's life.

'It's all about pressure,' said Paul. 'If you send a dog around the cattle, and it's a hot day, you should never make it so hard for the dog that he has to stop; you only send that dog to where you can see he can only go another metre, but you stop him before he goes that metre. You call the shot. If you let the dog go on, and it's too hard for him and he wears out, then that's when you have that situation where the dog has too much pressure on him and he birrs up. You've gotta realise sometimes that the dog doesn't want to stop, and he mightn't obey you, but you still have to stop him, so *you* put the pressure on. If you don't put enough pressure on him, and he keeps going, it will be harder next time and you'll have to put even more pressure on him.'

'It's observing, observing, observing, and being aware,' continued Annette. 'Pressure and release, pressure and release. That's how we handle our dogs, our horses, our cattle.'

And, it's how Paul and Annette handled Bernie.

'For example, he might have been on a crowbar,' said Paul. 'And that sun was shining down on him and I could see he couldn't take another big set, so I'd grab the bar and say: "Give me a go, you can't do all of this, I want a bit of a go." When you look at the bigger picture, Bernie was in a bit of a pressurised situation when he arrived, and we released that pressure by taking him in.'

After all his battles at school and college, twenty-year-old Bernie had finally landed in a classroom that suited him. It wasn't one founded on a culture of cramming in information for the sake of marks and grades but one that drew out a person's abilities in an environment that made the person comfortable, happy and eager to both learn and perform. Paul was the main teacher, but he gave little explicit instruction; instead, he led by example, and Bernie learnt to watch and listen closely.

'I realised really quickly that I had to pay close attention,' says Bernie. 'Paul would never go: "Righto, it's smoko time, now." He'd just pick up his hat and walk off. And it would be up to me to interpret if that picking up the hat was meant to mean smoko time, or was he walking down the fence to do something? I didn't want to be following him if he turned around and went: "What are you doing? Get back up there and hold that wire!" Most of his lessons were non-verbal. I'd say: "I don't know how to tie that fencing knot, Paul," and he'd go: "I've told you so many times." Well, he mightn't haven't said a word all day. I had to watch. Really watch.'

Accolades came with little emotion. Just an approving nod or a simple, 'Good work.' Not everything, though, went well. Today, there are sheep panels that bear the marks of very poor welding. 'Paul still jokes we'll go and fix them one day,' says Bernie.

Horses were the focus of much of Bernie's education. In appraising their farmhand's riding abilities, Paul and Annette tossed a few words between each other across the kitchen table – 'efficient', 'fundamentally basic' – before they settled on 'capable horseman'. While this may not seem a glowing A on a report card, it's nevertheless a solid assessment from a couple who, during their competition days, were champion campdrafters and endurance riders with some very 'tough and handy horses'.

'I remember the first time I saw old Rootsy compete,' says Bernie. 'I can't remember where, it might have been down Gundagai way. Anyway, he said to me: "Go catch that cream horse over there, and get me that black one as well, coz we're off to this campdraft." And he shod the horses himself, and I brought the clippers out to hog their manes, but he said: "Don't worry, we haven't got time." I'd come to hear that a lot. Then we rattled the horses into an old float and headed off. At the other end there were these fancy gooseneck trailers and shiny horses, and Rootsy had just brought these furball things out of an Adelong winter. Then it started raining and I saw him getting all excited. I asked him: "What's happening, boss?" And he said: "Well, won't we come out and put the pedal down now?" And that's what he did. He had the turbo on. While everyone else was pulling back, he had these horses skidding and sliding, but they knew what they were doing. I just watched him and thought: "Shit, check out this guy with the old farmer hat on. He's off the Richter scale." And yep, he wins the Open draft. And here I am living on his place; I just fell into "horse expert camp".

Campdrafting is a traditional Australian bush sport. It involves a horse and rider 'cutting out' or isolating a beast from a mob of cattle in a yard (the camp), and then working that beast, against the clock, through a course in another yard. A judge awards the horse and rider a score out of one hundred; in the case of disqualification, the judge, sitting on a horse, cracks his stockwhip. To an outsider, fascination in campdrafting may be lost somewhere between splintered seating and the bar, but for those enamoured with it, the subtleties and skills are captivating. The athleticism of the horse, the ability of the rider to simultaneously read the moment and think ahead. At their very best, they're in perfect symmetry, a Torvill and Dean on dust. With a statement befitting both a riddle and a wealth of experience, Paul says a 'good campdraft horse has to be able to do everything by himself and must be dictated to all the time'.

Watching from beyond the rails, Bernie used to 'light up' at the spectacle, and he yearned to compete, but it wasn't his time or place to do anything other than learn away from the spotlight. He loaded and unloaded horses; set up and pulled down electric fences; fed and watered; and shovelled shit. However, it wasn't all work. Campdraft weekends were social occasions where competitors sat and whiled away evenings by parking their denim on tailgates and fold-out chairs, drinking, eating, swapping yarns and speaking in reverential terms of horses from the famed Spinifex and Romeo bloodlines, some of which Paul and Annette owned. For Bernie, these were outings not to be missed. Make new friends, catch up with recently made ones, and 'chase girls' and 'hit the piss', although not necessarily in that order.

It was when he was back on Paul and Annette's properties that he had the chance to saddle up and further his progression from his childhood when, with the help of his mother, he once wrote a letter to his 'pop' (Denise's father): 'I hope you like my drawing of the brown horse in our paddock. I go to pre-school now.' In Adelong, the school was one of harder knocks. One Roots horse that Bernie rode, Balero, was an Arab Cross: 'Geez, it spat me out, some.' Also, Annette recalled the day in the 'triangle paddock' when Bernie wouldn't get off a young horse to pick up a piece of wire, and as he leant over, the bucking was of more concern than the barbs. Just another lesson among myriad others for a young man finding his way.

Throughout it all, Paul and Annette observed, observed, observed. Pressure on, pressure off. But most of all, they cared, and in doing so, a relationship formed that no-one expected when that diff was lowered into the one-tonner. 'Bernie became like a second son to us, and that's still how he is with us,' said Paul.

When listening to, and watching Bernie on his verandah chair, it's clear the feelings are mutual. 'Paul and Annette are extraordinary people. Was I lucky to find them? Well, it was just meant to be. I didn't think I needed a hand. Everything was going all right – but Rootsy and Annette, they knew better, didn't they?'

The relationship between them was layered further by the connection that Bernie had with the 'first son', Dave, an only child, who was in his early primary school years when Bernie arrived. Behaving as a protective older brother would, Bernie 'kinda put

Dave under my wing'. 'It was very special, like this,' said Annette, interlocking her little fingers. 'Bernie looked after him. He took him to sport and got him doing things like football that Dave didn't think he could ever do. It was incredible because young men at that age usually didn't want anything to do with kids, but Bernie was different. He always had time, *always had time*. And he always listened.'

While these kin-like connections were the pillars for Bernie's development at Adelong, two other bonds at the time were as invaluable as their influences were immeasurable. The first involved HOD. In the time-honoured manner of the dog never judging the man, the blue heeler was rarely far from Bernie's side. 'He used to cart it everywhere,' remembered Paul. 'He put it up on his horse, and he'd sit it on a gatepost. I bet there were a lot of conversations those two had. When you start thinking about things like that, we mightn't even have Bernie if it wasn't for his dog. It gave him comfort when he was needing it. You know, this fellow who knew nothing, fresh from Sydney, living in the bush. If he hadn't had that dog with him, who knows?'

Bernie dismisses the suggestion with a shrug. 'Dogs can know what you're thinking, what you're feeling. HOD did. He was a good'un. He played his part, but you know, I don't get too carried away with looking at that. He was part of what I went through. He was with me. We went through a lot together. The first dog I had on the road.'

The kilometres had begun ticking over when HOD was still a metropolitan dog, and also a witness to the early days of another bond, one that defined unconditional friendship. Riding chained up in the back of the HG with a couple of swags, he went away on trips to the bush, both planned and random, that Bernie and

Dusty took when they were at teachers' college. While the dog may have had the wind on his face, it was the two 'tight mates' in the front who were enlivened by the rush of the experiences, the joy of escaping. And there was also the strength and comfort gained from being in the company of a like-minded, wandering soul.

'We just used to get up and go,' says Bernie. 'Most trips were planned. We'd save up money and then just take off. For a day or two, a week, longer, whatever we could do. By the time I was in Adelong, Dusty – he stayed at college longer than me and was doing part-time work – would come down every now and again and he'd have a bit of a break, then away we'd go. I dunno how exactly it began, but we started playing this game, "Left and Right". Like, we'd drive a hundred kilometres out of somewhere, in whatever direction we chose, and then we'd take the first road right, then the next one left, and right again, and on we'd go. All sorts of fun and dramas, you know. We might end up in scrub somewhere and then we'd be sayin': "Is a fire trail a road?" "Nah, it has to be a driveable track." Just making shit up as we went along. This one time, I think we were out the back of Cessnock somewhere, and we were on this billy-goat hill country that just wasn't driveable. I wouldn't do it now in a four-wheel drive let alone in an HG. Anyway, we got stuck and the car was busted. Busted engine mounts, and all sorts of busted shit. We had to walk out, and we found this bloke, and would you believe it? He had an HG in his front paddock. He helped us out, but when we told him what we were doin', he said: "You blokes are coming through *where?*" Couldn't believe it. Yeah, we used to get into all sorts of spots. Through rivers, over boulders, big slopey slippery hills … crazy stuff.'

Fittingly, Dusty, who lives in northern New South Wales, was on the road on a family holiday in Victoria when he was interviewed for this book.

'We did a lot of driving in our younger days,' he said. 'If it ever got tough in either of our camps, Bernie and I'd get in a ute and go. It was those times when you didn't have to talk. It was just get in and drive. A lot of the time we had this agreement that Bernie used to drink, and I used to drive. This one time – I can't remember where we were going, but we were going somewhere – we bought a carton of beer before we left and then, off we went. Bernie had a few beers during the day, and we talked when we needed to. At the end of the day we got wherever we were going to, we pulled up and lit a fire and I said: "Right, I'll have a beer with you now." So, we had a beer. Finished it. "Can you get me another one, Bernie." "No, that's all of them." "You drank *twenty-three* beers and saved me one!" "No, I saved two: one for you and one for me." And that's how it was.'

Two mates and a dog; little imagination is needed to paint them in stereotypical Australian bush images. Swags, galahs, riverbanks, stars, trails of red billowing across scorched plains … Bernie, Dusty and HOD 'living the dream'. Occasionally others went with them. 'I remember going on a trip,' said Mel Phillips. 'They were both driving their utes. Dusty was at the front, and I was with Bernie travelling so close behind. We couldn't see the road; it was just a pillow of dust, and here was Dusty guiding Bernie where to go over the CB radio. We were travelling at speed. We got to the end and I said: "Never again will you do that." I could have killed them! That was the cowboy in them. Recklessness. No concept of what could happen.'

It seemed consequences were only to be considered after the fact.

One evening, when Dusty was back in Sydney, Bernie was driving into Adelong after a day's work at the Roots' properties. HOD, as usual, was in the back of the HG, but there was a telling difference.

'I'd had a few stubbies on the way,' admits Bernie. 'Down the Snowy Mountains Highway, and a policeman pulls me over. I'm gone for drink driving. Then the cop asks what's under the green canvas canopy on the back of the HG. "Nothin'," I said. But the cop says: "Well, I'm having a look." "Well, I suggest you don't." Then, he went and opened the thing and my dog bit him. And I went slidin' downhill from there. The cop thought the car was stolen. Of course, it wasn't. But I was a bit of a smart-arse to him, and that didn't help matters. I was put in the back of the bull wagon and taken to Tumut the back way on a dirt road. The trip threw me round like a rag. They threw the book at me; tagged me down, I think, for dangerous driving, neg driving, on top of drink driving. Anyway, I had to front up in court and I was a bit of a smart-mouth there too. Might have said something funny about the magistrate's name. I can't remember what I got. Maybe twelve months without a licence. Anyway, that fucked up things pretty quickly. And it wasn't the end of it, either. At some stage I went back to Sydney, and left HOD at my parents' place while I went away somewhere for a couple of days. I dunno, he must have got a bit anxious and did the "lookin'-for-the-boss-thing" and he jumped a fence. Never saw him again.'

Fickle fortunes. Bernie liked to drive, but he legally couldn't. He loved dogs, but he didn't have one. And he had a job, but it was hard to get to.

Paul and Annette Roots recognised the signs. They knew it was best for Bernie to move on and be given new challenges that would be scaffolded on the ones he'd had at Adelong, so Paul contacted their close friend Jimmy Matthews. Jimmy was a legend in the stock and station trade. More importantly, he was the same Jimmy Matthews who'd helped drive Annette to campdraft competitions after the death of her father. Regardless of blood, he was as good as part of the Roots family. And so was Bernie. It was time for two distant relations to get together.

6

The rectangular brick home is on a rural block called Warrah, and it's far enough away from Armidale to be a convenient distance from the distractions and potential dangers of town life. The yard, scattered with shrubs and gum trees, has a mix of plonks and placements. A dusty excavator bucket sits alone in a clump of yellowing grass; three ageing wooden dog kennels line up a few strides apart from each other; and an ample pile of cut logs conjures thoughts of snakes lurking in refuge. In the carport sit two plastic canoes, a ride-on lawnmower, a runabout boat on a trailer, a surfboard, a blue boxing bag hanging by rope from the roof, and a tired blue Kawasaki motorbike leaning on its stand or perhaps its laurels. Other bits and pieces lie in two tin sheds: horseshoes, a jerry can, rolled-up swags, fishing rods, bags and tins of dog food, and a Driza-Bone jacket that's crumpled with both sunlight and shade. There's also a small pool table, a table-tennis table and gym equipment … barometers of good times, and bad ones too.

The place smells sweet and smoky. A star jasmine overwhelms a downpipe on one front corner of the house, and out the back there's a fire pit. Right now, it's a quiet place. The seven boys who live here are at work and school, and the supervising youth worker is grocery shopping.

Inside, the house is clean and orderly. The kitchen holds no Vegemite-tinged knives in the sink or crumbs on the bench. The floor is swept. Nothing unusual catches the eye until, in the living room, a whiteboard dominates a wall. It is filled with writings in black and green.

The whiteboard has been divided into three columns. At the top of the first, 'AGREEMENTS' is underlined; even without reading below this word, those in the know realise a critical statement has been made: There are no rules in this house, only agreements that are decided upon by the boys. '3 min showers.' '<u>No</u> food in the lounge.' 'No TV till <u>all</u> chores done.' 'No smoking in rooms.' 'No youth workers to clean boys' rooms.' 'HANDS TO YOURSELVES. IF IT'S NOT YOURS DON'T TOUCH IT!' The final word in the column shouts out 'RESPECT.'

The third column poses the question: 'WHAT DOES WARRAH MEAN TO YOU?' The answers are poignant: 'Safe haven.' 'My freedom.' 'A place called home.' 'Something that can help you stay out of trobel [sic].' 'A place for everyone.' 'Second fam.' 'BROTHERHOOD/Mateship.'

Above all, the eye is drawn to a circle in the middle of the second column. Lines stretch away from it and point to: 'honesty', 'maturity', 'be honest to yourself', 'Respect what you got and don't ask for more' and 'U fuck it, U fix it'. The biggest writing dominates the centre of the circle: 'own your own shit'. Every resident knows these words aren't to be used lightly; they are the boys' mantra. And when adhered to, they help build characters who, in their own individual ways, are inspired by the words that sit in a square of sunlight near the top of the whiteboard: 'LIFE isn't about FINDING yourself. It's about CREATING yourself.'

Bernie sits on his verandah chair and reaches over to a small table that's draped in red cloth. He picks up a cigarette packet and searches for familiarity. Then comes the snap of a lighter, a flame, a deep inhale, and words drifting off a blue breath: 'Jimmy Matthews … legend.'

After spending 'kinda a year' in Adelong, Bernie had no intention of returning to a Sydney life. He'd periodically visited his parents, both of whom realised their eldest son was still very much exploring who he was. And the next stage, with the support of both the Shakeshaft and Roots families, was a move to Diggers Rest, a rural area about forty kilometres north-west of Melbourne, near the airport at Tullamarine. Bernie lived in a caravan in the corner of a hay shed on Jimmy Matthews' property Newman Park. He was again a farmhand, his central chores included 'chippin' thistles, shovellin' shit' and fencin''.

Jimmy Matthews, from East Malvern, Melbourne, was only a young teenager when he left school and worked as a clerk for a stock and station agent at the vibrant Newmarket Saleyards at Flemington. It wasn't a surprising choice of occupation; Jimmy's father was a butcher, so too a grandfather and some uncles, and all were regular customers at the markets, buying stock that would be sent to an abattoir before the meat made its way to sale. It was just a few years after the end of the Second World War, and the sight of sheep and cattle being transported in rail trucks was common. This was a time when the Australian economy was about to hitch a ride on woollen backs. Jimmy, with his kelpie under his seat, used to catch a train and tram to Newmarket. One day he was told to get his dog off the tram, so Jimmy put his mate on the footpath and whistled to it from his window seat; the kelpie ran alongside his boss until, showing too much devotion, he forgot to look ahead and ran into a pole. Jimmy jumped off, picked up his stunned companion and took him home. Both recovered to resume their roles at Newmarket. When Jimmy wasn't clerking, he earned extra money working mobs between the railyards and saleyards. By the time he was seventeen, he had his auctioneer's licence, and in the years that followed he and his partner built up a business that became the largest privately owned stock and station agency in Australia. After the Newmarket Saleyards closed in 1987, Jimmy moved on to work for Dalgety's (later Landmark) throughout northern Australia, a place in which he'd already had much experience. He was widely known, respected and liked. A smartly presented man, often characterised by his stiff cowboy hat, he had a firm handshake for both buyers and vendors.

'I'll tell you the type of man Jimmy was,' said his son, Ray, while taking a breather from breaking in a horse near Diggers Rest. 'He was up at Katherine Show [Northern Territory] and a fella approached him and asked him for some pointers about getting this particular job that was coming up. And Jimmy told him: "Yeah, well, have a look at you. You want to get that earring out of your ear, get your hair cut, get a hat, clean your boots, and look like a stockman." Well, that caused a few problems with the human resources people, but about three months later this bloke comes up to Jimmy somewhere.

'"How ya going, Mr Matthews."

'"Who are you?"

'"I'm the bloke who took my earring out, got my hair cut, got my boots cleaned, and got a hat. What do you think?"

'"At least you look like a stockman, now."

'That was my father.'

Jimmy and his wife, Dulcie, accepted Bernie without concerns. If Paul and Annette Roots wanted to help the 'boy' out, that was good enough for them. As long as Bernie worked hard and didn't cause trouble, there'd be no problems. In return, Jimmy would welcome the new lad into an environment in which he'd also helped ex-jockeys, ex-boxers, footballers out of work.

'Jimmy had a great skill of making everybody part of the family,' said Ray. 'The old man was: "Come on, we'll get in and do this, or do that, then we'll get you up to the house and Dulcie will give you a big feed."' And Dulcie did, although Bernie's tall, skinny frame prompted her to often say: 'You can't fill him up, this fella.' It was in this homey atmosphere that Bernie felt very much at home. At the centre of his existence were horses. Jimmy had racers, trotters, campdrafters, hacks ... he was passionate about them all, and he was willing to share this passion with Bernie if the 'boy' hung round long enough to listen.

'Jimmy had some really good horses; they won a lot of things,' says Bernie. 'It must have been in my first few days at Newman Park, and Jimmy wanted me to exercise this one horse on his trotting track on the place. Rap Dancer, he'd had his wins, but he was one of the greatest hoorangs you'd ever come across. His head just wasn't right; something must have happened to him as a teenager. I'd never done any of this driving-a-horse-in-a-sulky-cart thing. It's a complicated operation, harness racing, with leads and buckles, bits and pieces. So, I'm trying to work out how to get onto this sulky. It looked pretty easy, it was nice and low. So, I put one foot over it, and the horse knew, didn't he? He was thinking: "Aaah, I got a new player here!" Coz what you're supposed to do is first put your arse on the seat, and then slide yourself around. But one foot while standing up? As soon as I did it, old Rap Dancer bolted. All I was thinking about was a bit of advice Rootsy gave me at Adelong: "If you get thrown off a horse, whatever you do, don't let go of the reins coz it's a long walk home." So, we wheel around this corner a hundred miles an hour near the stables. The sulky spits over with me, one leg in, one leg out, upside down and the horse starting to pick up the turbo. *"Don't let go of the reins. Don't let go of the reins."* And they're long reins too, so I'm starting to swing out, and we're heading for this big corner post at a set of day yards. Well, I went one side of the post and he went the other side with the sulky. At that stage there was no holding him. My arms were killing me, but I ran after him up this long tree-lined driveway, a beautiful driveway, and we found him tipped over at the front gate. Then, it was back to the drawing board. "You have to get back on, boy. Look I'll show you." Jimmy was always calling me "boy".

'A couple of days later, once I knew how to get on the sulky properly, I'm starting to have this arrangement with this horse. We're out and we've had a couple of laps on the track, and now I'm starting to feel a bit full of meself with this experienced, wise and half-wild horse. We're halfway down the straight, and this prick grabs the bit and he's going, and I can't stop him. Things are blurring past, sand in the face, picking up traction, and we're firing towards this corner that's got a drop-off behind it and then there's about twenty yards to the boundary fence. If you've ever sat on a trotter, you get a different feeling of speed, and I've got no brakes, no steering, and this horse is going flat, fast as his laidback ears will let him. I'm bracing for going around this corner, but he's got no intention of doing that. He flies off the end of the track, launches off this drop, must have been half a metre, and we go sliding into the barbed-wire fence. Buster number two. I was so angry I could've killed him. I shouted at him: "This shit ain't gonna wash!" I've got crook arms, bark off from the first day's effort, a sulky is smashed, and I'm cranky as. I just laid it out to him right there in the paddock. "I might never be the boss, but we're going to have some fuckin' mutual respect here."

'Anyway, I went on to have the most wonderful relationship with that horse. I used to sleep in the stable with him. I can't remember why I started doing it, but it probably just comes back to gaining that connection. Just a swag and the pillow and the horse. We became mates and he used to lie down beside me. I was his go-to man at the races. I'd ride him out to the parade ring at Moonee Valley or wherever, and then the driver would get in. At Newman Park I could ride him bareback, just with a head collar. I used to take him down to the river and stand him in the water after races and workouts.

'I think the whole development between us was a bit like me with schoolyard bullies. I remember this one time when one of my mates was torturing another kid, telling him he was a poofta and all sorts of nonsense. I said: "Not on, mate," and I gave him a flogging. It was a good lesson. When you stand your ground, you don't do it in half-terms. Make sure you only have to do it once. Rap Dancer got me good twice, but we worked it out between us.'

Bernie pauses, as though he's comprehending what he has just said. His cigarette has long petered out and been stubbed in an ashtray, and his hands are now resting, with fingers splayed across his thighs.

'You know,' he continues, 'in hindsight, I learnt exponential amounts. Paul Roots, Jimmy Matthews, they were the guys that took me from boyhood to manhood. I look at the way they handled me. They put all the opportunities in front of me. Waited until I was ready for them. "We're not going to put you on that fancy pony; we'll put you on this thing first. Teach you how to ride, boy, how to fall." Until I met them, I had no idea about much.

'Jimmy, he was your average-sized man, but a mountain of a man. Of all the important people in the world he could go and talk to, he had time to sit and talk with me. He was the same when I went away with him and Ray to campdraft events. Like I was with the Roots, I didn't ever compete when with Jimmy, but what I learnt! Then there was that day he made me get on that racehorse in his round-yard. A big, fancy round-yard. And this horse used to tip up and rear over, and Jimmy says: "Boy, we're going to fix this today." And that got me thinking: "What part of *you* are in the *we*, Jimmy?" Anyway, he gave me an old Milo can with a lid on it. He'd filled it with warm water, and he says: "Sit on the horse, and wait until it gets to almost the top of its rear, then smash the tin on its head. Horses don't see colour, but this one will feel the knock and the warm trickle down his face and he'll think it's blood. And that's how we'll stop him rearing, boy." I nearly got killed that day. I'm on that horse – coz he only starts rearing when someone's on his back – and he's about to tumble over backwards and I know I need to bail, and Jimmy's there: "Now, get him!" That was Jimmy all over. And the trick worked.

'Another time with Rap Dancer. That horse had so many ... geez, he had some habits. He used to run off the back of his float. Knew the exact timing. The tailgate would go down and he'd come out, steamroll anything, anyone. Jimmy said: "Enough of this shit." They took the horse over to a trainer's place, and backed the float up to a swimming pool, and Rap Dancer heard the rattling of the chain on the tailgate, and he came flat-out of that float and launched backwards – into the water. It scared the bejesus out of him. He never charged off the float after that.'

These stories would, no doubt, anger some readers, but it's all too easy to judge the past. Different times, different ways. Listening to Bernie talk about them is also different. He's a storyteller, a yarn-spinner from the bush, a breed that has captured imaginations for generations, from horseback to campfires, shearing sheds to fence posts. Are they a dying breed? Not yet, but the image of a boot being placed on the bottom rail, arms crossed over the top rail, and eyes looking out over the country and the weather as much as they do the audience isn't as common as it once was. And that's why listening to Bernie on the verandah is a rich experience. He's smiling, and he winks when he says he rode most of Jimmy's very best horses, 'But don't worry, Jimmy wasn't there when I did.' One of the roles of the author is to push and prod the subject, but right now Bernie is so happy yarn-spinning that it's best to do as he has done with horses over the years: give him his head, let him go.

'I used to drive this old blue truck around to get sawdust at a timber mill. Never mind I didn't have my licence. And there were these boys there, and they were ripping up mounds on their motorbikes, and we get into this boy argument: Is a motorbike faster than a horse? There was this party coming up, so I was thinking I'd go across to this party. It was a twenty-first or something. It would take about half an hour to drive there by the road, but about the same time to ride on a horse through the paddocks, down through gullies and creeks, some pretty steep country. And there was this horse, Sally, at Jimmy's; she was a proper fancy expensive old racehorse that was being trained up for campdrafting. And of course, I'm not allowed to ride this horse, so I took her across to the party. This argument starts up again, and it comes down to bragging rights, a race between a motorbike and the horse. *Shakeshaft what are you thinking?* Well, obviously I wasn't thinking at all. The race wasn't far. It was over a few big things, though, bumps and tracks and gullies. I knew if I got in front of the motorbike rider, he wouldn't be able to get past me. I was just blocking him, really. I was rat-shit cunning. Anyway, I won the race, and I was a legend and drinking there until who knows what time. But it was late. And Jimmy's coming home the next day. So, I get back on the horse. The boys at the party told me a couple of weeks later that they didn't know how I got home, coz they reckoned I was as drunk as ten men. Apparently, I put the saddle on back to front. I don't know how many gates I had to go through, how many crossings. I have no recollection of it. But I remember waking up the next morning. You know, it was a really early start with all the horses to look after in the stables. I didn't even make it into my caravan. Fell asleep outside somewhere. So, I wake up, and then the slow-motion panic: "Where did I leave the horse? Fuck, where's the horse!" At Jimmy's, there was this big beautiful manicured rose garden, a big circular driveway around it, and here's this horse standing in the middle of the garden. She's eaten some of the roses, and the saddle is hanging on sideways for dear life. Talk about panic. I got twenty horses in the stables to look after, Jimmy's gonna be back and Ray's gonna be up soon, and I gotta try to disguise what's happened. The grass has divots in it! I'm scrambling, mucking stables, getting horses out, the works. Then I start thinking: "I went through two different properties on the way home. How'd you go with shutting the gates, boy?" Panic. Just panic. Anyway, Jimmy gets there. He must have known, but he never said nothing. Christ, how much thin ice have I skated on, but never gone through?'

If only the question could be asked to Jimmy. But he died in 2016, and was working cattle right to the end. Those who knew him in his final years remember, among many things, a man with colourful neck scarves who used an artificial speech-aid after he underwent surgery for throat cancer. It was a somewhat ironic contraption for someone so authentic, so self-made.

Jimmy helped make others, too. His actions, and the words that flowed either side of 'boy', heavily influenced a young man who had arrived at Newman Park without a plan. However, after nearly a year Bernie knew exactly where he wanted to go. His days in the south were over, and the north was yelling at him to come and have a crack.

7

It's a warm day, about thirty degrees Celsius. Apparently, there's a chance of rain this afternoon.

Apparently.

The ground in the paddock is hard. Some tussocks of dry grass poke as high as the shin, but more commonly they reach only the ankle; they crunch underfoot.

There are eight boys. Three are walking alongside a digger whose cabin is filled by the cowboy-hatted silhouette of a young farmhand. The others are behind a caged trailer that's hitched to the back of a LandCruiser Troopcarrier – call it a troopy – that Dawso is driving at a crawling pace. It's thankless work 'stick-pickin': bend over, pick up dead branches and twigs, throw them into the trailer or digger's bucket to be taken to large piles that will be burnt later. Yes, thankless work, but it needs to be done before barley or oats can be sown.

It's a week before Christmas. Earlier, in their familiar loose circle at the depot, Dawso asked them what they would each give everyone in the world if they were Santa. 'A skimming stone,' said one. 'A dog,' said another. When one boy suggested 'a hug', there was a chorus of cheerful groans.

As the stick-picking continues, the smallest boy, wearing maroon rugby-league shorts, drives the troopy. He's one of the younger ones here, but he handles the driving easily, giving the impression he first dropped a clutch long before he could see over the dashboard. Another boy, tall and lean, runs, stops, props, and launches a stick in an arc that ends on top of the trailer pile; nothing but net for an imaginary three-point bomb.

The boys and vehicles work their way downwards across a gentle slope. Conversations rise and fall: 'I used to play fullback. So quick. Scored a lot of tries.' 'Ham and pineapple's better than supreme.' 'Will I still get a present from Santa, coz Mum kicked me out of home a few weeks ago?'

The sun is high. Swigs are taken from drink bottles. Sweat and sunscreen sting eyes. But it's good to be out, doing something together. The digger grunts and sends a puff of black smoke into the air. And where's the troopy? A few heads turn to see the white LandCruiser bumping along. No attention is given to the driver; all eyes are on the trailer, where a smiling boy, ginger coils of hair springing off his shoulders, hangs one-handed off the side. He's holding a long stick triumphantly above his head: 'And Hufflepuff wins. What a victory! What a great day!'

The moment passes. Another boy, whose callused hands belie his years, lobs another stick into a pile, and continues his conversation.

'Yeah mate, I'm going to get me a start up north as a jackaroo. Get meself rich.'

The Northern Territory is a staggeringly beautiful place. Kakadu, Uluru, gorges, waterfalls, crocodiles, rainforests, unfathomable sunsets, deserts, Indigenous arts. But, chasing the gloss of tourist brochures isn't the only appeal for the visitor. The

NT is frontier country where time, distance and isolation can mean the middle-of-nowhere is only the beginning. It's also a spiritual place whose myths and mysteries can leap or seep into the imagination and soul; the NT is a place where people might go to find themselves or lose themselves. Bernie, however, was drawn by none of this. He just wanted to 'ride horses and be wild and crazy'.

Jimmy Matthews had greatly influenced Bernie's decision to move on, again. While at Newman Park, Bernie had listened intently to his boss's stories about life on the enormous cattle stations, many of which were more than a million acres, up north. He knew he had to go and experience the existence for himself. He just had to. Jimmy agreed, and it took just a phone call to launch Bernie on the next phase of his development. A job was arranged at Newcastle Waters, a vast station midway between Darwin and Alice Springs; media tycoon Kerry Packer partly owned it.

Bernie would join a stock camp as a ringer and spend most of his time mustering. It was towards the end of the state, territory and federal governments' Brucellosis and Tuberculosis Eradication Campaign, in which stock were tested and those that were infected were shot. This wasn't a life for the soft or pampered. Yet, boys and young men, often with little or no experience, came from all walks of life from across Australia and overseas to be hurled into the deep end, or more likely, the dust. Over the years, work practices had caused controversy, and when Bernie headed up, the memories of a tragedy in Western Australia's Kimberley region still echoed across the station industry. In late 1986, inexperienced teenage jackaroos James Annetts and Simon Amos went missing. Four months later, their bodies were found away from their bogged four-wheel drive, in the Great Sandy Desert. A coroner determined James died of dehydration, and Simon of a rifle wound. They had walked eighteen kilometres in search of help.

With little more than a swag and a notebook that Jimmy had given him, Bernie launched into his next chapter by taking a bus from Melbourne, and after too much 'going and going and going' he realised, for the first time in his life, how big Australia truly is. Finally, he arrived in Elliott, a dot on the map close to Newcastle Waters.

'I couldn't believe it,' says Bernie, leaning forward on his verandah chair. 'Some of the countrymen were living in these tiny little tin sheds, and the pub had Aboriginals on one side and whites on the other. It was pretty raw. I couldn't take it all in straightaway.

'At Newcastle Waters, workers were split into crews to work in stock camps. Most were just young fellas like myself. Mostly, the higher maintenance kids stayed closer to the homestead, whereas the others went to the outstations and camped in swags. It was worked out pretty quick that I'd go with an outstation mob, so they put me on a plane and flew me out to Humbert River Station south-west of Katherine. There was just a small crew, seven, eight or nine of us. Mustering nearly all the time. Wet and dry. Cows, calves, bullocks.

'Right from the start, Jimmy Matthews' advice was ringing in my ears. So many things he told me. When it came to horses, he, and Rootsy too, taught me how to survive in the Territory. I'll never forget when Jimmy said before I left:

'"Boy, when they ask: 'Can you ride?' What are you gonna say?'

'"Yeah, I can ride."

'"No. If you say you can ride you're going to ride every hoorang in the Territory. Tell them you can sit on a quiet pony if someone can catch it for you."

'And that was my first line when the head stockman came out drafting horses. I got these three or four old gold horses, coz I couldn't really ride, could I? Anyway, I reckon I put all of Jimmy's wisdom to good use. He'd told me I'd get a plant of about fifteen horses. Different stations have different horses, and when you go somewhere new you get drafted new horses. The horse-breaker is always out in front of you getting them ready. "Do you know what a greenbroke is, boy?" I had no idea. They were young horses that'd had a breaker do some rough Territory-style stuff on 'em. "Boy, you might be able to sit on them with a saddle, maybe not, but you're not going to have good steering or brakes, and they're going to buck." I was excited by that, but Jimmy screwed my head on tighter. "You're going to have to know each horse in your plant. Take the notebook that I gave you. Write all your horses down. Don't worry about names, just describe your horses. The way they look, their mannerisms, whatever will help you remember them. Coz when they run out a hundred-odd horses and you've gotta pull your lot out to the side, you've gotta know them."

'He also told me about jumping horses on and off trucks. Coz, when you're out in the sticks and they're moving the horses around from camp to camp, there are times when there isn't anything nice and proper to back the truck up to. No loading ramps. So, you find a bit of a slope if you can, or you could be looking at a three-foot drop from a ledge if there's nothing better around. And you reckon jumping off can be hard? Jumping on is another thing altogether. Lead the horse up, "Come on, mate, up you go." It can be pretty scary. I saw some awful busters. And you know what the alternative is? You've been in the saddle for twelve hours, and you gotta ride for another two to take the horse to the camp. Anyway, I was prepared coz Jimmy said: "Start looking at the horses, boy.

Anyone with scars on its hind legs isn't going to be a good jumper, coz he's had a jump, missed it, taken the skin off or fallen over backwards. On the days you know you're jumping, take an old horse who knows how to do it. Write it down, boy. Write it down."'

Bernie pauses and shakes his head, slightly. 'Jimmy Matthews. A lot of memories there.' The words are soft, though not whispered. A highly respectful tone. Bernie stands up and walks over to the verandah door. He lights a cigarette and looks out at Girl and Lou, who have barely moved all morning. Girl, 'the blind old senior citizen', feels her boss's presence and pushes herself up, her hips last to rise. She dawdles over, and nudges against Bernie's leg, then returns to lie in sunlight on the grass. Bernie continues speaking softly: 'Senior citizen, all right.' Then he returns to his chair.

'I was lucky. What I learnt from Jimmy and Paul Roots, I use with the BackTrack boys today. You know, making notes, knowing your dog. But we'll get to that, won't we? Anyway, Jimmy. Christ, what didn't I learn? "Get yourself a good saddle, boy. Look for cracks in the girth straps. Use two saddle cloths on a horse; its back won't go red raw and you might be able to ride the horse two days in a row." I was the only dopey bastard who knew all of that.

'And the whips. "Make sure you can crack the whip beside the horse before you run, boy. Don't wait to try it when you're in with the cattle. If the truck is leaving at five o'clock, you get up at three o'clock and take the buck out of your horse while everyone else is still asleep." So, day to day I'd get up before the other boys were out of their swags, and I'd be lunging my horse in the round-yards; take the pig root, the kick, the buck all out of him. Then, I'd put him in a big yard and wop it up him a little bit, crack the whip, see what he would do; even if he was bucking, I'd get to know that. I knew all my horses individually. Jimmy taught me good and proper about everything. He was all about getting the detail right. "Where are you going the next day? How far are you going?" "Where's the sun when you get up?" "Pay attention to the trees. The big ones, the whipstick ones, coz that sort of stuff you'll need to know when you're coming home. If you get lost, it's up to you to get unlost. Pay close attention." All that sort of stuff, he taught me.

'I put in all the time. Showed I could stick a horse pretty well; I was no Paul Roots, but even if the horse chucked me I've still got the reins: *"Don't let go of the reins."* I showed I could follow instructions, I could fence, drive the truck, if the cook got hung up I could cook for camp. Jimmy and Paul taught me to be very humble about it all. There were others wanting to fight and big-note; I knew not to big-note. Just do what I had to do.

'I still look back and think: "How the hell did we survive out there? We were working in different spots all the time. I remember driving from Top Springs to out on the West Australian border, and we were driving and driving for hours and we didn't even see a tree; then you go up to Humbert River and you're on the edge of crocodile country where you have these hills that are too big to ride your horse over – there'll be five or six of them running off in different directions – and if you get down into one of those valleys or gorges between them it's easy to get lost. And I did get lost a few times; I'm pretty sure everyone did. And that's where all those lessons from Jimmy Matthews were tattooed into my brain. Yeah, how did we survive, all right. The kids nowadays wear helmets and they've all got CamelBaks water bottles and radios. There'd be days when we'd pull up at lunchtime and my tongue was swollen from dehydration and I couldn't even smoke or talk. Hit the water bag! Ride all day in forty-plus, sometimes fifty, degrees. Get paid bugger all. Two hundred and forty-six bucks a week. Gross. Once a month with a cheque. I've still got some of the pay slips. The notion of the life was a lot more exciting than the reality of it.'

There was a perception, and not by any means an unfounded one, that the life of the Territory ringer had a touch of the American wild west. Among the other youngsters on Newcastle Waters at the same time as Bernie was the eldest son of high-profile advertising businessman John Singleton. Nowadays, Jack Singleton is also in advertising and media; rewind the clock to station life about thirty years ago, and the products that were most endorsed were those individuals who could handle themselves well. 'We were absolutely thrown in the deep end,' said Jack, laughing, in a phone interview. 'You go through an interesting period of your life. I remember we all went in the bull ride at a rodeo. Everyone got blind drunk because we were all shitting ourselves about our rides. And the bloke who was most drunk was the one who lasted the full eight seconds. The fights at the Elliott pub? Yeah, they happened. I got tapped on the shoulder once by a mate:

"Come on, we're going outside for a fight."

"What, me and you?"

"No, we're fighting these two other blokes."

'I don't remember who won or lost, but we all came in as mates after that. It wasn't Marquess of Queensberry, but you'd hold up your fists and get on with it, bare-knuckle boxing style. When you were working, there was both self-sufficiency and dependency on the mates you made. I didn't know a soul when I went up there. Such a different world. The skill of the Aboriginals. You're out a long way from anywhere and need a drink, and one of the blokes I really remember, he'd say: "Jack, you're thirsty," and he'd dig a hole in the ground and there'd be water there. Gee whiz, everyone grew up very quickly. Not that we all had a trouble-free existence, but I can certainly look back now and think: "Because I rode that horse or I was in the round-yard with that wild bull, I can cope with the day-to-day challenges.'"

Work all day under big skies, get your hands dirty, show you're tough enough to cop whatever comes both on and off the station. Spin words among the crackles of a campfire, sleep under the stars, get up before sunrise and do it all again. Day in, day out, for weeks at a time. Earn your dollar and your right to be a man. That was the notion. But, as Jack could attest to, it could come at a cost. His time in the Territory ended abruptly after he tumbled from his horse in a collision with a charging bull. He hurt his shoulder so badly he was flown out for treatment – and in search of another lifestyle – by the Royal Flying Doctor Service.

As he sits smoking in his verandah chair, Bernie talks of so many accidents and deaths 'up north over the years' that 'it's ridiculous'. Kids who shouldn't have been there. Bosses who should have known better. Bernie crossed paths with both. In his camps, most of which were dry (alcohol-free), and at others there was a limit of no more than two cans of beer per night, he became friends with 'good guys', but there was also the 'riff-raff wrestling and fighting'. He acknowledges he 'might've had two or three fights'; enough for people to realise he was one not to be messed with. These altercations untethered his own wildness, but as time passed he realised thrown punches weren't the most painful displays of human behaviour he experienced. Indeed, the very worst behaviours influenced him in ways that, like the death of the street boy in Calcutta, would have a lifelong influence on his attitudes and his work.

'I know now, the best thing I did was sidling up to the countrymen pretty quick coz they knew what they were doing.

They knew the horses, the paddocks. But the thing is, us white fellas weren't meant to talk to them. They even had to eat separately, and they had to sit in the back of the truck even if there were seats in the front. But, if I had to drive the truck somewhere, I'd pull up as soon as we got out of sight, around the corner or something, and then it was: "Hey guys, more comfy in here." They'd get in, we'd put a Slim Dusty tape on and away we'd go. I started eating with them too. Those actions can cause a lot of grief, but I still know the difference between right and wrong.

'When we were out there in those huge paddocks there'd be about ten of us, and we'd stay within eyesight of each other; if you didn't see anyone for ten minutes it was time to start getting a bit nervous. We'd start pushing the stock along, and the choppers would come about lunchtime and we'd start working with them. Big mobs of cattle, often in the thousands, and most of the time us white fellas didn't really know where we were going, but the countrymen did. I remember sitting one day with the white fellas and some of them were saying: "Look at the lazy coon riding over that hill to go and have a sleep." The racism was extraordinary, particularly from these kids coming out of cities. And these countrymen were riding in the worst gear; one fella used to ride in thongs, and some of them only had one stirrup iron, but they could stick any horse. The countrymen got all greenbrokes. Anyhow, they knew their stuff. There'd be us white fellas creeping around the paddock so that nobody gets lost, really, and we're talking about what wonderful cowboys we are, and then when the choppers start coming in and we've collected a tiny mob, here comes so-and-so over a hill and he's got a huge mob, hundreds on his own. Then someone else comes over a hill and he's probably got the same number. All of a sudden, we got a thousand or more head, and us white fellas might have contributed sixty! I got no idea if they were on the same pay as us, but they deserved more.

'Another time, there was a new set of yards that had been built at this place out near the WA border, and we were as good as lost. We had a big mob, in the thousands, of cows and calves and were trying to push them with just one motorbike and the rest were horses. The calves were just dropping back, couldn't keep up – drop off, drop off, drop off – they were often left to make it on their own. If we could, we picked them up and carried them on the front of our saddles, but we couldn't get them all. Every couple of hours a plane would fly over and then in a line to the yards where we had to go. But we had no idea; spent most of our energy just trying to stay on our horses. It's getting pretty serious. The sun's going down, everybody's fucked – horses, us, the cows are still trying to go back to their calves – and we just can't find these yards. Everyone needs water, and the plane's not coming back, and these brahmans are getting cranky. Eventually I ride over to one of the countrymen and asked him:

'"You got any idea where these yards are, boss?"

'"Oh yeah, just a little bit over that way."

'"How do you know that?"

'"We been watching the kangaroo tracks; they come in this way in the morning and go out that way in the afternoon. And emu, he just went through a little bit further. It's near water, that's where the yards are."

'Nobody took the time to ask them.

'Follow the animal tracks! The head stockman didn't want to believe me when I told him. Of course, the yards turned out to be where the countrymen thought they'd be. We nearly lost the whole mob by not asking them. How stupid! Another lesson for me. The more I paid attention to the countrymen, the more I was embarrassed to be a white fella out there.

'About halfway through the season I started to get a bit disillusioned. The treatment of countrymen; dying calves; not showing guys how to get horses onto trucks. I'd seen a few accidents, too – serious ones, head injuries. I was thinking: "Someone could die out here." By that stage, I'd hooked up with a horse-breaker. I really liked him. A wiry little thing out of Queensland: sandy kinda hair; proper old bushman look; would have been about thirty. He had this presence around horses, like Rootsy did. You'd see him after three hours with a new horse and he'd be standing on their back. I just knew I had to hang around him as much as I could. So, I'd be helping him after hours, and he'd come out riding with us on musters, and we'd be talking all the time. He told me he was putting a team together for a big droving job, all on horseback, in Queensland. I said: "I'm in!" It was a couple of months away. By that time, I'd been mustering for about six months. So, I put my resignation in. And then, I had the buster. That changed everything in a hurry.'

A dog barks from behind the homestead. This time it's not Gibson. 'Hey Billy, sit down.' There is silence. Just for a moment.

'Yeah, a bad buster,' continues Bernie. 'I was on a day off, but I was still riding anyway coz there was a campdraft coming up. I'd done a couple of them and was keen to do more. This bullock comes wheeling out of the bush, and I was after him flat; we were seriously travelling. The beast is just a couple of metres ahead of me, and then he just collapses. Bang over some fencing wire no-one could see in the long grass. A split-second later I'm down too. Bullock, horse, man, wire, dust and blood. A big slide, and I'm still sitting in the saddle, and the horse is on top of my right leg. When I got up, I knew I was in trouble. Felt like a proper good corked thigh. I think they might've had to put the horse down as well; we were all busted. We were in a bush-blocks camp and had a couple of weeks to go before we were back at the homestead at Humbert River. My leg just got bigger and bigger. I tried putting Dencorub on it, but that didn't help. I couldn't even get on a horse, so they put me in driving the truck, but I couldn't take my foot off the accelerator. I couldn't bend my leg at all; it was locked solid. I worked out a way to push a stick down on the accelerator and still use my good leg to do the brake and clutch. Talk about pain. I kept telling my boss: "This isn't good." Eventually, I got sent back to Humbert River and then to the nurse at Newcastle Waters. This was over about two weeks. Couldn't walk by that stage.'

Billy barks again. Bernie turns his head and looks in the general direction of where all his dogs, bar Girl and Lou, are tied up. 'I'm warning you, Billy.' Then he rubs his thigh.

'I got back to Newcastle Waters. They looked at me, and decided to send me to the closest hospital at Tennant Creek two hundred and fifty kilometres away. But that was no easy job. After dinner one of the fellas took me to the station mailbox on the main road; it was a good way away from the homestead, dozens of k's, I think. Then they left me there, coz the next bus didn't come through until early in the morning, maybe two o'clock, and no-one would've wanted to drop me out at that time. I got there and just waited. The bus came and they had to rearrange the seating coz there were only window seats left, and with my leg I couldn't get into them. I finally got to the hospital and saw the local doctor. He examined me and reckoned I was right to get back to work. I thought: "You're fuckin' kiddin'." But nah. So, back to Newcastle

Waters. Got tipped off the bus in the middle of the night and waited until someone came out to do the mail run in the morning.

'I wasn't sure how I was meant to do anything. As it turned out, I'd met some nurses in Tennant Creek, and they must've been a bit worried; any idiot could see there was something seriously wrong with my leg. These nurses must've made a complaint to someone at the hospital, so there was a note waiting for me in the Newcastle Waters mailbox. It said another doctor wanted to look at me back at Tennant Creek, and a ticket had been booked for me on the next bus. So, I sat and waited. I'd got to Newcastle Waters at about midnight, then got back on another bus at two am. And I was hurting; even a gutful of rum wasn't pulling up the pain.

'So, back to hospital, and this time a specialist who has come in from Alice Springs looks at me: "This is no good." They flew me to Alice Springs immediately. Five hundred k's on a Royal Flying Doctor plane. They operated on me that afternoon, took a pint-and-a-half of blood out of my leg. The injury had started calcifying. I'd snapped my anterior cruciate ligament in my right knee. We're close to three weeks after the accident by now.

'Then I was in a backpackers' joint in Alice Springs for, I don't know how long. Three weeks, a month. It wasn't a bad time. By then I'd got to know some of the nurses. Think about it: a good-looking ringer, new guy in town, funny, entertaining … Then I got the all-clear to go back to work, but I'd resigned, so I was in a bit of a pickle. I got put back in a stock camp at Newcastle Waters. Back in a swag. Me and me matchstick leg. I should never have gone back.'

The knee gives Bernie trouble from time to time, but the aches and pains are 'manageable'. As he continues talking, he reveals another injury that marks his memory like a blink-and-you-miss-it town on a road trip. After returning to work he was caught in 'no-man's land' with a 'wound-up' bullock in a yard. Safety was the top rail of a fence about three metres away. He ran for it and stumbled. The bullock smashed into him and launched him over a gate. He broke two ribs, and his face 'looked as though it had been a few rounds with Muhammad Ali' – but never mind, incidents like that were 'a weekly occurrence out there'. Indeed, he thinks he remembers it only because he's digging deep to reconstruct a timeline that 'gets a bit messy about now'.

'So, I'm back on the station at Newcastle Waters,' says Bernie. 'And I get this phone call from England: "You're going to be a father." It was a nurse I'd had a fling with in Alice Springs. Jayne. She'd gone overseas with her best friend. Shock! I don't know how I pieced that into my life's equation. Well, I didn't. She was this smart, beautiful thing, hippy, an environmentalist, and I was a wild, fighting, horse-riding, rum-drinking Territory ringer. Two opposite worlds.

'Jayne came back to Australia, and I met her and her friend at a campdraft at Daly Waters. She was already getting morning sickness. And she was adamant she was going to have the baby. I wasn't sure about it, but if she was going to be a mother, how could I not be around to be the father?

'Up until then I'd been counting down the days until I went droving with the horse-breaker. Then, just to throw in another inswinger, I got kicked on the side of my crook knee by this little heifer. It wasn't much – you could get a hundred of them in a day – but this one was in the wrong spot. It dropped me, and I was screaming. I was taken back to the homestead in the back of a ute, bouncing round everywhere. The nurse gave me a big shot of morphine – "Oh, thank you!" – and I'm off with the Flying

Doctor to Alice Springs, with all my gear coz there's no coming back this time. You should have seen the X-ray. A spiral fracture right up my femur. So, more surgery.'

And that's the way Bernie finished his time as a ringer. He'd arrived in the Northern Territory chasing adventure; any trepidation had been sheltered beneath his enthusiasm, and the knowledge and wisdoms passed down by men who'd travelled many more miles than he had. But now, as he looked ahead, understanding what it meant to be a father and a partner wasn't as simple as knowing how a greenbroke behaved.

8

Sparks are flying in the welding shed. Two boys are cleaning horseshoes with angle grinders, while a third has just finished tidying up a join on a dog cage. He pushes his protective visor back then meanders around some benches and arrives outside. He puts a hand up to shield his eyes from the sunlight, and a rolled-up sleeve on his oversized protective jacket slides back towards his elbow. He then flails his arms as though he's one of those inflatable stick figures that bend and floss at used-car yards. He stops and notices something a few metres away. He walks over and starts jumping up and down on metal pipes that lie on the ground. Clang, clang, clang, clang, clang ...

'Joe, get off there,' says youth worker Matt Pilkington. Matt's voice is firm, but seemingly not firm enough. Matt repeats his request ... and again.

Joe finally does what he's told. Then he goes and tries to start a mini quadbike near some rusting machine parts and fencing wire. He kicks and kicks and kicks, but who knows how long the bike has been dormant.

Joe pushes the quadbike forward a few metres, then sits on it and starts rocking it. Another boy comes over and puts a hand on Joe's shoulder. He is tall, lean and freckled. Above all, he has the respect of his peers.

'What happens if that falls over on you?' he asks Joe.

Joe shrugs his shoulders, dismounts and walks away. A few other boys push the quadbike back to its usual place. Meanwhile, Joe is trying to balance on an old piece of 4x2 timber that has some nails driven into it.

'Joe! Come on!' Matt says.

Joe turns and looks at Matt as though he has only noticed him for the first time. He slides his visor over his face, walks back to the shed, and resumes welding.

Matt shakes his head and smiles wryly.

Later, Joe goes out again and flicks a pebble across the depot car park, with a broken fishing rod.

Here, every day has its surprises.

James Shakeshaft was born at the John Hunter Hospital in Newcastle on 25 April 1991. Anzac Day. What better nickname for the boy than Digger? And what an excuse in the years ahead for Bernie to celebrate by playing two-up with his closest mate, Dusty. Nowadays, Bernie might joke about the timing of the birth, but this belies the 'turmoil' he and Jayne experienced after they first told their families that Jayne was pregnant. 'Everything went into meltdown,' says Bernie. 'The shame of a child out of wedlock for Catholics. I can't remember the finer details, but there was a bit of a family upset.'

Bernie also had a 'ding-dong' with Jayne's mother, and he recalls being told: 'There's no way you're having a baby with my daughter.' All the friction only made the parents-to-be defiant, and despite the prospect of 'having a baby before having a relationship',

Bernie adopted a 'stuff-you-all' attitude. His and Jayne's position was made worse by the pressure of finding somewhere to live. They left the Northern Territory and initially stayed at Bernie's parents' home; at the time Denise and Joe were away on holidays and coming to terms with Bernie's news. Denise had even struggled to tell Bernie's youngest brother, Mark, who was still at school, that he was going to be an uncle.

After staying just a few weeks in Sydney, Bernie and Jayne moved to Stroud, a small bushland town seventy-five kilometres north of Newcastle. Jayne's mother, Anne, owned a house there, and although she had misgivings about Bernie, she opened her doors to a young couple who had nowhere else to go. At the time, though, Anne was living in Tennant Creek.

For the first few months money was scarce because Bernie, recovering from his broken leg, was unable to work. When he finally could, he picked up casual jobs, including fencing and cutting oyster stakes, until eventually he was offered a full-time position at the new business venture of two of Australia's most famous television stars. Brothers Mike and Mal Leyland enthralled viewers with their unconventional travel programs that became so much part of Australian culture in the 1970s and 80s that their opening title ditty is still remembered by people today: 'Ask the Leyland brotherrrrrrrrrrs.' In late 1990 they established Leyland Brothers World, a theme park on the Pacific Highway, about an hour's drive from Stroud. It included amusement rides, a museum and a bush camp for school students. However, its centrepiece was a large kitschy replica of Uluru that caught the eye of many passers-by.

'Bloody enormous, it was,' laughs Bernie. 'In its day the park was big, people everywhere. I used to ride an old farm bike to get there; it wasn't far as the crow flies. On the back roads, stay off the highway. Mike and Mal were just like they were on TV: "What do you think, Mike?" "I'm not sure, Mal." That's how they talked to people.

'My job was to drive their truck on their nature circuit. They had an old Blitz wagon with a trailer. I had to conduct the tour as well, through a microphone: "And look, that's a koala and that's a kangaroo." We had to go through a swamp area, and with a crash box I was double-clutching, triple-clutching, revving, and boy was it difficult to stop! I couldn't believe we didn't have any accidents.

'Then all of a sudden, da-da-da-daaaah, Jayne and I, we've got a baby. It was an exciting time, but there was also some "What the hell?" mixed in with that. We'd had no practice at this baby thing. Not much practice at the relationship thing, either. Living in Stroud, working for the Leyland brothers. What had my life become?

'But, I loved fatherhood from day one. Did that on my ear. Always a hands-on dad with James. Changing nappies. It was easy. I think it was part of me, really. When I look at it now, parenthood reflected a lot of my life. If you look at what I've done many times, was I ready? Shit no. But could I stick it? For sure. And could I make it work? That's what I had to do, that's what I did.

'James coming along made the connection come back with Mum and Dad, too, after all the hoo-ha of the pregnancy. They had a grandchild. We all had to take a different position. The magical power of a baby. We all worked it out in our ways.'

Reflecting from her Sydney home, Denise acknowledged the turbulent time with a telling economy of words: 'Bernie and Jayne were very young. Very, very young.' She and Joe visited Stroud regularly and played a strong role in the development of their grandson. So too did Maree Shakeshaft, whose support for Bernie and Jayne had never wavered. She recalled: 'When James was born, I had this feeling of, "Oh my goodness!" Seeing him for the first time, there was a really strong feeling of, "He's mine, he's part of my family."'

All the while, Bernie and Jayne tried to build a relationship. Inevitably they had their times of 'toughing it out', but they both persevered and were determined to make it work. And work was a focal part. Double-clutching and guiding tourists were never going to be enough to provide for a family with growing needs, so Bernie started looking beyond the artificial red rock on one of Australia's busiest roads. What he found was a job that, if fate was real, most certainly played a hand in: with a nod and a handshake Bernie and Jayne were suddenly 'parents' to more than one child.

9

The boy sits on the armrest of a sofa and puts his back against the door that's ajar in the smoko room. He wears a jacket, cargo work pants, tan boots and a cap. He is strongly built. He holds an unlit cigarette between his right index and second fingers. A smoker's grip, but right now it seems more like he is gaining strength from a security blanket. His head is down, his face is half in sunlight, half in shadow. He says nothing, plays no role in the morning circle other than being there.

Bernie steers conversation around the circle of seven boys and many more staff:

'Rate the start of your day out of ten. Ten for off-the-chart fantastic, one for low-as-you-can-go.'

'Six.' 'Five.' 'Eight.' 'Seven.'

The numbers lead to the boy at the door.

Nothing. Just a vacant expression, eyes to the floor. The heater on the other side of the room hums.

A discussion begins about what it's like to have a 'shit day'. Dawso says he needs space and might try to go for a run. Some of the boys say they like listening to music, or playing with their dogs, or finding mates to hang with.

Energy is high, banter is rich. The meeting comes to an end after half an hour, and everyone trails out. The boy follows the others. His head remains low.

Ike, a staff member who walked a rocky adolescence, stays behind and talks to Bernie about the brooding boy:

'He was a one at the start of the previous day as well. But I put him out on a work gang with some of his friends and he came back a six or a seven. I could've told him to sweep the shed, but that wouldn't have done him any good.'

Bernie nods but doesn't speak. He just watches from the doorway. Watches the boy join a group that's chatting near the welding shed. It's only then that the boy lifts his head and talks. Bernie nods again. Silently.

House parenting. Bernie had never heard of such work, but if it offered good money and free rent, why not try it? The De La Salle Brothers had a farm near Tarago, a short drive from Goulburn in the southern tablelands of New South Wales. Wool-growing country. But the only fibres Bernie and Jayne needed to pay attention to were ones of moral making. They accepted jobs caring for a small group of troubled boys, 'busted ones' carrying horrific mental scars from 'fucked-up' childhoods. It was a substantial, if not dramatic, change for someone who had no professional experience or formal qualifications in any type of welfare field. Considering his own broad streak of careless abandon, was Bernie the right type of person to protect and nurture such children? He relished fatherhood, but could caring for others elicit the same sense of responsibility and behaviours that having James did? Until he began the job, he honestly didn't know. But in his past, melded in with street races, flung fists, skolled rum and all other moments in which preservation of self (and sometimes others) was neglected, there were those many times when empathy, sensitivity and a spirited belief in social justice ruled who he was and what he did.

'We've got this very complex character, but I don't think he ever lost that need to reach out to others,' said Denise Shakeshaft. 'I remember when Paul [Bernie's second-youngest brother] won a scholarship to a new school. He was a very quiet kid, a very gentle boy. A teacher recognised he needed a little bit of extra guidance, being a new boy. Paul used to talk about this teacher quite a bit. Then this teacher went out and committed suicide; he'd had a very bad accident years earlier that had affected him. Paul came home from school, and he was absolutely shattered, and he withdrew into himself. I told Bernie I was worried about him – Bernie had finished school by this stage – and he said: "Just leave him to me, Mum." Then he borrowed our car and took Paul to the beach, and they just walked from one end to the other and talked.'

Bernie just had a way about him. Connecting, understanding, feeling. Perhaps he was the perfect type to be a house parent? Again, he didn't know. But he says there was one certainty: 'I didn't ever sit down early in my life and think: "What am I going to be?" I think I had sharp intense blocks that came where I went: "Shit yeah, I'm doing that." Like listening to Jimmy Matthews and thinking: "I'm going to the Territory!" Nothing early on was ever planned out; I'd just get an idea and if I felt like there was enough drive in it, I'd go and do it. From getting in the car and going to the Snowy Mountains or trying teachers' college. If I didn't like it, well, I didn't continue. I certainly never went: "I'm going to be a youth worker." But a theme did develop after I left school, maybe when I was with Paul and Annette Roots, when I started thinking: "If I'm going to do something, whatever it is, I'm going to be really good at it.'"

So, Bernie launched into his new job with questions still to be asked, but not one was about his commitment.

'It was a big farm, commercially run. We were put with the boys in a house, a kit-home type of thing on a hill. Four bedrooms and a granny flat on the end. The brothers lived higher up in a very similar house, and the school for the kids was another of these buildings a few hundred metres away. I think the old teacher was a German fella. They had a few sheds, bits of machinery, motorbikes, horses. There was some pretty steep country, lots of little tracks, and a billy-goat track to get into the place. Must have been about ten gates here and there.

'Jayne and I rolled up on our first day, and the brothers were giving us all sorts of instructions. One of the things they said was: "The boys will call you 'Mum' and 'Dad'." We both hit the uncomfortable button pretty quickly on that one. When we met the kids, they'd obviously been briefed, and the "Mum" and "Dad" thing started; I was looking for a hole to crawl into. So, we sat the boys down and said: "Look, maybe while the brothers are around you can carry on like that, but when they're not here don't call us 'Mum' and 'Dad'. You got a mum, you got a dad; you mightn't know them, or it mightn't have worked out with them, but we're not your mum and dad. We're just some sensible people giving you a hand. So, my name is Bernie, this is Jayne, and this is James."

'These boys weren't little tackers, but they weren't old teenagers, either. They were late primary school, early high school. My job, with Jayne, was to look after them, mostly out of school hours.

In the mornings and evenings, we'd cook meals with them, and we'd get them up and going, and ready for bed at the other end of the day, and then we'd do stuff with them on the weekends. They had some pretty scary stories. Just so sad and scary. Sexual abuse, whatever. You'd hear them, and then you'd look down at your own little kid and think: "How the hell do you get from that innocence to where these kids are?" Violent, going to jail. What happens? I don't know, maybe it was those kids who started teaching me about only looking ten per cent behind you, or ten per cent into your past. It started to become a very personal choice for me not to go back there too much. It's good to know, but you know what? In general terms I didn't want us to get bogged down in it. "So, boys, let's go and ride some horses, or motorbikes or do some spotlighting." Do something useful and have meaningful conversations about it.'

Bernie, who pauses often while speaking, takes a longer than usual break. Ten, twelve seconds …

He looks nowhere specifically, apart from into his own thoughts.

'It was the serious start of my youth work, I reckon. And I was good at it. Four boys, five. I used to take them out chasing rabbits. Kids love spotlighting. Doesn't dent the population, but it dents a few cars. For the first few times, I'd just let them jump off the ute and chase the rabbits, coz you can't catch them when you're just chasing them. So, this went on, and these boys were full of hot air about who was going to catch a rabbit and smash it and kill it; they were having punch-ups over who was going to kill the first rabbit. One night I felt it was the right time: "We'll do it a bit different tonight, boys. We'll sneak out and chase 'em back towards the light." Coz if you do it that way, you can catch 'em easier. Before you know it, they'd caught this rabbit that they said they were going to smash and bash. So, I made them stand in this circle – I'll never forget this night – and I said to them: "Don't drop it." But of course, it's a wild animal that they've just caught, and it has got teeth and claws. It's ripping, biting, shredding these boys and their hands are covered in blood and I'm telling them: "Don't you drop that rabbit." But they didn't even know how to hold it; if you get it with the flank it can't get you with anything. So, I grab it. "Righto," I said. "Where did we get up to? Who's gonna kill this fuckin' rabbit?"

'They couldn't do it. None of them.

'And I said: "You guys were punching on last week about how you were gonna do it, stomp on its head, use a bar, so here's a hammer, here's a rock, who's going to do it?" They couldn't, and they were all in tears. And they let the rabbit go. Then we talked about it. What it meant to kill an animal. Later on, we did kill some. But I taught them to do it the right way. With respect. I taught them how to skin the rabbits too. I reckon everyone who eats meat should at some stage kill something. They need to understand the whole process. Everyone should look after an animal at some stage too. Makes them better people.

'It was a learning time. Not only for the kids, but me and Jayne too. Learning to be parents, learning to deal with these wild boys, coz they used to have some wipe-outs, you know. I guess the brothers were in charge of the rocks through windows, that sort of stuff. They were pretty strict. Didn't tolerate a lot of swearing, but they were all right; they used to come down and have a wine with us. There were a couple of good ones and a couple of cranky ones. Good fellas. Anyhow, all that wild stuff with the kids never kinda worried me. Never frightened by it.

In those days we were highly conscious of James – he took his first steps while we were there – but, and here's something really interesting, he was like a pup with those kids. He was a circuit breaker. They were extraordinary with James. I don't know. Something to do with trust, maybe? They included him. There was that sense of belonging.

'I wish I knew then, what I know now.

'I'd be lying if I said I remember the exact details, but we were in this burnt-out patch one day. I was doing whatever I was, around firewood it might have been, and I looked up and there was this brown snake going right towards James, about ten metres away. I properly killed it, [but] it wasn't before one of the kids walked between James and the snake. Pure protective instinct.

'That same bloke dropped into the BackTrack depot a couple of years ago just to say g'day. I was looking at him thinking: "I know that walk." Then it came to me: Scott. I've got his contact here somewhere. I reckon he might be worth talking to for the book. Tell you a story or two.'

—

The town is small. Its features are similar to other places in the backblocks: the silo, tallest construction for miles around; the pubs with first-floor verandahs prettied by iron lace; the wide main street with rear-to-kerb angled parking; the war memorial honour roll with surnames that have never left the district … This town is where Scott lives. After passing through the outskirts it took me only a few turns to reach a small red-brick home. A woman, with a young child propped on her hip, was waiting near the front gate. Beside her stood a man, slight, sinewy, bald, and with a goatee beard. He wore blue tracksuit pants and a black T-shirt that opened the imagination to tattoos that poked above the neckline.

Scott smiled and shook my hand strongly. 'Good to meet you. Come in.'

We walked through his house, passing a snake aquarium that contained three pythons. 'My daughter loves them. She's smarter than Bindi Irwin, I reckon. But I'm her dad, I'm biased.'

We sat on two chairs outside the back door that led to a modest gravelled yard flanked by Colorbond fencing. It had a stroller, an upturned toy cart, some plastic balls and a few sparse runners of grass. Over an introductory chat, Scott rolled himself a cigarette.

'There is no doubt Bernie made me who I am today. I have probably got more now than I would have ever had,' he said.

Scott then unravelled his past. It was a difficult one, painful. Yet he talked about it without resentment:

'I was in and out of trouble at school in Sydney. Like, I wouldn't go to school. They flogged me off to here and there. Me nan and pop looked after me. Me dad died, when I was about eight, from alcoholism, and me mum wasn't much chop at the time. Some of us were going out stealing cars. I remember robbin' a candy store. In and out of trouble all the time. Every second night I was being brought to the police station, being a real little …

'I ended up doing a bit of time in detention. About three months. In the back of a prison bus going down there. I was only thirteen. Pretty scary at the time. The magistrate knew me well. She was always letting me off, but she eventually got sick of me going in there to court and she said: "Nah, you're not going home." You see, Nan would get up and lie flat to her face: "My boy wouldn't do anything wrong like that."'

Scott shook his head.

'I probably racked up twenty or thirty charges before I was fifteen; I was pretty lucky to get off a lot of them. You know, a kid that doesn't have a mum or a dad, living with his grandparents, you're pushing the edge every day. I didn't mean to hurt me nan and pop, out on the streets carrying on like I did. But a kid doesn't know about that at that age. He just wants a stable life. I met bad people. I ran away from home all the time, and out on the streets I saw shit I shouldn't see. People getting stabbed. I saw a lot of shit like that. I used to stay at Kings Cross as a young boy. Would stay in alleys or with mates that I knew. It was pretty dodgy. Sometimes sleep in stairways. Anywhere. On cardboard. And then the coppers would pick us up and drive me back home. I was really mixed up. Things you shouldn't really have to do at that age, or experience, you know.

'Then me pop died. Then me nan died. I got shuffled around a bit, got separated from my brother, which was hard. Then I met Bernie and Jayne down there on the farm. I can't remember everything, but I can remember more good times than not.'

Scott's mood lifted noticeably. He re-lit the rollie he'd barely puffed. He then spoke about class times, 8.30am to about 3pm, and darting with the other boys 'off down the paddock' to smoke at recess. He also talked of the brothers, 'top-notch fellas', and Jayne, with whom he had some disagreements, but she was a 'good person'. Most of the time, though, he reflected on Bernie.

'He was very funny. I don't know, he just had that wit about him, he always had some line to come out with. But he could be hard when he needed to be with us kids. I don't think I gave him much trouble; I'd say we would've had our arguments, but I can't remember them.

'I think it was every Wednesday Bernie would take us all horse riding. He gave me a cracker of a horse named Athena. I still remember this horse. Napoleon was another one. It would have been about sixteen, seventeen hands high and I'd never ridden a horse before. I couldn't pull it up and it just took off, and I ended up going over a fence. I got worse done to me growing up in Sydney. I was always getting into fights, getting bashed up, so falling off a horse was nothing compared to that. And it wasn't the horse that hurt me; it was the ground. It was great fun. I love horses now. If it wasn't for Bernie I'd be scared of them, but I ended up working on horse studs for a while.

'He taught me how to drive in this old Nissan Patrol ute. When we went spotlighting, us boys would take turns holding the light while someone else drove. Bernie taught us how to trap. There were never any rifles, which I was disappointed about back then. We'd go down to the shearing shed too. We learnt to shear and crutch, and we drove tractors, plenty of tractors to drive. I wanted to ride bulls. That's another thing Bernie taught me. He put me on a few steers and a few sheep, lots of sheep. And after school we'd get on the dirt bikes and go for a ride. You're making me miss that place. I just loved it so much. It shaped me. It made me the man I am today. Bernie put that much work into us. I'm sure he pulled me aside and gave me words of wisdom and edged me on. I held him up that high he was a father figure to me. If I didn't meet Bernie, I'm a hundred per cent certain I'd be in jail. Or dead. No doubt about it.'

Scott and I spoke for half an hour. When I left, his daughter was asleep on his partner's lap in the living room. 'I can't wait for Bernie to meet them,' said Scott. 'To show him the man and the dad I've become.'

—

Back on the verandah, Bernie takes time to answer a question I have asked about Scott and the many others on whose lives Bernie has had an impact. In contemplating his response, he repeats the question: 'How does it make you feel? Um … Oh, proud, knowing that if you're just doing something right for the right reason pay day can come a long way down the track. I enjoyed Tarago. I didn't think much about it, back then, but I suppose we were making a difference in our own little ways.'

Sometimes at Tarago, Bernie's influence lay much closer to home. Mark Shakeshaft, who acknowledges that he, like his older brother, 'wasn't the most well-behaved teenager', used to visit the farm while he was still at school. 'It was a good environment for me to hang around in,' said Mark over the phone. 'With nature, the open spaces, always doing active things, and Jayne and Bernie were so easygoing about it all. That was the first time I saw Bernie with a social carer's hat on. He was very good at it.'

Tragically, the farm was eventually deemed unsustainable, and it closed. With the gates shut, the boys who'd been there stared at wretched uncertainty. Fortunately, for Scott, the road ahead would again lead him to Bernie. But first, the young Shakeshaft family had their own issues to contend with. After about a year at Tarago, they moved to the Southern Highlands where Jayne took a job as a cleaner and Bernie a gardener and stablehand at a distinguished private home and horse stud. It proved the wrong fit. The money was poor and the housing less comfortable than at Tarago. Also, there was the exacting matter of preparing the gardens for an upcoming public open day. The problem was, Bernie had little more experience in horticulture than catching the occasional snippet of Allan Seale on ABC TV.

'The garden was exquisite, but I had no idea,' says Bernie. 'It was nearly a full-time job on just the mowing. Then a couple of weeks before the buses were going to come rolling in, one of the owners, the old lady, asked me: "Where did you plant the bulbs this year?" Uh-oh. I was meant to have planted them all in these fancy-pants arrangements, but the best I could come up with was: "What's a bulb?" Fail! So, they had to cancel the flower show.'

Bernie leans forward in his chair and giggles as though he's a kindergarten child sharing a joke in class without the teacher knowing. His shoulders hunch and his eyes fill with mischief. 'Yep, that was going nowhere fast.'

By then, Jayne and Bernie were married; they'd had a ceremony in St Brigid's at Raymond Terrace, the same Catholic Church in which Bernie's maternal great-grandparents had tied the knot. The officiating priest was Father Liam, the Marist chaplain who'd taken Bernie to India. Nowadays, Joe Shakeshaft laughs at the memory: 'Father Liam said to Bernard [at some stage] before the wedding: "You better go to confession," and Bernard said: "I'm never going to do that!"'

But what would he do as a husband and father? As his short career as a gardener came to an end, he realised he and Jayne were as good as broke. James was about two years old, and as a marker of how quickly time passed, he would soon enough be going to school, playing weekend sport, and being invited to birthday parties that had take-home sponge cakes wrapped in napkins. Time never slowed. And this meant Bernie and Jayne had to consider their options without delay. They would go wherever the work was. And wherever could be a long way away.

10

The location isn't important; for the moment, the only thing that matters is the fire. The boys sit and stand around it. Some are quiet, their faces aglow as they stare into the flames. Are they thinking? Or have they switched off entirely so that they've lost a sense of themselves and all around them? It's a beautiful place to be. Warm and comfortable. Safe. Other boys chat with visitors, marketing types who've come from as far away as Melbourne to see for themselves what the boys (and girls) do, and who they are.

When he thinks the time is right, Dawso gains everyone's attention and steers the boys through conversations that introduce them to the larger group. Only the occasional crackles of wood can be heard above them. One boy was kicked in the head by a horse when he was a small child, and as a result he has some learning difficulties. 'He's come a long way,' says Dawso. The boy grins and then feels his body shake when a mate wraps an arm around his shoulder. Another boy talks of cutting rap music, and someone else mentions growing up without a father. The marketing types soon join in, and a ring of vulnerabilities and hope is exposed.

Bernie, holding a bottle of beer, stands, listens and watches from afar. It's what he likes to do. As he so often tells the boys: 'Two ears, two eyes and one mouth. Use them in that ratio.'

Up north again. The Territory. The place of wild happenings. Yet this time, Bernie didn't arrive with the urge to be crazy. Instead, he went with a thought that Jayne had instilled in him over time: 'What you think is what you get.' Because of his reckless approach he had conditioned himself to wonder when the next broken bone would come along, but with some re-shaping Jayne had taught him he could still go hard and be somewhat wild without landing in plaster and slings. 'It might've had something to do with parenthood as well,' says Bernie. 'New responsibility, the need to grow up, but I reckon at that time I was still a work in progress. Old habits and all that.'

Jayne had a job training health workers at Anyinginyi Congress, an Aboriginal health service in Tennant Creek. The town, with a population of about 3000, was a troubled spot renowned, among other things, for its high crime rates, domestic violence, substance abuse and poverty. In the Barkly Tableland, where Mitchell and Flinders were known as plentiful grasses, not explorers, it was also the hub of vast cattle-growing country. However, Bernie had moved on from a stock-camp existence, and after he and the family moved into a rented house, he went chasing whatever work he could find beyond swinging into a saddle. For a while he joined a gold-drilling contractor taking core samples in the Tanami Desert for mining companies. The long days, starting in light and finishing in the dark, consisted of either diamond drilling, which was 'wet and muddy and slow', or RC (Reverse Circulation) work in which a hammer piston, powered by a 'smashing big air compressor' drove a drill encased in pipes.

'There were only two of us, the boss and me, and then we had two geologists who tested the samples,' says Bernie. 'I had a few jobs. Lifting the head, about a hundred and twenty kilograms, onto the drilling platform; starting the compressor; loading and swinging pipes off the truck. It was hot and dangerous, tough men's business. Everything was big and scary. I remember the thermometer going over fifty-five degrees on some days. I could be holding a pipe with a forty-eight–inch Stilson in each hand, no gloves, and the pipe snaps and the Stilsons go flying. Lots of pressure. I'd come home covered in hydraulic oil and dust. Used to hose off in the backyard before getting in for a shower. But, in comparison to working on a cattle station, it was more money than I'd ever seen. Always paid in cash. I didn't like the boss – hardest man I've ever worked for – but we needed the money, so I just shut-up and hooked in. We ended up having a big blue over safety. I ended up walking off through the desert and up to the nearest road and waited for the geo guys to come past. I jumped in the back of their ute, back the hundred and fifty k's into town, and that was the end of that little job. Had it for four or five months. Toughened me up. I was tough at the end of that.'

So, it was back to looking for work again. In the downtime, Bernie cared for James, and almost invariably he had another member of the family at his side. Sandy was a black-and-tan kelpie that Paul Roots had given Bernie a couple of years earlier in Stroud. She was a good all-rounder, could work sheep and cattle, and bring in horses 'quiet and gentle, to have them in a good place'. 'She was a bit unusual for a kelpie,' remembers Bernie. 'Coz she really blended in with the whole family. They normally don't do that. Normally they lock on with one person.' Sandy was 'a cracker', a companion for all seasons and moods. Put simply, she was a dog doing what dogs can do, or as Paul Roots said: "You can talk to your dog, you can kick your dog, you can feed your dog, you can not feed your dog, you can love it, you can hate it, and the dog will always be there.'"

And so it was that Sandy was alongside Bernie when he started his next job, teaching young men basic mechanical skills that could be used to maintain Anyinginyi's fleet of vehicles. The position renewed Bernie's connection with Indigenous Australians, a connection he'd been 'intrigued by' since his time at Newcastle Waters. He didn't quite understand this fascination, but he felt he needed to find out more. While tinkering over engines wasn't an ideal time for exploration, one person he met led him far away from the garage and into a world that would change his life forever.

'Anyinginyi was where I first met Brody, a guy about my age. He had a special presence about him. One of the Warumungu people. Around Tennant Creek was their traditional home. Because of Jayne's work, and mine to a smaller degree, we were pretty embedded in the Aboriginal community, but I was surprised when Brody wanted to take me hunting. I knew it was a special thing for me. I'll never forget the first time. We went out into one of those stony deserts to track a perentie; I didn't even know what a perentie was. We were going for what must have been hours. Brody is just walking along carrying this rifle, and he'd stop and painstakingly try to show me tracks: "Can you see that?" I could see some stuff, but not much; I needed a full-on track laid out good and proper for me to see. But Brody wanted me to see everything, all the small details, like rocks pushed slightly out of place, and trails of a tail. He wanted me to see how this animal walks and thinks. Along the way he showed me plants, too, for tucker and bush medicine. So much knowledge. A special man.

Anyway, we got to this waterhole in a rocky gorge and Brody says: "We got him now." Clearly, I wasn't seeing what Brody was. To me, there were no signs at all. Then we got to the edge of the water, and he says: "See it." Oh yeah, now I do. Big tracks in the sand. Dumb old me got that. Then Brody just propped his rifle on the ground, sat in the shade and said: "Now we wait him." I was asking all the stupid questions:

"'Where is he?"

"'In the water."

"'But I can't see him, where? How's he breathing?"

'Suddenly this little head pops up and *bang*, got him! Brody's into the water and dragging out this bloody dinosaur of a lizard. I'd never seen anything like it. He would've been at least two metres. Now, *that's* a perentie. A huge goanna. Enormous tail and claws. Stand as tall as a man. Welcome back to the Territory, Shakeshaft.

'So, we took him back to the Aboriginal camp, and all of a sudden Brody is the hero. I was already in awe of him. That day, either coming or going, we'd got a flat tyre and we didn't have a spare. "We'll fix him," he says. Then he pops the tyre off and starts jamming spinifex into it until it was solid enough to drive on. Albeit not very quickly, but we got where we had to go. Extraordinary. Just so resourceful.'

—

A rooster crows. Shadows over the garden are long. It's the second day of intense interviews on the verandah. Bernie was up early feeding dogs and horses. Now, he sits in his chair with a cup of steaming coffee. Behind him a row of jeans, shirts and underwear

115

hang along a line and catch some late winter sunlight. After a few minutes of general chat, he waits to be thrown a question. All that's needed is a reminder of the tease that Bernie finished with the previous afternoon: 'We'll get into the deep stuff tomorrow. Things you can't explain. That's why I reckon this book is being written. I still don't reckon my life is that interesting, but the things you can't explain are.' It was a statement worthy of Paul Roots, and now, as Bernie puts down his coffee, he begins with a familiar 'uuuuum'.

'You know, resourcefulness is just part of it with Aboriginal people,' he says. 'I dunno, sometimes you see stuff, and whether other people believe it or not doesn't really matter, coz you've seen it, and you know what you've seen. Even if you can't explain it. You know "sorry business", don't you? The mourning period after someone passes on in an Aboriginal community. In Tennant Creek sometimes we heard old women wailing for days. Sad but beautiful at the same time. Intense. A lesson to respect the grief of every culture.

'Someone close to Brody passed on and Brody went away for a couple of weeks. What happened? I don't know. He just went. But before he did, he told me: "I want you to go out with these two old men." They've passed on now, so we can't say their names. They used to make whip handles, boomerangs and other tools out of mulga. Brilliant craftsmen. Brody wanted me to drive them out into the bush, cut down the branches they wanted, then bring them and the wood back into town. "No worries," I thought. But as Brody walked off, he added: "You bring 'em running shoes, eh?" He smirked in that countryman way, then off he went. I couldn't work it out. I'd seen these old men. They shuffled, they didn't walk. Why would I need running shoes?

'So, I take them about twenty k's out of town into the mulga scrub, and by the time I've taken the chainsaw out of the ute and turned around, hey presto these men have gone. I'm standing there "cooeeeeing" like a stupid white fella. No idea where they've gone. Eventually one of them comes back and he's not speaking any English but I can tell that he's cranky. He starts pointing at the ground. Rough translation: "We showed you where we were. Have a look at the tracks we left you!" Yeah, fair point. After he pointed it out, I could see their bare-foot imprints in the sand; it wasn't that easy, but for these old fellas it was: "For God's sake, dopey!"

'Anyway, later we came across these dingoes. I don't know where they came from. We'd be walking along, and I'd look across and: "Shit there's one under that tree." And we'd go a bit further: "There's another one!" I got a bit jittery coz these are wild dogs, and I'm wondering if we're going to get jumped. Seven dingoes. I try to ask the old men what could happen, but they're pretty relaxed and are laughing.

'The next day we went out in a different direction, and what's the first thing I notice when we're walking along in the bush? "There's a dingo!" One, two, three ... seven of them. They couldn't be the same dogs as yesterday, because we were in a different place. Next day we go out again. Hey presto, dingo bingo, the same seven dogs. Now I'm paying attention. This goes on for about a fortnight and every day I'm going: "How the hell do those dogs know where those old men are going to be tomorrow?" North, south, east, west, thirty k's this way, forty k's that way. I was amazed. Counting the dogs, looking at their markings. The same dogs every time. And these old men were just nodding and smiling. What the hell was going on? So, I spoke to Brody, and he came out with us when he got back from "sorry business", and he's just nodding too, giving the impression, "What appears to be the problem?" I asked him how the dogs knew where to go. The old men could see that I was interested, and they wanted to explain it to me, but the language barrier was too much. So, Brody has a go, and after talking backwards and forwards a bit he says: "The dogs don't find the old men; the old men find the dogs. They can touch a track and describe that dog. They'll tell you whether it's male or female, its weight range, and then they'll tell you a story about what it's doing." Just by touching the track. What they say – and I'm trying to be simple here, coz there's still a whole lot of stuff I don't understand or know – is that you look at the tracks and there's a whole storybook there, it's like Googling Wikipedia. And once you know from those tracks what the dog was doing yesterday and today, you can see where it's heading tomorrow. Envisioning it, seeing it out in front of you. Using that energy and the stories from the tracks. But it's not just the tracks; it's also getting into the dog's mind or spirit. It's so hard to explain. And I don't know if I have the authority to tell you more. All I know is that it happens because I saw those old men, and others, do it over and over again. Those old men, they were putting the dogs where they wanted them to be; a bit like me saying to you: "Let's catch up at the St Kilda pub on the fifteenth." At that time, I didn't fully understand it, and still don't, but those two old men really started me thinking. I don't talk about it much, coz I reckon people might think: "What's he on? Bernie's on the magic mushrooms." But … well, it happens. So much we don't know.

'When James was about three, he got really sick. All his stomach started blowing up, like a cow with bloat. Doctors looked at him and wanted to take him to hospital. There was an old fella, Rossy, I used to knock around with. A super-wise man in his fifties or sixties. James was in this fever and we were really getting worried. Nobody could work out what was going on. We were about to take him to the hospital and Rossy says: "Hang on a minute, get all the meat that's in your freezer" – coz meat is a big barter thing up there – "and we'll go and visit this old man." We take our meat to this camp on the edge of the bush; I'd been in the camp a hundred times but never seen this old man. I stay in the car, Rossy goes and speaks to him, and then this old man gets into the car and we take him home. I don't have eye contact with him, don't speak to him. We get back and I try to explain what's going on to Jayne. I don't even know what's going on, it's all trippy with an energy and intensity that I can't put in words. We take him into the room where James is, and then Rossy tells us we have to leave. That really freaks us out, but we do what we're told. Rossy stays with the old man, and from outside we hear this singing coming from the room for, I reckon, ten minutes. Then we're allowed back in, and the fever had broken, the swollen stomach is down, and James is half-alert. And the white-fella doctors couldn't explain it. And off he went. Medicine man. Our thank you to him was the meat. I still get the shivers thinking about it all.

'We don't know what had been wrong with James, but I have a fair idea: I'd been in the wrong spot at the wrong time during men's business. Sacred, spiritual goings-on that I had no right to experience. It's incredibly powerful. I should've known better. Not listening to someone. I won't say any more. Except that, lesson learnt: two ears, two eyes, one mouth, use them in that ratio. I hadn't been using them that way, and I was punished.

'Another time I was with Rossy driving some old men to Alice Springs. We stopped in Tennant Creek at the servo – the trip was five hundred k's on the dot – and I remember Rossy talking with another old man on the edge of the servo. Then we go on to Alice Springs, have a stop for five minutes at Barrow Creek, and keep going. We get to Alice Springs in three-and-a-half hours – pretty standard up there with no speed limits – and there's the same old man sitting at another servo. What? How? And I say: "Isn't that the same old man?" And Rossy just gives me this little look. And I know to shut-up. How does that sort of stuff work? You'd think there's a logical explanation. Was it real or was I imagining things? You can dismiss a one-off, but I went on to see dozens of those sorts of things. Things you can't explain. I don't know, do you put that stuff in the book? Bernie and his magic mushrooms.'

The intensity in Bernie's eyes is magnetic. Just watch him and listen. Be drawn into a life story that's as unpredictable as it is irresistible.

Bernie, Jayne and James lived in Tennant Creek for about a year before they moved to Alice Springs because of Jayne's work. They left behind a place that had opened minds to the powers and practices of tradition and mystique. Bernie had many questions, few answers. But he believed. And he knew he had been in a privileged position. The Barkly, with its flowing grasses, had been a place of great personal exploration and discovery. Yet it also presented its hardships. The harshness of Tennant Creek was felt in untimely ways, including when meat baited with 1080 poison was used by various people, from rangers to those who took the law into their own hands, to curb populations of camp dogs. One day, Sandy took one. Perhaps it was thrown into their backyard or maybe she'd picked it up when she was out with Bernie in the bush. It didn't matter. The result was the same: 'The poor girl didn't make it to Alice Springs with us,' says Bernie. 'She was a good'un, but I try not to get hung up on that stuff. She was one of my best, though. Had her strengths. Special in her own way. I've never really thought about it, but I've rarely been out in the bush without a dog. I've had some good ones. Just dogs being dogs.'

The next came after Bernie arrived in Alice Springs: Ben, an alsatian–cattle dog cross. Another dog just being a dog, alongside a bloke who was just beginning to understand how little he knew and how much he had to learn.

11

He stands by himself in the car park at the BackTrack depot. A class has just finished, and most of the boys are sitting and chatting on the table bench not too far from Bernie's office.

This lone boy is a little different. Yes, he's as sociable as anyone – if not more so – but he also likes his own space. Especially when he reads. It's one of his favourite pastimes. In the shade. On a couch. The back seat of a car during a lunch break. Science fiction and fantasy, mostly.

'Reading takes you places. A book is just one big adventure, really.'

Right now, though, he holds nothing in his hands. Yet they've caught the eye. Literally. On one hand he has drawn an eye on each inside middle joint of his fingers. Red texta. Bright and bold against his skin. Why? Just doodling, perhaps? Boredom in the classroom? He shakes his head. Then he smiles and moves his fingers back and forth quickly.

'Look,' he says. 'They're all winking at me. I like doing that. Reckon it's pretty cool.'

By this stage of the verandah interview, Bernie has on several occasions exposed one of his greatest weaknesses: he's not good with numbers. At times when I've asked for the year of an incident, or a person's age, including his own, Bernie has answered with: 'See, there you go, tricking me up with all that maths and numbers stuff again!' Memories of his experiences in Alice Springs are a further example of this: 'Geez, a lot happened up there,' he says shaking his head. 'Big years up there. *Big years.*'

Bernie and his family's introduction to 'The Alice' was an uncomfortable one. They moved into a house with one of Jayne's colleagues and his wife at the 'rougher end of town'. Almost immediately, they were harassed. At night their roof was pelted with rocks and fruit, and by day locals would loiter on the street out the front and stare at Bernie whenever he appeared. Another of Jayne's co-workers, who lived nearby, made some subtle inquiries and found out the cause of the problem: the previous inhabitant of the house was a committed sex offender, and the locals mistook Bernie for him. Once the mistake was realised, there were no more worries.

About a year later, the young Shakeshafts bought a house only one street back from the Todd River, the famous ribbon of sand that barely and only briefly carries water. It remains renowned for its annual regatta, in which all sorts of home-made boats are raced on foot. However, to Bernie, whose keenness to observe human behaviour was growing after the mysteries of Tennant Creek, the Todd was more a place for 'all the countrymen to come into town and get drunk'. At times the tragedies of Aboriginal alcoholism blended with racism, pathos and absurdities. Bernie saw it all:

'There was always some sort of humbugging going on. Some people got humbugged. Some people didn't. We didn't. There were these white fellas who lived close to us. Big drinkers. And they had these three savage dogs that were Indigenous-mad. They trained them for that shit. They did some weird things, like putting the dogs in a sack with a countryman's shirt and then they'd flog the crap out of the dogs. So, the dogs learnt pretty quick. Awful stuff, but I didn't want to interfere coz I had the family, and you just don't know, do you? Anyway, these guys were so cocky about their dogs that they had their fridge out on their front verandah, a big house, where people walking past could see it. Talk about that for temptation for anyone who doesn't have any money or is up for a free carton. So, I watched this old countryman one day. It was lunchtime. The dog owners were all at work. The dogs were going ferocious but this guy, he's got no flinch in him around the dogs. He just walks along the front fence, opens the gate, and as the dogs come out to savage him, he slips through the gate and then shuts it behind him. So, the dogs are now out on the street with no way back in, and the old fella takes a carton of beer and keeps walking out the back through the swamp. Then the owners got a fine for having unrestrained dogs.'

Bernie laughs and sucks deeply on a cigarette. 'Dog stories, eh.'

Bernie's dog, Ben, had his own to tell. Originally, he'd been used as a guard dog at a pet shop in which Bernie had been working part-time. Like the dogs that were supposed to protect the verandah beer, he could be ferocious. When it was announced the store was closing for good, Ben's future looked bleak. 'So, I took him,' remembers Bernie, 'Just another busted thing.'

Animal welfare. Human welfare. The two had become recurring themes that drove Bernie both consciously and subconsciously. Perhaps it was inevitable that at some stage he would return to youth work. His time at Tarago had taught him he had skills that he could apply in many different contexts and communities. He found a job as a youth worker with the Alice Springs Youth Accommodation and Support Service (ASYASS), an organisation that helped street kids, offering crisis refuge and day programs. It was a job that he would have on and off again over several years.

'It was hard,' acknowledges Bernie. 'It was three-quarters paperwork. Great kids, and I'd do bits and pieces with them, but not enough. Not everything sat right with me. I remember some workers there. The cops were looking for some kids and these workers let the kids sneak out the back door. I don't know when it started, probably somewhere after school, but I've always been big on owning your own shit, and that just wasn't right.

'There were some funny times, though. Now I'm jumping ahead a bit, but who came to visit? It must have been Queen Elizabeth and the Duke came to Alice. Early 2000, it was. A big royal visit. This youth service was upstairs in a building and it had a pretty good view from a verandah. Good to watch a royal visit from. Straight down the Todd Mall. Well, these kids were arguing about the extra cops in town. And I was going: "What do you mean the extra cops?" I could see Federal Police, Territory Police, and it was pretty clear which ones came with the crew from England. But these kids were going: "No, there's another mob here, too." They were pointing out these guys wearing bum-bag sorta things. "Why have they got them?" The kids reckoned they'd seen them all over town. I hadn't spotted them and wasn't really interested, to be honest. Anyway we were standing on the verandah when the royals were coming along the mall. This verandah had one of those trestle tables with the fold-up legs leaning against the wall, and these boys couldn't care about who the Queen and Duke were; they just wanted to work out who these undercover super-cops were. One kid just flicks this table and it goes "Bang!" on the floor not far from where the royals were walking up. Instant echo. Half these guys with the bum-bags turn their heads, and the kids are going: "There." "Over there." "There's one." They picked out all these guys with the bum-bags. I was amazed. No surprises we got a visit from some of them straightaway: "Oh sorry, mate, it was just a table." It was hilarious!'

Bernie again laughs at the story, but beneath the mirth is admiration for the 'street-smart nature' of the kids he was trying to help. From the time he first arrived in Alice Springs, he worked hard on establishing relationships with Indigenous communities. Often, it was the little moments, those ones that could be overlooked, that had an impact. Denise Shakeshaft, who visited Alice Springs with Joe on several occasions, said one such moment stands out in her memory: 'It was when James was still a little fellow. I'd either just gone or come back from shopping, and I walked out of the house to find out where everyone was, and here's Bernard sitting and talking with an old Aboriginal man on the road, and James was beside him. That said a lot about Bernie. The time he spent with people.'

While he worked on new relationships, an old one also demanded attention. After the closure of the boys' home at Tarago, Scott endured more hardship. Initially, he returned to school, but was expelled when he was in Year Ten. He then went 'downhill a bit'. Drugs and 'this and that'. He drifted – Sydney, Brisbane, other parts of Queensland – and he searched, but he really had no idea what he was looking for. Finally, he arrived in Alice Springs.

'Jayne and Bernie kept ringing me and asking if I'd come and help them fix their place up,' said Scott during the interview in his home town. 'I jumped on a bus and got up there; they paid for me ticket. They didn't treat me any different from anyone else. If I needed a good kick up the arse they gave it to me. It was a lovely place. I loved it. I had a caravan out the back. There was an annexe and I slept out there under the stars with the geckos. I helped Bernie out in the yard and I did a few trips with him, and he took me out to a place called the Simpson Desert. It's a pretty famous sort of place, isn't it? It was brilliant. Then he took me out to this little Aboriginal community in the middle of nowhere. It was just one of them things you've got to see. Houses, and cars burnt and dumped. Anyway, we were teaching them how to fence. It was a cool experience. All that stuff stays with you. It's part of who I am now. I owe it all to Bernie and Jayne, pretty much. In the end, it probably didn't work out too well up there. I went to a cattle station and drifted a bit again. I lost contact with Bernie and Jayne after that. I had to do me own things.'

Again, it wouldn't be the last time Scott would turn to Bernie, but the next meeting would be many years later, when both had progressed to very different stages of their lives. When he took Scott into the bush Bernie was working with the Institute for Aboriginal Development (IAD), teaching land management to communities. Most of his working hours, though, were spent at ASYASS, where he was strongly influenced by two colleagues: Will MacGregor, a man raised on hard knocks – he now runs BushMob, a community-based service for high-risk youth, in Alice Springs – and Antoinette Carroll, whose background included juvenile justice work in Dublin, Ireland. Bernie's and Antoinette's primary job was helping young, long-term unemployed Aboriginal men find training and employment.

'We also looked to support young people and their rights in the criminal justice system. Giving them a second chance, a fair go.

Trying to find pathways,' said Antoinette in her phone interview. 'Bernie may have seemed casual on top but there was an intensity underneath him. He took things to heart and had this really strong sense of justice and fairness. He had the ability to make everybody feel very comfortable by using humour and not taking himself too seriously. One of a kind, that's for sure. I think the great thing was his ability to gain mutual respect with the young fellas. Instead of coming in with a punitive approach he would go, "We're doing this together. We're going to hang out, kick back." But then if he had to hold someone to account, by God he held them to account.

'In our line of work, you go to a lot of meetings and there's a lot of collaboration and often it is very like *Groundhog Day*, and you're thinking: "Here we go again." But Bernie had this great capacity to cut through that and get things done. So, while there was a lot of negotiating about who, where, when and why, he would just go, "Right, just organise it." So, we would creep off and have a chat over a Guinness in the pub and work out what we needed to do and then we'd come back with solutions. There was one project we got off the ground, working with young men doing horticultural activities and fencing. We handpicked a small group of young fellas. The idea was that they would engage in a short program with the aim of potentially providing some with traineeships in businesses around Alice Springs. One of the big things about it was Bernie's approach to how the boys were chosen. Some of the boys were: "Yeah, I'll do that." But Bernie was: "No, *we'll* decide whether you do it, and here are the rules around it." A couple of boys did go on to get traineeships. It was very much Bernie's initiative, and I think an early sign of what he would go on to do with BackTrack.

'We were together for three years, and we definitely had a lot of fun. We could still have a laugh about what was a very serious job. We clicked. We had the same level of enthusiasm and creativity, the same sense of humour. His swearing, though, could be out of control,' laughed Antoinette. 'Young men would come and tell me they were embarrassed for me having to listen to the "f-this" and "f-that", and they'd hang their heads down with shame out of respect for me. I would tell them: "I know, but I can't stop him."'

It was Bernie being Bernie, yet again. In return, Bernie looks back at Antoinette and his youth work in Alice Springs with similar warmth. 'Here's this crazy Irish woman who taught me as much or more about youth work than anyone else. The way she worked with those kids. Hard kids. She never flinched under any amount of rapid fire. And she got, I got, we all got into some pretty scary positions. I remember going to this one house. There was all sorts of stuff going down. A domestic-violence situation. I got the girl out somehow, but this bloke had me cornered upstairs. He had a knife. A big history with violence. He was eighteen, nineteen. Talking about going to cut me up into pieces. The silver tongue got me out of trouble. We all had moments like that.

'Antoinette always knew what to do. Again, it was watching and listening, for me. The same with Will MacGregor. A tough man. Call a spade a spade. Still a mate of mine. So much of it comes back to how do you treat people? You have your own ways and then you've gotta learn from others too. It's not cheating if you copy someone else's tricks or techniques. It's common sense, if they work. Good management. Good people management. I dunno how many times Antoinette, Will and I would argue with the bosses and different workers: "What's this solving? You're only making us look stupid to the cops." We were always thinking about how we could do things better. Never be satisfied. You have to keep looking. Looking for where the gaps are in the services, and how existing services can be run better. Will and Antoinette really made me think about that stuff.'

Antoinette, who was new to Alice Springs when she first began working with Bernie, was also welcomed into the Shakeshaft home and family. By then, Jayne and Bernie had a young daughter, Maeve, born in 1997. She and James were sometimes on the sidelines as Dad played soccer in a senior social team, the Storm Birds, which he and Antoinette established, and invited some in their social circles to join. 'I'd played soccer all my life, but here was Bernie, who'd never really played that much, but of course he gets in there, he names the team, he organises it and goes to all the training sessions. And I was thinking: "What the hell, you don't even know how to play properly." He was just very good at doing. He was a doer. I hope he has managed to slow down a bit now,' said Antoinette.

The influence of soccer on the family grew as James kicked through his primary-school years and discovered a love and talent for the sport that would take him all the way to trialling for junior-age Territory representative teams. Bernie was his coach, and what he lacked in knowledge about the finer points of soccer, he more than compensated for by encouraging the social values of sport and community. 'We'd have these barbecues at our place, and all the teams would be invited over,' recalled James in a phone interview. 'Even from a young age all my friends knew Dad as well. He always had the group thing going on. It wasn't just about showing up for the games; it was about spending time, sometimes whole days, playing soccer and other sports. Getting that feel of team bonding and social interaction that's so important to learn when you're a kid.'

Bernie too continued to further his own education, both formally and otherwise. 'Somewhere in the middle' of his youth work, he returned to TAFE to study for a Certificate 3 in Lands, Parks and Wildlife. This didn't necessarily mean he hoped to change professional direction; it was more a chance to explore his interest in the outdoors.

'One of the reasons I was interested in the course was the many volunteer hours I had to do. There were lots of ecologists doing field work for universities in the national parks and on cattle stations, and they always needed helpers. I got a start, with a couple of others, working with a camp doing feral-cat research. I was a volunteer for some chief scientists. But what really caught my attention was the trapping done by this Victorian fella. He was getting cats, foxes and dingoes. Straightaway I was onto it like a rat up a drainpipe. It just fell into a dream space for me. Animals, traps, and you remember I'd been knocking about with countrymen learning about tracks, so it all came together. I didn't know if any sort of long-term opportunity would come from it, but I wanted to show that I was ready if one did happen. So, it was going back to those old lessons that Jimmy Matthews taught me. Who was first out of bed? Bang! Who made sure the camp was right? I did the stuff that nobody else wanted to do. Packing and unpacking vehicles, going through checklists, making sure the bird books were there, filling the bosses' water bottles, checking all the data collection sheets were done. I was busy. Putting my hand up to do anything. Washing and cleaning vehicles after everyone else went home.

'I hadn't been around dog and cat traps much. They were all new-age things with rubber faces; you couldn't use anything with steel anymore. This was in the early days of that stuff. I knew about old rabbit traps and how to catch possums in cages, but not this new way of doing things. So, I rode shotgun with this trapper guy and milked him for every single piece of information. How to tune the traps, how to peg them. And this guy, he was a good trapper. His gear was meticulous, so I learnt how to de-scent traps too.

'Here's what happened. Number one rule: use gloves. Cats are really choosy about smells, and we know dogs are off the Richter scale with what their noses do. I'd seen other trappers use their hands, but, boy, if you wanted to play A-grade, put your gloves on. Now, let's de-scent the traps. Make up a forty-four–gallon drum full of tannins off the barks – your wattles, tea trees, whatever's in the area – and boil it with water for days until you get this black molasses kinda soup. And then make sure the temperature is right, coz you don't want to melt all your rubbers. But it's gotta be on the simmer. Then you put the traps in there for, I don't know, half a day. And that heats the steel, opens the pores, and then as the traps cool down all the tannins are sucked in. Right, you're ready to go. But don't forget your gloves!

'We were doing other types of catching, too. Reptiles, small mammals in pit-fall traps. That's where you dig a hole, put a bucket in the hole so it's flat level with the ground, and then you've got shade cloth that you run out for a few metres one way, and a few metres the other; the animals come through the bush, through the channel, and *Boom!* into the bucket. The next morning you come along and key them out [identify and record]. We had these little Elliott traps too. Aluminium traps with two fold-down doors and a little treadle plate. You make up a ball of peanut butter and catch spinifex hopping mice, and other small fauna. Fascinating stuff.

'But back to the cats. The research I was working on was their diet. It was a big sample size. We had three different sites out on the station, Hamilton Downs. Go to each site and work for two, three, four weeks. Traps in the mulga, some on the flats. We were picking up thousands of scats and sending them away for analysis; you could tell from just one hair what type of animal had been eaten. So, we were picking up all this cat shit, and I was onto these cats; I could see their tracks, could find where they hid their shits, could tell the difference between their shits and dog shits. I learnt that stuff.

'Then, you won't believe what happened. Right at about the time the course finished the researchers wanted someone who could do field stuff, and just like that I was in. Working for Parks and Wildlife with people I'd got to know well on another cat project. There was Rachel, a PhD student – we'd become really passionate about keying out skinks and scorpions and some of the smaller animals – and her partner, Steve, although he was away on another project too. Another guy who'd been volunteering got a job as well.

'It came at the right time. I was having a break from the youth work. Just needed to get my head round what I wanted to do, and I reckoned this was perfect for me. Under the job description I was a field assistant, but as it turned out I did all the cat trapping too. The deal was I had to catch them, put a tracking collar on them – without getting myself shredded or harming the animal – record their details, and then release them again. The aim was to work out the home range of each cat, what they were eating, how far they travelled, what interactions they had along the way.

'Now we get to the good bit. These days, GPS collars are used, but back then it was a bit more complicated and we had to triangulate radio signals. UHF or VHF, whatever it was. I forget how many cats we had out, maybe five or six. So, we were out on these ranges, not very high but wide. And we put up towers on top of these hills to do the triangulations. By then we had the next course of volunteers coming through. The cats' locations had to be taken every fifteen minutes, twenty-four hours a day. Four-hour shifts. We were pretty busy, but forget about that, think about the country. It's just gorgeous, central Australia. The cats are out in the mulga woodlands, and here you are on night shift looking up at the shooting stars like you've never seen before. The sunrises and sunsets, all the colours changing. And you're perched on the side of a hill with your headphones on. A ticket in the front row to the best show in town. Sensational.

'I got on well with all the guys I worked with, and because I was handy at a few things I started to get sent out on all sorts of jobs outside the cat camp. Counting camels from an aircraft; go and look into a population explosion of kangaroos in the Barkly; spotlighting for foxes in the Mala Enclosure, that predator-proof fence near Willowra out in the Tanami Desert. Just a crackly old radio for communication: "Return to base, there's a fox in the paddock." I even took some Indigenous kids out there to help me work on the fence. Great kids. So often, I was just driving on these busted roads, off into the spinifex, just two-wheel tracks. Beautiful country with emus, bush turkeys. I got to do things all over the joint and saw some of Australia's greatest country, living through wet and dry. Loved it. Working hard. Often out on my own all day, on a quad counting tracks. Kangaroos, foxes, cats, birds, lizards. Recording everything. Then wipe the sand clean with a steel-fangled thing that kicked off the back of the quad, so you could make new records the next day. And at night, go and do some spotlighting. Long hours, but how could you complain?

'Out in the desert, brand new LandCruisers, make your own tracks, enough fuel to drive to Perth and back across extraordinary country. Just unreal. And the money was insane. On one of my earliest trips I got back into town and the workmates said:

'"You gotta go and collect your TA."

'"What's that?" I had no idea.

'"Travel allowance, coz you get paid for being out bush."

'I thought they were taking the piss out of me. "Tell me how this works. We get a salary, we get to drive a brand-new car, get all our tucker paid for, we're sleeping in swags, then we come home and get extra cash just for being away? Oh, and you pick it up from the Motor Registry, do you? Yeah, pull the other one."

'But I was given a little pink slip, and everyone else had one too. So, I tentatively creep up to the Registry one afternoon looking for the bastards trying to set me up. Can't see them. I go up to the front desk and say: "I was told I had to bring this slip here." And the cashier processes it, no questions asked. But I'm still looking over my shoulder, thinking the cashier's in on the joke too. But nah, I've got this wad of cash and it's mine. Won the lottery. "Right guys, when are we going bush again?"

'So much happened during that time. Snake catching was an added bonus of the job; I never had so much fun. I'd get call-outs to go and catch them in and around homes in Alice Springs, and then I'd take them out into the bush and release them. I've got no fear of snakes. Shit no. I'd catch them in the double-pluggers [thongs], not a problem. Actually, I got another good double-plugger story to tell you. Remind me of it later.'

Bernie pauses just long enough to watch me make a note, then he's away again.

'I remember this poor lady one night. Her husband was away. And she had four different snakes at different times. I kept getting messages from the same phone number and I was thinking:

135

"This can't be happening." But it was. The last one was an eastern brown. The dogs had killed it. A thumping big snake. I told the lady: "I don't know what's going on here, but if I were you, I'd go and book into a motel somewhere." Because I had a sense those snakes were going to keep coming all night. You know, it would be interesting to have a look in an animal book and see what snakes mean in your life, wouldn't it?'

Again, Bernie pauses, as though he's contemplating an answer. When a study of concentration gives way to a grin, there's no knowing what wick has been lit in a stirring mind.

'So, my pager goes off. I ring the lady back:

"We've got a lizard in the backyard. A goanna."

"How big is it?"

"Two foot."

'Then I thought: "Righto, it'll wait, I'm off to lunch." But I tell the lady: "I'll be there as quickly as I can. Just keep an eye on it and don't worry too much about it." But the pager keeps going off: "How far away are you?" This lady is getting half-hysterical. I get there, and she's shaking. I'm expecting this two-foot-long thing and I've got my little snake bag and catcher, coz goannas scratch and bite. The lady tells me to look behind the garden shed. I walked towards the back end of this shed and then I stop. She's not kidding! Two foot is the tip of the thing's tail. Oh my God, it's a perentie! Remember what Brody tracked and caught? A crocodile on land! It's the middle of summer, it's hot, and this fella is all revved up. I tell the lady: "Go inside," while I'm thinking: "How am I gonna do this?" Soon as I move closer – we're talking a couple of feet, not metres, from him – he's on the hop and all cranky. He runs around and keeps slamming into a window, then he starts up the glass, gets to the roof, flips over and comes back down again. Does that about four times. By now I'm thinking, but I'm not really thinking clearly, though: "What if a man is to get his snake bag and kind of scoop this thing's head when he comes back off the roof?" Coz he was kind of falling every time. He was longer than me, must have weighed twenty-odd kilos. All claws, jaw and tail. I'm shaking like a leaf knowing this has got to be in my all-time top ten of dumb ideas. But we'll give it one crack. See, I'd already tried to chase it out of the yard but it wouldn't go. Anyway, this thing flies up the glass, hits the top of the roof and I've flown in like Steve Irwin with me snake bag. Got him. Great, we're going well here, but then his head hits the bottom of the bag and those big black legs aren't even close to going in. They're hanging out the top. So, the bag's not gonna work. Now what? So, I wrestle this thing. Slapping and bashing. Hissing, kicking, scratching, fighting. I was lucky I had a ute with a canopy and I launched the big fella in. I went and got Jayne and said: "You gotta see this." I drove it out bush, crawled up on the roof, opened the door and let it go. Out he went, and I took a breath. Yep, that was really dumb, Shakeshaft.

'Not as good as the Indigenous kids, don't worry. There was this bunch from a long way out. They were visiting Alice Springs, and were taken to the Desert Park, a great tourist and education set-up not far out of town. I was working there, and I get this call on the radio: "Get back to the office, we've got a problem." These kids had spotted this perentie, peeled branches off trees and they killed it. I'm not sure anyone really knew what had happened until these kids were walking out and they've got this giant lizard with them. You could imagine the bureaucracy needed to handle that one. Should the kids get into trouble? No way. Just let them take it home as a trophy and we'll go out and catch another one.

No problem at all. And for me, more lessons. Don't judge people until you know the reasons behind their actions. Their culture, upbringing, values … all that stuff. But sometimes we just jump right in. "Oh that's awful." "How could they?" "Naughty children." The Northern Territory can be a wild place, coz it *is* a wild place, but it's one that … well, if it wasn't for the Territory I don't think BackTrack would've happened, and we wouldn't be here now having this chat for a book, would we?'

Forthrightness is one of Bernie's strengths. This is one reason he has, so far, been an easy subject to interview. But, there are some difficult subjects, including very personal ones, that are still to be discussed. Nevertheless, they are likely to find their place among further cheerful recollections of adventures up north. Adventures that left indelible footprints on a philosophy that has shaped and saved countless young lives.

12

A boy wearing a Parramatta rugby-league jumper arrives at the BackTrack depot. He is late. The morning Circle Work has just finished, and he stands at the exit to the smoko room as his mates pile out. He high-fives some of them. Hip-hop is playing loudly on his phone.

Bernie walks over to him: 'Morning. Good to see you could make it. What are you up to?'

'Dunno,' says the boy, 'I just got here.'

'And,' says Bernie, slapping the boy on the shoulder, 'it's a good place to be.'

Tracks. We all make them. Footprints on beaches, trainer wheels on wet grass, hooves on the oval loop at a country showground. To most of us, they're rarely anything more than fleeting impressions of moments that have passed. But after spending time interviewing – let's still say *chatting* with – Bernie, there have been too many references to 'signs' and 'signatures' to dismiss with the wind. As little as one imprint can lead someone on a timeless journey. And Bernie is such a someone, opening both mind and soul to worlds and possibilities that are far removed from his day-to-day existence. When these come from Australia's Indigenous culture, he chooses his words carefully. Just as he believes he was in the wrong place before James became ill in Tennant Creek, he feels it's not his place to reveal all he does know.

'Absolutely, I am a spiritual person,' he says, nodding. 'But not in a ten Hail Marys kind of way. I guess my view is if you look at too much of the trouble and conflict in our world, religion pokes its head in there somewhere. I reckon it's a simple, straightforward thing: there is a power greater than yourself. But as for all the "We're right, you're wrong, join our club" stuff that goes on with religions, I find that a bit ludicrous.

'I remember hearing something in Tennant Creek. It was an old fella that told me. Their belief for that mob is that when you pass away, a third of you goes up into the stars into the spirit world; another third stays in the middle level, whether that's in a plant or stone or animal; and the remaining third goes back to mother earth. That kind of resonates with me. It's a little bit of heaven and a little bit of reincarnation and a little bit of this mother earth. The thing is, we walk around on mother earth but we forget to respect her a lot of the time. Then, you watch these old fellas, these countrymen; when they go somewhere new they rub their feet in the soil and they touch it with their hands. It's about connection. But it's so easy for us white fellas to lose that connection. And that's one of the biggest things I learnt from my time in the Territory. Although I didn't know it when I was in the thick of it, this connection was part of the bigger picture. It was helping me build the platform for BackTrack, step by step. Then throw in all the other stuff: youth work, animal research, tracking, the countrymen, my own parenthood ... all of them were building that platform.'

One of the most significant moments in this development came after Bernie 'won the lottery' and was given a job tracking and monitoring dingoes, for the Parks and Wildlife Service. At first, he worked with Steve, the partner of Rachel, the PhD student he'd got on so well with on other research projects. Among their aims was to examine the effects of 1080 baiting on dingoes. The project spanned three properties, which were divided into baited and non-baited areas. Beasts that came through the yards were checked for dingo-attack marks; most attention was paid to calf predation, and in a result that surprised Bernie, victimised stock was found in greater numbers in the baited areas.

'I learnt an extraordinary amount about baiting and dingo behaviour on that job,' says Bernie. 'But it was so much more than that, coz that job was when I really started to fine-tune my tracking skills, and that took me on to other dingo jobs. Even when I wasn't out working, I was practising tracking in the sand behind home. Out in the Coolibah Swamp. It was like a classroom for me. Lots of different animals. I spent time looking for the minutest tracks. That's a bird, that's a centipede. And then when I came to something big like a dog track it was easy pickings, it was like seeing it on a big screen in 3D. I always kept working on the detail in practice and in the field. What does a mouse track look like? Compare it to a spinifex hopping mouse that has a brushy tail that leaves a flick-mark in the sand. Or the dingoes are in season, and what's the difference between a male and female track? The male has worn claws coz everywhere he pisses he does the raking thing. You can see that in their tracks. And what's a scorpion's track look like? And that's what it looks like when it's going backwards. Over and over and over again. I just kept doing it. Practising. Getting every tiny detail: the blade of grass that's laid down, the sand that's been pushed back by the wind, and that stone that's back half a roll. What caused that? The wind? No, too heavy. A strong animal. Echidna? And then there's the age of tracks. So, I'd go out at all different hours. And I'd get Ben to walk through at night, and again in the morning, and in the afternoon. Then in another week. In three weeks. Get him to walk through water.

'You know when you learn to read you go through this painful process of learning the alphabet and all its sounds, and then at some point it all comes much easier? You go from reading little cardboard books with not very many words and lots of pictures and then later on you're good enough to read novels? Well, reading tracks is the same. Practise, practise, practise, and if you do enough of it, you'll start seeing things and understanding them without knowing you're doing it. Just like reading a road sign. It just happens. When I was tracking – and it still happens – nothing else in the world matters; I am just in that moment. I go into a space. In the zone.

'But there's something else. And it's here – well, it gets a bit tricky. But when you really start to know each track, you start to *feel* them. Each animal has a different frequency. It can get hotter and colder. It's like a little radar. So, you touch the track, and once you get that feel it's, "Right, here we go." Paul Roots knows what I'm talking about. He does it with wild cattle. He'll tell what the cattle are doing by what he sees on the ground. How fast are they travelling? When did they last eat? How long ago did they walk through here? He sees things in different ways. But then you get the countrymen, and I've watched them do it, and realised I don't even have half an idea. People like Puppa Wati. He's done things I could never explain.'

Puppa Wati, the 'dog man', a nickname that Bernie and Puppa gave each other when they worked together on dingo jobs. They'd first met on a camel survey where they were flown over thousands of kilometres day in, day out, and spent hours on end looking out windows and tallying the numbers and mapping the locations of the animals they saw. At night, back at their base in Curtin Springs, they shared stories over steaks and beers. A close bond developed. Men from different worlds drawn together by their love for the outdoors, and all the realities and mysteries it holds.

Puppa Wati is from South Australia. A Kokatha man. After a childhood that included tracking and hunting native animals – a way of life that wasn't accepted by some local farmers – he made his way to the Northern Territory to further his education and employment prospects. His tracks eventually led to Uluru, where he worked his way up from a traineeship to become a chief ranger. It was here he not only connected with the land and its people but helped guide the rich and famous, including Jennifer Lopez, Bill Clinton and Morgan Freeman, around one of Australia's most internationally famous and spiritual destinations.

Nowadays, he lives with his partner and children in Victoria. Their home is close to bushland. Tall timber, mist, the echo of a whipbird's crack. We sat down for the interview in his lounge room, where some didgeridoos stood in a corner, and a black-and-white autographed photo of Lionel Rose, the first Indigenous Australian to win a boxing world title, held court on a wall. Puppa Wati was casually dressed – jeans, T-shirt, thongs – and his hair and chin-stubble had those errant greys that sneak into a man's mid-life. He began his recollections of Bernie and their work together with an ice-breaker. It was the day after the 9/11 attacks in the United States, and Puppa Wati was woken by a knock on his door. 'The planes have gone down, they've hit the buildings,' said Bernie from outside. It made no sense to Puppa Wati, but soon enough he joined the rest of the world staring in disbelief at footage of falling people and tumbling towers. Later, he and Bernie did as they so often did: they boarded a little propeller plane to begin another day's survey work. However, once airborne they were soon told by the pilot, who was tapping his instruments, that there were problems. They returned to base, and problems were indeed discovered with the alternator and belt. Although there was talk they would take off later in the day after repairs, Puppa Wati and Bernie had no intention of going anywhere but to the pub. 'Call me a superstitious black fella but I wasn't going up there again that day,' recalled Puppa Wati, smiling.

Superstitions.

Beliefs.

Cultural interpretations.

Secrets.

Puppa Wati's character is influenced by them all. And this was one of many reasons that Bernie was drawn to him. Here was yet another Indigenous man who knew and *felt* in ways that intrigued Bernie and made him search for a greater understanding of life. This search was itself a track, one on which dingoes left a trail of questions for him that were encouraged, in part, by Puppa Wati's heritage:

'My family has connections with the dingo and its connection to Uluru,' said Puppa Wati. 'There's storylines. The dingo used to come across from the west to Uluru; it ties into similar stories to Azaria Chamberlain's. There's a lot of old stories where young children and women and men were attacked and eaten by the devil dog. Ancestral stories. From Uluru it travelled down south into Kokatha country after it had conflict with other ancestral beings. There are stories there where we hunted that devil dog. There are only certain things I can say about it; it's a big part of my culture. My boys and children, I've got to pass this knowledge down to; they will look after those ceremonial lines when they go through their rites of passage. Bernie and me, we always talked about some of this; it would be nice one day to go back into the desert together.

'I had never met a person who was that keen on working with the dingoes. He had more scientific knowledge, whereas I had the cultural knowledge, which he wasn't privileged to. But he still saw things that showed him.

'We flew over some special places. There are some sandstone rocks, giant boulders, a few hundred klicks the other side of Uluru, south-west. And there was this one huge marble-shaped one, a couple of buses high, and on top of that was a dingo looking up at us. And I'm saying to Bernie: "Is that a wild dog?" And he said: "How did that dog get on that? It's got me buggered." I said I reckoned it was an old fella who was obviously watching us while we were out there. This big old dingo just sitting there watching us. Do we record it? Or was it a spirit one? Bernie and me, we always talked about that dog.'

It was all 'part of the journey, part of the learning' for Bernie. And, it was all fun. When trapping dingoes, he and Puppa Wati used to bet about which foot would be caught in the trap; it was a game that Bernie says his colleague 'had down to a fine art'. But then came the greater challenge of handling the dog.

'A dingo only has two thoughts when it's in a trap: fight and flight,' says Bernie, sitting in his verandah chair. 'We have just taken flight away from him, so he only has one thing left: to fight. He's a wild animal, he understands domination and submission. He understands that he's in a shit position. He's jammed in a spot and suddenly I'm the alpha dog. He sees me as a dog. Nothing else. So, now we go back to Paul Roots. Pressure on, pressure off. Exert that presence. Let the dog know I'm the boss, you're the subordinate; if you attack me, you die. It usually takes about five minutes for that dog to lie down and be calm. Pressure on, pressure off. Then you put the lick of electrical tape around his mouth, just in case, and do your recording, and whatever else from there.

'Of course, it didn't always go to plan. I was doing this job at Ormiston Gorge. There was a hybrid bitch and it had bred close to the campground. The aim was to catch her, shoot her, and leave the pure dingoes behind. I'd had it all worked out. I could see her tracks – every dog has a different footprint, the same as every person does – and I was going to catch her in front of her den on this rocky slope. So, set the trap, and it's at night when the howling begins. Got her. Now, working with dogs in the Territory you gotta carry a firearm. I'm clambering up this slope, stumbling about with a young ranger new to the job. We've got the torch on. And there's the dog. Get it to submit, yep no worries. Now to take this thing out of the trap. I put the firearm down, a twenty-two. Then I slipped – it was really steep – and I must have misjudged the length of chain on the trap, coz the dog just came alive and *whack!* It had me on the left hand. Oh no, I'm going to lose my thumb here. It was shaking me around and I was thinking to myself: "Just breathe and don't pull. If you want your thumb, panic slowly." So, I'm there panicking slowly and there is blood running everywhere and this dog, it's not letting me go. And I'm telling this ranger she'll have to shoot the dog, but she's upset, in tears I think, and I can't reach the rifle. Every now and then the dog goes quiet, and then all of a sudden it goes for another rip. Panic slowly, panic slowly! Don't pull your hand away. Eventually the ranger nudges the rifle over to where I could pick it up, and I try to cock this thing while the dog is shaking me. It must have gone on for minutes by the time I killed it. Then, we had to get rid of the pups, coz they all had hybrid in them too. I kept one, black and white with white spots, for a while at home. But it wouldn't get on with other dogs, and I was the only one who could handle him. God, the number of people he bit! I tried to pat him and say: "Isn't he a cute little fella?" But *crunch!* I ended up having to get rid of him. Dingoes, they're super-smart, super-athletic. But they're just so hard to keep.

'I still felt connected with them, though. Admiration. Plenty of admiration. Puppa Wati and me – I was by myself and with others sometimes – we used to go out in the Toyotas, and we had this vinyl chair that we could put on the back when we were spotlighting or we'd put it on the bull bar at the front when we were tracking. We'd sit on it, drive along and do our work. Comfortable enough. One day, I saw this dingo. Beautiful animal. Strong, sleek. And he was in this area where the dogs were going to be wiped out. But he kept coming back, kept showing up when I was around. Was it the same dog? Yep. I looked at his prints. Same dog, all right. Wherever I went. We had that special connection. I can't explain it, but I felt it. So, I taught him how to survive. I used to fire rounds over him or under his feet every time a vehicle came along. And every time he came in too close to me, I'd shoot near him. Just to make him aware. Tell him what trouble could be. But he kept following me on and off for a couple of years. I'd be camping and he'd come and camp not too far away. How did that dog know to go there when I could've been two hundred kilometres away? Back then, I was still working this stuff out, but I have my thoughts now. He was a spirit dog. Yeah, people can call me a weirdo. I'm happy for people to say that. But I know what I felt. And I reckon I helped that dog stay alive. That was my gift back to him.

'There were so many things I didn't know back then. And there still are. But I reckon I know why a lot of it happened. It was preparing me for the future, and what I could use at BackTrack.'

Significantly, it wasn't only Bernie's dingo education that remains strong in Puppa Wati's recollections. At the simplest times of their work together, they shared stories, drank beer, stared into campfire flames, and ate rabbits they had trapped and cooked. But there were also the complexities of broader relationships in environments that were burdened with racist attitudes and cultural ignorance.

'He was a diamond in the rough,' said Puppa Wati. 'In the Northern Territory if someone didn't like you because of your race or your background, it was pretty evident. Bernie wouldn't hang around and take crap. People that weren't genuine, he wouldn't spend time with. He had the bullshit radar. He didn't mind getting in blues with a few people because he'd always be there to defend people who were getting the rough end of the stick. It didn't matter if it was about race, background or position in life. We'd go into a white-fella bar, and we'd hear all the comments about me not belonging in there, but Bernie would be: "Get stuffed." Then I'd take him into a blackfella bar and it would be different: "He's like one of us." He was well known in Alice Springs and around the Aboriginal communities. He was respected.'

However, as uplifting as many of Bernie's relationships may have been, they couldn't fill the cracks in the relationship at the centre of Bernie's life. During his several years working with Parks and Wildlife, Bernie split from Jayne a number of times. He moved in and out of the family home and lived in places including a bus in a friend's backyard. Not even the birth of Maeve could heal the unpredictable rifts.

In any interview, discussions about personal relationships can be difficult to broach, and I warn Bernie before we start. He shakes his head and says: 'It's okay. It happened. It's part of us. I was probably a hard bloke to live with. Absent a lot. And drinking. It's not very difficult to work out some of the angles that would have caused problems. But I always would've done my share of the parenting. Maeve was too little to know what was happening. And James, he was at school, I was coaching his soccer. Things between us were pretty good really, but Jayne's and my relationship was always going to come to a head. And when it did, Jayne took the kids and moved back to New South Wales, Raymond Terrace; her dad was really sick there and needed lots of care. It was a ratty time. I was thinking I should've got a job back in Alice Springs and James should have stayed with me. Eventually he did. He hadn't been going well at school down south and he needed his dad, so back he came.'

James was used to coming and going between the states. In the years before the marriage break-up, he had often spent school holidays in Sydney with his grandparents Joe and Denise, and after the break-up he was taken back on a brief trip to Alice Springs with his aunt, Maree, Bernie's sister. Finally, when he returned to Alice Springs to live with his dad, he felt as though he had arrived home. 'It's where all my friends were,' said James. 'It was good to be back.'

During his interview, James sounded very much like Bernie. Similar intonations, long pauses, punctuations of thought with 'you know', the unusual use of 'proper' as an adjective. When I told James this, he laughed wholeheartedly.

'Yeah, a lot of people say we have a few similarities. My old man, I always remember he would take me out bush. He taught me how to drive out on the roads in the middle of nowhere. He took me spotlighting, and he taught me how to track the dingoes. I kind of took it at face value at the time, but I now look back and go, "Wow, man, there were a lot of skills there, especially about the Indigenous culture." You know, I was brought up to have a lot of respect for that way of life, and that left my mind open. There are definitely some special things that go on out there. It was Dad's life back then. Apart from soccer, they were the lessons he was giving me. There was no taking me to the local fair or the show; instead it was going out bush doing things.'

Bernie continued to spend long periods, often weeks on end, working away from Alice Springs. During those times James was cared for by a couple, Jo and Gerard, who were close to both Bernie and Jayne. One of their children was the same age as Maeve, and they were close friends. Gerard was a 'wise soul', a good sounding board for Bernie, and apart from occasionally offering advice about fatherhood he gave other tips that Bernie valued. One evening Bernie whinged to his friend about how his boss, a 'good guy', was annoyed by Bernie's lack of regard for clothing regulations. Bernie used to cut the sleeves off his Parks and Wildlife uniforms; it was a very 'ringer-ish look' but not very professional.

'And that's where the next double-plugger story comes in,' says Bernie, grinning. 'I used to wear them a lot at work. It didn't matter what the situation was. But the boss was into me about it. Gerard told me, and spot on he was too: "Look, you idiot, look at all the things you do, and all this bloke is concentrating on is your thongs. Whatever you do, keep wearing them." I've got no doubt I was forever stretching the rules, with my shirts, or going to work a bit late, so if the thongs were the only issue the boss could see, that wasn't too bad. So, Gerard taught me the "thong lesson", the distraction theory.'

There was, however, no disguising the difficulties of being a single dad trying to raise a boy approaching adolescence in a remote desert town. And what of a young girl growing up with a single mum in a densely populated coastal corridor? In his answers Bernie looked beyond the geographical distance to the emotional distance. For a man whose cross-cultural experiences had given him a deeper understanding of connection, he knew and felt that his family needed to be closer together. He spoke with Jayne about this, and after spending about ten years in the Territory, Bernie decided it was time to make tracks back south.

PART TWO

Education is not just sitting in a classroom learning to read and write and count. I could get a bunch of city fellas to walk in bare feet through a frosty paddock, and their toes are about to snap right off, but I reckon none of 'em would know to go and stand in a fresh cow-pat to keep their toes warm. But I know a lot of country boys who would. We all learn differently, and we must realise that. No-one is always right. No-one is always wrong.

Bernie Shakeshaft

13

There are thirteen staff at the meeting in the smoko room. It's late afternoon. Jannelle opens proceedings. She talks about upcoming dog shows. There's discussion about logistics. Which boys will go? Who will drive them? Where will they stay? It's a gentle start.

After that, talk turns to 'the incident'. It happened the previous day. Ugly. A fight between two boys. One of the worst moments ever at the BackTrack depot.

Ike, a former shearer, rubs a hand across his blond stubble. As a youngster he'd hurled his share of knuckles. He stresses one of the most important 'agreements' of BackTrack: 'Leave your crap at the gate.'

Heads nod.

More talk.

Opinions. Observations. Solutions.

The mood is serious. Arms are crossed. Worry weighs down on brows.

Then, another troubling topic. It seems one boy has been fudging the truth about a particular issue.

More heads nod before Bernie jumps in: 'You gotta shine light on that stuff when they're not telling the truth. These kids will eat you alive with stories. Makes my fuckin' blood boil. Makes me fuckin' swear too.'

Finally, there is laughter.

The cigarette smoke that hangs over Bernie is like a cloud from detonated words. F-bombs. C-bombs. The verandah hears them all. They erupt midway through the second day of interviews. It's now that we have arrived at the reason Bernie's life has begun to attract so much attention: BackTrack, the organisation whose website opens with rolling images from a widely acclaimed documentary that is layered with the words: 'HELPING YOUNG PEOPLE GET BACK ON TRACK.'

Simple words, yet incredibly difficult to implement and uphold.

For the past fifteen minutes Bernie has spoken about his move from the Northern Territory. He said it was tough. He thought he was going to be up north for the rest of his life. But 'things happen, and responsibility comes tapping you on the shoulder'. Move on, do what you have to do.

Bernie and James arrived in Gunnedah, then a town of about 9000 people in north-west New South Wales. In the language of the local Kamilaroi people, it is the 'place of white stones'. It is also one of coal and fertile soils, and the divisions between mining and agriculture run deep in an area that partly inspired Dorothea Mackellar's iconic poem 'My Country'. Bernie secured a job as a youth development officer with the local council. Was it a single-minded plan to return to youth work? No. It was more a case of knowing he had the skills and experience to get the position. Furthermore, Gunnedah was only 180 kilometres south-west of

Armidale, the town of childhood memories that Bernie was feeling increasingly drawn to.

Over about eighteen months – 'but don't get me started on numbers and dates again' – Bernie and his colleagues did some 'really cool stuff with the Gunnedah kids', including fishing at the nearby Namoi River, and running a youth council whose headquarters was in a community centre off the main street. But Bernie was also frustrated: 'I was working with some pretty busted people, but I think I probably spent too much time doing fairy-cupcake sort of stuff and play groups in the school holidays, rather than working on the kids who really needed help. I felt I was just a babysitter.'

It was a busy and evolving time for Bernie. He was back being a hands-on dad to both James and Maeve, because he and Jayne were together again. They were living in and renovating a house, 'a falling-down type of thing' they had bought cheaply. Jayne was also studying Natural Medicine, and was often at college on the central coast, four hours' drive away. Even when she was absent, though, there was an affable reminder of her presence: a long-haired half-collie named Missy, with whom Jayne returned home one day. Missy, however, didn't have Ben for company. The pet-shop shepherd had been with Bernie on many Territory trips, but in his old age was more a fan of sitting on a lounge chair in air conditioning; he was to see out his final years with a woman from whom Bernie had rented a flat in Alice Springs.

As he juggled family commitments with his work in Gunnedah, Bernie began searching for more. Again, he can't remember how exactly it happened, but a new job offer came at just the right time, and unquestionably, it was the right place: a youth worker in Armidale. Soon enough the Northern Tablelands town was again home to a Shakeshaft family.

'I don't think Armidale had ever really left me,' says Bernie, with smoke hanging over him. 'I still had good friends there, like Flinty. And knowing the streets, the houses, the schools, it all seemed like a good fit. Nothing much had changed since I left, really. A bit bigger, and a set of traffic lights, that's all. I knew I was being drawn there. There was a reason.

'So, I get this job, and it's a good one. The high schools in town, Armidale and Duval, had got together and decided to do something about troubled boys. I was put in charge of about ten of them from each school. The powers-that-be said they weren't going to reach or finish Year Ten, but it was my job to try to get them over the line. It was a joint program with TAFE. I thought: "I should be able to tackle this." But these kids, they were a pretty intense little crew. Some from one school wanting to go the biff with some from the other. Pulling knives. Yeah, pretty intense. But that's okay. They were wild, and I felt more at home with wild kids.

'I challenged people straightaway. Challenged conventions. First up, I got some senior school staff and the TAFE guys, and we did a workshop with the kids. And I said: "We're not going to have any rules down here." Well, you should have seen the meltdowns. They were asking: "What do you mean we're not going to have any rules?" Simple. "We're *not* going to have any fuckin' *rules*." Everything was designed to catch everyone's attention, especially the boys. Because if you don't have their attention, you can't move ahead. I said: "Instead, we're going to have agreements. So, today, we're going to work out what those agreements are."

'The kids started writing down things like "Ya gotta have respect."

'And I'd hit back: "That's all nice, but what the fuck does that *mean*?"

'"Don't punch any cunt in the head."

'"Excellent, everybody happy to have that agreement? Give a show of hands for it."

'Hands go up.

'"Right, agreement number one: Sorted."

'The whole idea behind the agreements – and we still use them all the time at BackTrack – is to get the kids involved. They're the same sorts of things you'd come up with for your son, or I came up with for my kids. You know: pick up your own mess, clean up after lunch, don't swear at teachers, don't punch people, show up on time. But the difference is that you put it in their words in a way that they can understand and own it. And you make sure the onus is on them. I'm not the principal, the magistrate, the parent of these boys, and I'm not telling them what to do. They have to tell themselves that. It's not that there aren't any rules; it's just a different way of approaching the problem. Using the kids' words and the way they think. The language can be offensive but we have to try something different because we're in the business of keeping kids alive – the non-offensive rule book gets put aside to do that.

'So, onto TAFE. Let's get this program happening. Youth Links. Every Friday, and later on it grew to Thursdays as well. On those Fridays we had the whole of TAFE to ourselves. I can't remember the exact order, but I reckon we started with welding. I could street weld, but nothing more. It was hard, you know. I think the first teacher is still on stress leave. I'm not sure when it happened, but it was certainly early on: one kid made this bomb out of the oxy bottle and a cigarette lighter and he blew a hole in the roof. These were bouncy kids, ricocheting off walls, hitting each other, chucking stuff. It was just a struggle to make it to lunchtime.

'Then we tried art. Had a decent teacher. The boys were making sculptures out of those Hebel blocks and other bits and pieces. But, most of the stuff was rude. Like, giant penises. "Okay, instead we'll do something with clay, do something fine with our hands." Then a police car pulls into the driveway with a big clod of clay in the middle of his windscreen. So, we got moved on from art, and I'm thinking: "This is *not* working!"

'Where did we go after that? Computers. Education Department computers. On the first day those boys downloaded enough inappropriate material to start a state inquiry. So, kicked out of the computer room too. It was bedlam. Thank God we had these agreements; at least we weren't punching each other in the head.

'It turned out to be a hell of a year. Shit, we were bucking down the flat! I was enjoying it, though. Having a great time. Oh, that's right, here's another thing that happened. The TAFE had its own climbing wall, and I thought that would be super because the boys would have to take risks and look after each other. Belaying and all that sort of stuff. Well, lunchtime on the day we've done the climbing and the boss man at TAFE comes down and issues me a "please explain" about what my class is doing on the roof of a building. I said: "From here it looks like they're playing touch football." You see, they used the climbing wall as a stepping stone to get up higher. Oh shit! Things like that were happening all the time.'

We both laugh loudly. It's impossible not to. I ask Bernie if it would be possible to find some of the boys from that time. I say: 'They'd be great to have for the book. They'd add another dimension.' Bernie nods. 'Won't be a problem,' he says. 'We'll sort out a couple of them. You can explain to them what it's about, and then it's up to them if they want to talk. But I reckon Andrew will. He's a good place to start.'

—

Andrew had a blocked nose the day of our interview; a cold he'd caught from his kids. Upon entering Bernie's office at the BackTrack depot, he took off his cowboy hat, and placed it on Bernie's desk. His hair was matted in sweat and his hands were callused. He wore a blue BackTrack work shirt, jeans and boots. Throughout our chat he periodically leant back and swivelled on a chair. It was Bernie's chair. Andrew appeared very much at ease.

'I was failing at school, so I was suspended almost every week. I was smoking, fighting, wagging, drugs, all that kind of stuff. I didn't want to be at school, really. The only things that were going well for me at school was that I found the love of my life and football. That's probably why I was there so long. Rugby league. I played five-eighth, then moved to lock. A bit of ball play, and when I wanted to run hard, I just ran hard.

'And then I was called up to the deputy principal's office one day, and I was a bit blown away because I was thinking: "I haven't stuffed up, what the heck is going on?" When I got up there a few other boys in my year were up there too. A few of me mates.

'The deputy principal explained what was going on. There was a guy coming in to give us a proposal to try something different. And then Bernie walked in. And there was a connection straightaway, I think. He put a proposal on the table: "You boys are struggling at school. You've had some hard times in your life. We want to show you some ways to make it a bit easier for you, and probably school at the same time." But we didn't think that. As it turned out, some of it worked, some of it didn't.'

Andrew laughed.

'The metal work went well with a lot of us. Not all of us. Some things were set on fire. But that's probably one of the biggest things we took out of it: learning to weld and using the power tools, like grinders and drills. It was pretty good when you got to melt bits of steel with the oxy. So, it started working once we got into that. Bern thought, "The boys are getting their hands dirty, so this is the way forward."'

———

Having a way forward was central to Bernie's philosophy – the past had happened, and it was no place for the boys to dwell. Some of their histories were horrific. Bernie and I spoke about them and decided most of the more troubling details would be left out of this book. There were 'too many better stories to tell'.

The initial intake of Youth Links boys included one youngster, Michael, with whom Bernie felt a 'very strong connection'.

'A most extraordinary sportsman,' says Bernie with obvious admiration. 'But, I didn't think we were going to be able to help him. And he certainly wasn't going to be able to help himself. He was a busted, tormented, troubled little soul. I didn't think we'd ever keep that kid alive. He was either going to kill someone or be killed. He was a real dilemma, that boy. Had a beautiful, wonderful nature, a help-anyone-do-anything kind of kid, but a pile of damage underneath it all. He was wild. Definitely in my top five wild. Tough and streetwise. And could he fight! And the trouble with the cops … oh shit … he was as clever as. I know kids who've done two per cent of what he did and got locked up, but he managed to avoid and evade. Then again, when you know his past, you can understand. When he was about seven, he used to go to a takeaway shop in the evening and get chips scraped out of the oil in the bottom of a fryer. That was his food for the day. When I first got him …'

Bernie shakes his head and lets out a long, whistling breath.

'I reckon he'll be difficult to catch for the book.'

He was. There is no interview with Michael in these pages. But that's not a reflection on Bernie, nor Michael. They remain in contact; a long-distance connection that, over the years, has seen Bernie go to extraordinary lengths – including overseas – to help him.

'There were plenty of times when I had the biggest showdowns with him,' says Bernie. 'I did with many of the boys. It was part of the process. Many of them had the: "I'm a freewheeling, swearing, fuck-you tough guy" attitude. Well, okay. But they had to know I wasn't a soft-cock teacher type. So, I showed them that blokey stuff. Probably not too much at TAFE, and not one to tell TAFE either. But, my oath, I did a bit of hands-on stuff with them. If you want to have a bit of a stand-up-and-spar against a soft cock, bring it on. If you want to close a fist against me close it, but I'll tell you what, you'll get to understand that I won't back down to standover shit.

'It was about challenging them, right from the start. Have conversations. How do you treat women? There were times when we were driving along, and someone would holler something out the window at a girl and I'd slam on the brakes and say: "Get out! What did you just say? Can you imagine if that was my daughter?" You have to make an immediate impact. You have to get into their world. They'd rarely hear me raise my voice, so when I did – shit, listen up boys, what's the message? Communication is only ten per cent words. So much is in the delivery. "And anyone who didn't have your seatbelt on, we'll talk about that later, coz you just whacked your fuckin' head on the dashboard." Because when I say I jammed the brakes on, I jammed them on. Immediate impact. "Get the fuck out of the car. All of you." Now, I've got their attention. "Imagine if that was your mother?" Coz one thing that really pushed them was saying something about their mothers. I did that sort of stuff all the time, but the key was to talk about it. Think about it. And come up with a solution to the problem.

'So, that's when I'd bring in the deeper talk. I wanted to get the boys to put their names to things. To own their behaviours, and to question them. The rights and the wrongs. We'd just get in some sort of circle and talk. I'd steer the conversation if I had to. Other times the boys would bounce it along. We decided on the name of it right at the start. Someone said: "Circle Work", and it stuck. It sorta had a connection to guys getting together, spinning their utes and then hanging out. Circle Work. I didn't know back then how important it would be; we still use it to start the day, sort out issues through the day, and finish each day. We use numbers with it; that's an idea that a youth worker, Peter Slattery – a huge help to me over the years – had when I first met him when I was in Gunnedah. "Okay boys, we're going to go around the circle and rate how your day's been going. Anyone having a fuckin' shit, fucked off, fucker of a day? We'll call that a one." And if you're having a one or a two, what helps you with that? Do you like someone to come over and have a talk? Do you like us to poke fun at you? No, just leave me the fuck alone, okay. "Okay, we're going to have an agreement here if someone is on a one or a two, we'll leave them the fuck alone." And they get it. That's how we get them to own their shit and look after each other and respect that we all have bad days. And on the flip side, if you're having a smashing day, the best day ever, then you have a ten out of ten. It's all about getting the conversation going. It has become second nature to the kids we work with.

'So, getting back to the yelling-out-the-car-window-at-a-girl. It was important to dig down. "How would that make you feel if I said that to your mother? 'Come on, show us your tits!' Tell me, what are you feeling? I don't want a description, I want a feeling." Someone might come back with anger. "Right, there we go," I'd say. "Now tell me what that feeling is?" Make the big points with them. Talk until their ears bleed. Then they get to realise: "This shit is important." Too right it is. It's *very* important. Any of that sort of rubbish talk, anywhere, I'd jump on it, stomp on that crap. No place for it. Racism? Same thing. Any topic. If the talk and actions didn't fit with what I considered good behaviour and attitudes, I'd jump on it. Called them out every single time. "When you shake someone's hand, make it a firm shake, look them in the eyes. If you can't do that, boys, get to the end of the line and try again." And if they didn't want to do it? Well, we'll just wait it out, and no-one's going home until we have a crack at the lesson. The power of positive peer support was enormous.'

Much of what Bernie has said so far about Youth Links suggests it was a school of hard knocks. If a cartoonist were asked to portray it, there might be an image of a red-faced man, with sweat flicking off behind him as he raised a sledgehammer while chasing a spindle-legged cloud of dust out of which profanities, lumps of clay and big penises were hurled. But for those who witnessed Bernie at work, the picture was very different.

Carolyn Lasker was the head teacher of wellbeing at Duval High School during Bernie's time at Youth Links. We spoke over coffee at an Armidale cafe.

'The most noticeable thing for me was Bernie's natural affinity with kids. Any kids, really,' said Carolyn. 'It didn't matter if they were hard to work with. He wasn't the sort of person who, if there were adults around, would divide the two and let them each get on with their own things. He had a real ability to be able to bring kids into the picture and could really relate to them in a very adult way. And that made them feel a bit special about themselves. He still applies that wonderful quality to all the kids that he works with. And he's probably more effective with those kids who are a bit on the outer. Those marginalised kids. The Circle Work. Just drawing stuff out. That was really impressive. It was the start of him getting the tag "The Kid Whisperer".'

Many who knew Bernie used the nickname with some degree of banter, but this didn't belittle the deeper meaning. It was a title that had been earned over much of a lifetime. The great empathy he'd shown since his early school years had been strengthened by his own experiences of recklessness and personal disregard. He could relate to the boys in Youth Links because he too had endured struggles that warped his view about the value of life and the importance of building a future. Although he hadn't hit the depths that some boys had, nor had he suffered through tragic family upbringings, there was no doubting he shared one commonality with every boy in the program: he hadn't liked school. And amid the boys' reasons for this, there was again an overarching theme: each boy generally had poor results in the classroom, and hence was considered a poor student.

The more Bernie spent time with the Youth Links boys the more he sought answers to the question he had first pondered at length with Dusty when they were at teachers' college: What is education? His life continued to teach him that too many kids were still being shoved into boxes in which they didn't fit or belong. Yet these boxes were the ones ticked by the conventions of society as being best. In all too many situations sitting up straight, getting that good mark and gold star remained the benchmarks for success during school and in the years afterwards. That way of thinking was misguided, misinformed and a mistake. So, how best could Bernie shape education to best suit the Youth Links boys? While he continued to sift through ideas and discuss them with people whose input he respected (including the boys), his ability as the Kid Whisperer was tested in a way that no amount of planning could ever prepare him for.

Several months into the program, in July 2005, one of the boys in Youth Links was killed in a motorbike accident. He had turned sixteen just a month earlier.

'The boys were shattered,' says Bernie, quietly. 'He had some close mates in the program. Boys will cry if you give them the right opportunity. And better an empty house than a bad tenant. So, let's get it all out. We encouraged that. You don't need to hold it in. You don't need to do this supposed man stuff by showing everyone how strong you are.

'We handled that death the same way we've come to handle everything else at BackTrack: by talking about it. We went out to Paul and Annette Roots' place near Ebor. I'd never lost touch with them, and what a great bit of luck that they'd bought a cattle place not too far from Armidale. Their neighbour, Dave, helped the boys make a cross out of rosewood – it didn't matter if it wasn't the greatest bit of work, but it was important that the boys had a hand in it – and then we went to the accident site on the Old Kempsey Road. Beautiful country up there. We put the cross on the tree that the boy had hit, and we planted a happy wanderer, a pretty native with a purple flower. Then we had a conversation around that tree. We spoke about the accident and how they felt. "What happens when you die?" "Where do you think he is now?" "Can you feel it?" "Do you think about his spirit?" Absolutely, we spoke about that stuff. "What are you thinking? Let it out." "What do you think about wearing helmets on motorbikes?" We talked about it all. Painful. We were used to seeing these rowdy boys running around bashing each other, throwing rocks, annoying each other, but we didn't see any of that around that tree. Taking them back to the accident site. That was the power. No use tiptoeing around death; it's the ride we're all going on. If you know for certain that you're going to die, you better start working out what you think happens to you. And if you think it's nothing, that's not a problem; at least you've thought it through. Heaven and hell? The boys spoke about that. Questions and answers. Lots of thinking. "What happens if you and your brother, one goes to hell and the other goes to heaven? Will you be eternally happy?" Making them think. Making them think about how they felt.

'And hugs. All this garbage about males shouldn't hug each other. Some of these kids had gone through enormous trauma in their lives, and this death was just another kick in the guts. So, give them a hug. Forget the "I'm a big man, I don't do that." Forget all those images of toughness. Give them a hug. Give them that warmth and shelter. Let them be vulnerable. There's no weakness in showing it.

'We had a smoking ceremony, too. I'd seen them lots of times in the Territory. Big ceremonies where the whole house is smoked, and out in the bush with old men and animals. I think as long as the intention is pure, there is nothing wrong with borrowing something so respectful and meaningful from another culture. Releasing the spirit. You can feel it go.

'Yeah, that time at that tree ... boy ...

'We went to the funeral, too. Welded a horseshoe that was screwed to the coffin. Tough times. But ones to learn from. Who said: "You never let a good crisis go to waste."? Truer words have never been spoken.'

The death was a defining moment of Bernie's time at Youth Links. Boys being challenged by their emotions and thoughts, and being confronted by the realisation that puffed-out chests and swaggers meant nothing when teenage invincibility stood toe-to-toe with mortality. To Bernie, it was yet another time to learn, to better grasp the needs of the boys with whom he had begun to develop strong bonds. Above all, a triple-pronged mantra churned in his thoughts: 'First, we have to keep them alive; second, we have to keep them out of trouble and out of jail; and then we can work on their hopes and dreams.'

But how to get to that point? Part of the answer lies in the sunshine outside the verandah. Girl and Lou are curled like commas on the grass. They are asleep, oblivious to the soft mentioning of their names, and the roles they played in an integral team of youth workers.

'They were both part of that litter,' says Bernie, nodding in the direction of his two old ladies. 'Somewhere along the way Jayne and I put one of Rootsy's super-dog collies, Tie, with our Missy, the one that Jayne had found in Gunnedah. So, we had this litter of pups – Girl, Lou, Zorro, Leo, and a few others – and I was starting to think: "What would happen if I took these pups into TAFE for the boys?" I went through the whole bureaucracy thing. You know, have the dogs been vaccinated? Who's going to do the risk assessment? It made me angry. "Look at these kids I'm dealing with, and you're worried about whether they get worms from a wormy pup?" Seriously! So, I thought about it some more and decided: "Right, let's do this Shakeshaft style. If I can't take the dogs in, well, let's test that theory. And let's see what happens; it's easier to ask for forgiveness than permission!"

'So, in we go, and I toss the pups on the TAFE lawn. And I keep my distance, and I'm looking out through this window at all these violent kids, being as gentle as you've ever seen, sitting and holding these black-and-white pups. The boss was still worried about all the management side, but what I saw going on between those boys and the dogs was good enough for me.'

—

Sitting in Bernie's office with his blocked nose, Andrew smiled when he recalled that first day with the pups.

'That's when Bernie really opened my eyes up. That's when I really started enjoying what we were doing. I was from town, and before then I hadn't really had much contact with working dogs. I had a house dog, but I wasn't really interested in dogs that much. But Bernie's pups ended up taking us places. They helped us. Humans can judge ya, but a dog never will judge ya. I had Girl first. The first dog I became mates with. I got to train her. Teaching her to sit, wait, lie down … all that stuff. And just hang out with her. That day Bernie put the pups on the lawn didn't change me from being what I was, but it did make me think.'

Dogs that didn't judge and boys who'd all had countless judgements made about them. An unlikely mix in education? Or a natural relationship that society too often overlooked in its haste to tick the boxes of convention? After Bernie put his pups on the TAFE lawn, he knew what he must do: he had to keep doing things Shakeshaft style. Unfortunately, though, he felt fenced in by red tape. Sitting in his verandah chair, he sighs. It's a statement all on its own.

'I kept the dogs in the program, and I honestly can't remember how much trouble I got in for doing it. Maybe a few blind eyes were turned. But I do remember having a distinct gut feeling about dogs and boys. The year kept going, and we tried our best within some limitations. They were obviously not academically inclined, so why not be doing other things instead? In a bizarre way, the death of our one boy taught others about the values of welding and how it wasn't just about making things. It gave them a purpose, and that's something they couldn't find in a classroom doing algebra or spelling. The aim was to keep those boys at school to the end of Year Ten, and we did that. But then the program finished, and we started with a new crew. That's what I couldn't understand. There was no chance that those first groups of boys we'd worked so hard on were ever going to get jobs. They weren't ready. Our work hadn't finished. We'd built them up and got them somewhere, albeit slowly, but we were gaining traction. And then what did we do? Kick them out of the program. Righto, see you later boys, have a nice life. It didn't make sense. So much more had to be done.'

And it was.

14

The sunlight is sharp and wintry. In the shadows, mist rises with spoken words.

'Don't worry me. It's not cold,' says the boy as he sits down on the table bench near Bernie's office.

He's dressed in a black T-shirt and jeans that hang loose enough for the hip band of his underpants to be seen. The soles of his sneakers offer more slip than grip.

He says his journey to BackTrack began when he was in late primary school. That's when he started mucking about in class. First, he stopped listening to the teacher. Then he started swearing at her. Then? He skips a few stages in his summary and arrives at 'got suspended'. After that, he did as all too many troubled kids do: 'I fell in with the wrong crowd.' He began smoking 'yarndie' (marijuana). A gram a day: 'Not much.' To support his habit, he and his crowd started 'creepin'', breaking into shops and houses to steal money. Cop trouble followed. Others in the crowd are now locked up. But this boy, who is now looking down and scuffing his shoes in the dust, was lucky: he linked up with BackTrack.

'I love it here,' he says. 'I'm getting sorted out. It makes me feel proud.'

As for the help Bernie has given him?

'Yeah, he's heaps good coz he tries. He cares.'

This boy doesn't want to go back to school. He wants to get a 'good job'.

It's too early to say what the job may be, but he does like working on properties 'coz they're nice and quiet'.

For the moment, though, BackTrack is the way forward.

The boy is fifteen years old.

His father died when he was four.

'I think Bernie is like an inspirational dentist with bad teeth,' said Kevin Dupe, laughing over the phone. 'He doesn't look after himself. He's a bit of a rogue, a tearaway, but that's partly why the kids can relate to him.'

Kevin Dupe is the CEO of the Regional Australia Bank. He has lived in Armidale for more than twenty years. When he first met Bernie at a party towards the end of 2005, he was CEO of one of the Regional Australia Bank's predecessors, New England Credit Union Mutual. He was a man with a professional lifetime of business experience and connections.

'I made the mistake of asking Bernie who he was and what he did, and about an hour-and-a-half later, he drew breath.'

Joke as he does about that meeting, Kevin was affected by the presence of the drinking, smoking, swearing stranger whose vision and energy were out of the ordinary. Bernie said he wanted to establish a place where troubled kids could 'drop into' and perhaps learn a thing or two, such as welding and other manual skills. The idea was swirling in Bernie's thoughts and was far from settling, but he knew he could do something that could make a difference.

In fact, he *had* to. Kevin listened to the heartfelt delivery. And at the end of the unexpected conversation, he felt he too *had* to.

The exact details of the chronology have been lost to the years, but at some stage, not too long after that meeting, Kevin contacted Rosemary Mort, a journalist and media-relations professional who was widely respected in the community. He said to her: 'I want you to help this guy who wants to work with kids. I think it's a good thing that he's doing.' And out of that conversation, further phone calls followed until Bernie saw a number that he didn't recognise on his mobile.

'Shit, talk about things falling into place,' says Bernie in his verandah chair. 'Here's this Rosemary Mort on the phone. Who is she? Says she does some work for the local state politician Richard Torbay. I didn't really understand what she meant, but then the ears prick up. A meeting has been arranged for me with Rosemary, Richard, Kevin Dupe and Peter Ducat the mayor of Armidale. Down at a coffee shop. Wow. All right, then.

'I roll into this meeting and they've got the keys to the old Dumaresq Shire depot on the edge of town. See, there used to be two councils, Armidale and Dumaresq, but they merged into one, and this depot is not being used. And they say: "Let's go and have a look at it." Next thing you know, I'm walking through this old shed, garbage everywhere, big holes in the roof, wire in the yard, just a bloody mess. But Kevin says: "Here's a shed and a place to get you started." Right. Wow again. We're off and going. I rang Flinty, Jayne and a good mate of ours, Simmo. I also called Gel [Geraldine] Cutmore; she'd been working on this other thing I was doing at the time, Street Beat. I told them: "Guess what? We've got a shed! Now, what?" Well, there was a massive clean-up to begin with. Then we started a bit of a welding program for some of the boys. Just on the weekends to begin with. Gel, Jayne, her sister, Sally, Flinty, lots of people helped out. Gee, that time was a blur. A lot started happening.'

On its own, Street Beat was a blur. Or perhaps, a bleed; one involving youths cut from the mainstream and transplanted to the precarious edges where disobedience, cultural divisions, ignorance, boredom, low self-esteem and the exercise of power were all among a flow that could turn turbulent at any time, usually after the sun went down. Street Beat, run by the Eastern Area Community Health Service, involved paid workers driving through the streets at night and picking up wayward kids and returning them to their homes. Gel Cutmore was often alongside Bernie. She'd first met him at Youth Links when she was the Aboriginal Education Assistant at Duval High School.

'There were some very funny moments at Youth Links, and some embarrassing ones too,' she said during a face-to-face interview in Armidale. 'One of the things the boys needed to know about was sex. I mean, they knew how to have it, but did they know how to respectfully have it with girls? And did they know what to look for in sexually transmitted diseases? I showed them pictures of infected penises, what chlamydia looked like. They were squirming, and I could sense their unease. Bernie was all for it. He let me have that conversation with them.

'One of the first things I remember about Bernie at Youth Links was he asked me what I thought about the boys going off to smoke. I told him it didn't worry me – actually I would have said stronger words than that – and I said there were more important things we had to do with them. He agreed. It was about which battles we wanted to take on. And we continued that at Street Beat.'

It didn't take long for Bernie to realise he had an incredible ally. A strong, effervescent woman whose parents came from Indigenous communities in Moree and Kempsey. She was one of seven children, but 'really I had twelve older brothers because I also grew up with my aunties and uncles, and those brothers knocked some sense into me'. During the interview, her smiles frequently exploded into high-pitched laughter; a distinctive trait in a character who also knew when a few loud sentences laden with expletives could be frightening tools of persuasion. When working on Street Beat, the kids they picked up, mostly boys, were drunk or wandering around either causing or looking for trouble. Throwing rocks at windows, smashing glass bottles on footpaths, pulling antennas off cars ... lots of petty street crime, and occasionally, more serious offences such as break-and-enters, theft and assault. The boys were found under bridges and houses, in cubby holes they made in parks, in dark grandstands of the sporting grounds ... anywhere but at home.

'Sometimes there'd be huge parties,' recalled Gel. 'Lots of kids, and the police would call us and ask us to pop up and take the kids. So, we'd get there and take them, or one of us would stay to control things. The relationships we forged with a lot of those kids was just incredible. The boys would do anything for Bernie. They'd walk over hot coals for him. Bernie was pretty solid. Not much riled him.'

However, one thing most certainly did: the police. Bernie had run-ins with officers, particularly with those he considered were too verbally, and at times, physically aggressive. There were moments when he argued heatedly with them about how the kids should be spoken to, and how they should be physically handled. It was a sensitive, sometimes brittle relationship that was influenced by different attitudes, experiences and ages. When recalling some incidents Bernie acknowledges his anger at perceived 'injustices'.

'It was some of the younger cops I had trouble with,' he says. 'If the kids had done something wrong, yeah sure, they had to be taken through the appropriate procedures and channels, but over-reactions were a problem. I saw and heard things that I didn't consider necessary. And I still don't. One thing I really remember is when new counter-terrorism laws came out, and the cops started strip-searching kids on the street at two o'clock in the morning. I didn't like it one little bit. We were forever right in the confrontational zone: pissed kids, cranky cops, late nights. It wasn't a great environment for happy endings. We now have an unbelievable relationship with the police, but it wasn't always like that. There were some very tough and I think unnecessary times.'

Country policing is very different from metropolitan policing. Firstly, in cities such as Sydney, command areas may have just one or two stations in a small geographical area, whereas a country command, stretching over hundreds of kilometres, can have a dozen or more stations; notably some of these may have just one or two officers. Also, city commands usually have much easier and quicker access to a greater variety of resources than the bush does. The incidents too can be different. Theft of stock, hay, grain and fuel; heavy vehicle inspections, the monitoring of log books; farm accidents; and a higher frequency of road traumas.

Arguably, though, the most important difference concerns community culture. As opposed to many police in cities, country officers nearly always live in the command areas in which they work. Potentially, they may play sport against someone they arrest that same night, or they may be called to an incident, such as a domestic dispute, where they personally know the offenders and victims.

When police live in the area in which they work, their knowledge and understanding of individual people and circumstances in their community can be much deeper than in city areas. A country cop may walk into a local pub on a Friday night and know who he's likely to see, and who is in no fit shape to drive home. He's also likely to know at least some of the backgrounds of the people in the pub. Perhaps one is going through a divorce. Another may be on the final warning at work for not turning up on time. Maybe there's a mum renowned for driving her daughter's netball team to carnivals all over the state. How does such knowledge affect the officer's behaviour? Or should it? Does the officer immediately go and wait to breath-test the potential rule breakers around the corner? Or does he warn them? Does he take their keys, or offer to drop them home? Country policing is not a law unto itself, but it does know that the letters of the law need to have some flexibility according to the situation. This, however, can be a difficult practice for some police officers, particularly younger ones, fresh and eager but without the knowledge and experience of their hardened seniors.

Matt Lynch has seen both sides of the line. He grew up in Sydney, and after graduating from the NSW Police Academy he embarked on a twenty-eight–year career as a cop. He spent his first fifteen working in Sydney, during which time he earned promotion to sergeant. Coincidentally, one of the stations he worked at was Eastwood, the area in which Bernie had strayed during his adolescence. In 2000 Matt 'jagged an inspector's job' in Armidale and headed for a tree change with his wife. Officially, he was Inspector of Police of the New England Local Area Command, based in Armidale. In simple speak, he was 'one of the bosses'. It was in this role that he met Bernie and the two developed a respectful working relationship. During the Youth Links and

Street Beat days they occasionally saw each other when Bernie went into the police station to support boys in trouble or to attend meetings with various parties about youth crime and behaviours. Then, when Matt heard Bernie had acquired use of a shed at the old Dumaresq Council depot, he became both a strong supporter and interested observer of what was happening, while also playing devil's advocate among some of his sceptical colleagues.

'When Bernie started the welding program I could see his vision,' said Matt in an interview in the very shed in which the program began. 'But getting the street cops to have that view would take some time to gather trust and confidence in the program. In the early days some of the cops were thinking: "Right, here's another hoodlum centre where the bad kids will be in the one spot. A de facto juvenile detention centre where they'll pick up ideas and be able to plan more." I was trying to instil in the troops: "Let's just pull back a bit. It's something that's hands on. Let's just see what happens."'

Regardless of the outcome, Bernie was trying to do 'something positive' in a country town that, like other rural settlements, had its issues with youth crime. Finding solutions was discussed at Chamber of Commerce meetings where business owners complained about vandalism and thefts, and inevitably stories appeared in the local media. Bernie was very aware of community feelings, but at that stage he still didn't have any intricate long-term plans. It was more a case of 'let's work it out as we go'. It was an approach that reflected Bernie's lack of attention to finer details. As Carolyn Lasker, another to help during this time, noted: 'Bernie was the most disorganised person in the world.'

But he was also a visionary. Over the years, 'run at me' has been a common phrase used by the boys with whom Bernie has worked. Its origin is from the footy fields. An invitation, but more emphatically, a statement, spat out by a defender challenging an attacker to take him on. At the BackTrack depot it has morphed into a cliché that can cover any physical, and at times, mental confrontation, either serious or light-hearted. As he fought to gain traction with the welding program Bernie had all sorts of metaphorical giants hurtling towards him – money issues, attitudes, resources, the boys' ongoing behaviours – yet he never lost sight of a bigger but far-from-clear picture: he and his small but devoted band of supporters could improve young lives, and if all went well, change them for the better forever. So, run at him.

'I can't give you an accurate blow-by-blow account, but shit it was hard going,' says Bernie. 'At first, it was just basically boys hanging around because they were so grog sick from the night before. We just gave them somewhere to come. But the welding stuff eventually started to take some sort of shape; the boys kept turning up and we got a bit of confidence from that. I got so much help. Gel Cutmore was like my right-hand man. And Rod Day [Rocket], a welding teacher from TAFE, he taught the boys. Then we had this real big, massive steering committee. Just three of us: Kevin Dupe, Rosemary Mort and me. I dunno how many hours we clocked up at our dinner tables working out what to do.

'Somewhere about that time, Gel and I also had a meeting with Flinty and Simmo, his wife Dympna, a whole lot of close friends. We got together to work out what more we could do. Not just TAFE or welding or Street Beat or mucking round with feral pups. And out of that, we came up with the idea of this organisation that could look after a whole lot of projects. We didn't know what the projects were, but we were going to look after them! And that's how we came up with BackTrack. Ever since the days watching

Joe and Denise Shakeshaft were Catholics whose five children, Maree, Bernie, Anthony, Paul and Mark, grew up in an era when 'just make sure you're home before dark' gave a lot of scope for adventure. Bernie was always 'adventurous'. . . and into cars very early on.

Bernie wasn't the most studious high school student, but a trip to India (above right) at the end of Year 11, including a visit to Mother Teresa's Hospice for the Dying, was the first real turning point in his life – there would be a few of those.

Jimmy Matthews (top left) was a mountain of a man who, along with Annette and Paul Roots (opposite page top with Skipper), gave Bernie opportunities and helped him grow from boyhood to manhood. It was after working for both these men that Bernie headed north, to the Territory. There he worked as a dingo trapper and ringer. He'd chased adventure … and found it.

Denise and Joe Shakeshaft are proud of all their kids. They are all different people who have followed their interests passionately. Bernie also has a much larger family now – thanks to BackTrack.

Bernie and his kids, James (left, with Sandy in Tennant Creek) and Maeve (above). Parenthood is a lifelong journey – and one that is teaching all of the time.

With a family to support, Bernie took a number of different jobs. One, as a research assistant, meant he was catching and tracking dingoes and feral cats. Before GPS, it was down to triangulating radio signals in the middle of nowhere. Or counting animals from planes. Before he left the Territory, Bernie started to work with kids, and he gained an understanding of the way the system was letting them down. His time in the Territory would inform a great deal of the work he would do at BackTrack.

In 2014 Bernie was presented with a gift that certainly enhanced his educational journey: he was awarded a Churchill Fellowship. It seems particularly apt when you consider this quote from the man himself: 'What is the use of living, if it be not to strive for noble causes and to make this muddled world a better place for those who will live in it after we are gone?' Bernie was definitely striving to make things better for the kids at BackTrack. His idea to team boys with dogs was the first of many successes that would see the Armidale community support BackTrack – the rest of Australia soon followed.

The Duke and Duchess of Sussex, Harry and Meghan, are just two who have seen up close the magic of the BackTrack team. Governor Hurley and Mrs Hurley (below) have also responded to that magic: they are two of its biggest supporters.

Bernie and his partner Francesca – both are passionate about the land, animals and giving young people a hand. In the classrooms, in the paddocks, in the workshops and on the road, Bernie and the hard-working team at BackTrack always keep their three aims for the youth they work with in mind: keep them alive, keep them out of jail, and encourage them to chase their hopes and dreams. And the mix is working. You only have to ask the kids themselves to know that.

the old countrymen at Tennant Creek, I'd had that word in my head. And all the questions that came with it, that came with the principles of tracking something: What was it doing yesterday? What is it doing today? Where is it going? Unless people know or have experienced it for themselves, they might say: "Hang on, what does all that *mean*?" But once you know it, you realise it's about getting just enough information from the past so that you devote most of your energy, eighty per cent of it, to where you want something or someone to be down the track. But the key is not to spend too much time looking at what's happened. Once you have the details you need, move on. If you spend too much time analysing, you can get tangled up in never going forward. People look at BackTrack and might say: "Ah, it's about getting troubled kids back on track." That fits, but it's not the real story behind it.

'I think by then, I'd also got the boys together at the local McDonald's and I said to them: "Right, what are you gonna call yourselves?" At the time there were ads on TV about Nutri-Grain Ironmen, so the boys tagged onto that, tossed around a few ideas and came up with Ironman Welders. So, Ironman Welders and BackTrack kicked off at about the same time. Great, what's next?

'Rosemary, Jayne, Sally, Carolyn, Gel and Myf, a researcher from the University of New England, wrote submissions for grants, and Rosemary, being the media wiz, got positive stories into the paper. Photos too. It was seat-of-the-pants stuff. No outside money at first, just digging into our own pockets and unlocking the depot gates on the weekend to see if it was worth going on.

'Then, it all just began building up. Businesses – the Armidale City Bowling Club, the New England Credit Union, some fellow just walking through the gates – they all donated money. A thousand dollars, five hundred, two hundred ... put it to good use, boys. Other people gave their old tools, and bits and pieces. Scrap metal, buckets, brooms, whatever. I took down every tool I had, and then someone else donated a big steel bench. Things were happening. Small wins, but things *were happening.* And best of all, the boys just kept coming. They could see something real was happening. It was for them. And they wanted to be part of it.'

And so did the small but devoted band of helpers. No-one got paid, no-one could have known how successful BackTrack would become, but they all believed in it. Their recollections of a period that Kevin Dupe described as both 'awesome and raw' revealed a group of people who weren't only determined to support a community that they all loved, but rally around a man who, despite his warts, they all greatly admired and respected.

'From the very get-go Bernie had a sincerity and integrity of purpose,' said Rosemary Mort. 'He might have appeared to have had this laidback approach but at the core was this extraordinary determination. His enthusiasm was like a virus for others to catch. Once you were part of it you were part of it because you believed absolutely in it. There was no other purpose, really, other than working with the kids and *for* the kids. That has remained integral to BackTrack all the way through. The kids come first in every decision that's made.

'Bernie has always said that if you offer opportunity, and keep offering the opportunity, the kids will take up that opportunity. They are hungry for it. And Bernie really pushed that at the start. And while he did that, we all saw how he handled the kids in such a positive and may I say, loving, way that was best for the kids. He was quite strict. They understood that. He wasn't a pushover, but there was something special about his understanding of where the kids were at, and what their needs were. He knew where they were at and he wanted to take them where they needed to go.'

Gel Cutmore, who said Bernie was always the 'alpha dog', expanded on Rosemary's comments by pinpointing a vital part of the BackTrack philosophy.

'You have to remember none of these boys were choir boys,' she said. 'We were dealing with kids who had incredibly complex trauma, and a lot of people didn't know how to work with that. I think what's brilliant about what we did is that we never thought of the kids as victims, and we didn't have that welfare mentality about who the kids were or where they came from. At the start, most of the kids we had were white, too, so there weren't those big society labels about Aboriginal kids.'

Matt Lynch had more reason than many others to pay careful attention to what was happening. And what he saw gave him reason to be cautiously optimistic.

'I could see right from the start that Bernie had a "never give up attitude",' he explained. 'He was always looking out for the kids, doing what was right for them. But a really important point was that if a kid did something real bad Bernie would still help them, but he wasn't going to blame it on anyone else. Some kids, when they get into trouble, will say it's everyone's fault except their own. You know, "It's the copper's fault for locking me up." But Bernie had that understanding. He had a really good objective approach. It wasn't: "You've done it, you've stuffed up"; it was "Why have you done it? What caused you to do it? Is it a one-off? Were there any mitigating circumstances?" He'd take it all into consideration and show empathy and compassion where needed. He was never telling us: "Throw the book at that kid and put him away." He was always learning from the kids, talking with them, and talking with the cops too about alternatives, and what could be done at BackTrack to ensure we could all reduce the incidents of recidivism.'

Sitting on his verandah chair Bernie follows a pattern that seems committed to muscle memory. Flip lid on packet, pull out cigarette, snap lighter, take long deep suck, stare into the distance with squinted eyes, and … this time, as opposed to the C-bomb clouds, the smoke drifts through the gauze windows and disappears. I ask him if he wants a break – he has been chatting for a couple of hours – but 'No, I'm still firing on all cylinders.' In his relaxed way he appears keen to talk about what lies ahead.

'As I said, keeping the kids out of jail was one of our main aims, and I was always thinking about ways to do this. Then, something, *bang*, came out of left field. I was on the piss at this barbie at someone's place – might've been Simmo's – and James rang me from the Armidale Show. "Dad, have you seen this dog high jump, thing?" They were about to start this competition, and James told me a bit more and I thought: "Why not have a go at this?" So, we grabbed every hound we could within a few blocks and ended up with five or six of them. And down we go to the showground. We'd never seen this jumping before, had no idea what to do. It was all about getting your dogs to jump – could be a bit of a scramble too – up a portable wall of horizontal boards. If they made it to the platform at the top, great, slide in another board and see if they can go higher. We didn't take it too seriously. We were all full of beer and being a bit smart about it, but next thing you know, we've won the Armidale Show dog high jump. Won it with a collie called Jordie. Anyway, it got me thinking: "This is one for the boys to do. Give them and the dogs a purpose. Let's give it a crack." And that meant we had to take the boys to shows out of Armidale on the weekends. We thought, "Hey this is part of a solution. Friday and Saturday nights. High-risk times for crime. So, let's get the boys out, give them a purpose, look after them and see what happens."'

When recalling that time, Matt Lynch, a cheerful man with a horseshoe of grey hair ringing the back of his head, sat in his chair and laughed.

'When Bernie told me what he was doing, I first thought: "Bloody hell, Bernie, you're taking the ball up. It's going to be a hard slog!" But I was also thinking: "If he's getting the hoodlums off the streets at the peak times, great!" We'd seen some of these kids coming into the police station like they were going through a revolving door. Day in, day out, the high-risk offenders that the police knew and targeted because they were constantly causing grief in the community. But try taking them out of play, then the community isn't suffering, there's less victims of crime, there's less people making complaints to the cops … a good thing. But knowing the kids at the time, those playing up the most, I was worried they'd look for a good free time and then get back to their normal ways. I thought they might milk it for as much as they could.'

Yet again it was 'let's see what happens'. From gaining use of a shed for a 'peppercorn rent', Bernie and his helpers had developed BackTrack enough to suggest that though its future wasn't yet bright, at the very least it had an opportunity to grow. And opportunities were what Bernie thrived on.

15

There are five collies alongside Francesca's great dane, who's at an age at which snow appears on the snout. It's a black-and-white morning. The magpies are singing from the eucalypts, and instructor Phill Evans is lecturing the boys (and Francesca) on the do's and don'ts of handling.

'If a dog breaks from that position, first response is "No!"'

Phill Evans has been involved with dogs all his life. He knows what he's talking about. All except one boy listens to him attentively; the exception has his head down and neck arched in that all-too-familiar adolescent posture: he's texting.

Phill jokes: 'Hey Pete, I'll message you with what to do.'

The boy doesn't respond. An observer might think the behaviour is discourteous, but for Pete, like the dogs, what he does at times is a matter of taking tiny steps. Not so long ago, this boy was so shy that he sheltered in a dog cage and wouldn't participate in training at all. So, texting in public is a statement that reaches beyond words.

The session continues. Hands are raised, commands fly, tails wag … then Phill asks everyone to sit their dog in the yard's dust. They form a line, each animal a metre apart from the next, and dare not take their eyes off their bosses as leads are unclipped and strides are taken to the shade of the eucalypts a decent stone's throw away.

Phill walks over to a fence to the side of the dogs. He says nothing. Eyes remain on bosses.

'Meeeeeow,' says Phill with a theatrical high pitch.

Ears prick. Some heads turn. But the dogs stay put. They can't be swayed by such a meek distraction.

'Meeeeeow, meeeeeow.'

Muscles near the hips quiver. Weights shift onto front paws. But still no dog breaks the line.

A few seconds of silence, then ...

'Where's the puppy? Where's the puppy?'

Chaos. Dogs running in every direction. First to Phill. Wagging, smiling, barking. Are you happy to see me? Isn't this fun? Here I am, here I am ...

Then to the boys. Here I am, here I am. Look at me ...

When order is restored, a magpie flies from a eucalypt and lands on a hay bale that's on the back of a quadbike. It's as though it wants a better seat for round two.

In this age of digital footprints, there is a drawer in an office at the BackTrack depot that throws back to a previous time. In it are scrapbooks and loose plastic folders. They've not been meticulously maintained; rather, they represent a zigzagging journey between dried glue, Cellotape and newspaper articles that capture bits and pieces of BackTrack history. When he showed me the pile on my initial meet-and-greet trip to the depot Bernie shrugged his shoulders and said: 'We started getting so much press that we couldn't keep track of it all.'

The articles that have been kept, though, show how quickly BackTrack gained recognition, not only within the Armidale community, but all the way to New South Wales's corridors of power. The year after Bernie and crew took over the council depot and shed – 2007 – was the breakthrough time. Donations increased, but none was greater than the time given by Bernie. He juggled his paid job at Street Beat and Youth Links with his unpaid devotion to overseeing Ironman Welders while also developing BackTrack. Towards the end of the year, his commitment was rewarded when the state government announced $60 000 in assistance, part of which enabled Bernie to be employed as the official coordinator of Ironman Welders.

At that time the Ironman Welders were working on their first major commercial contract: making a hundred service hangers for the local Hillgrove gold mine, which the boys had already visited and from whom they had received $1000 donation. The boys, who were at various stages of studying for certificates through TAFE, needed to work twelve-hour days to ensure the order was met. And when it was, there was just reason for pats on the back. Afterwards, Bernie told *The Armidale Independent* newspaper: 'There is nothing like a real-life application to finish a job, ensure the quality and deliver it on time … It was a big test for the boys and the way they worked the long hours so willingly is a great indication of their commitment. They came through with flying colours.'

The impact of such news in the local media was tremendous. It not only created a feel-good factor that could potentially spread across the community, including to those people who remained sceptical of BackTrack or knew nothing about it; it also uplifted the boys who kept turning up to the shed and having a go.

'We did masses of publicity, especially when anybody helped us in any way,' remembered Rosemary Mort. 'It became a way for us to express our gratitude to the community. For instance, when the Armidale City Bowling Club first gave us some money, we took the kids down to meet the CEO and personally thank him. I wrote a story about that, and it turned out to be a very successful formula because the bowling club got some recognition, and they were also impressed by the efforts the kids made. So, we repeated that with a lot of people who helped us. We did group photos like you wouldn't believe because the kids all wanted to be in them.

'And an interesting by-product of this was that the parents of these kids, who were so used to being told about all the negatives, were suddenly seeing their kids in good, positive situations. They were doing something admirable and the parents felt very proud. It was a long process but the stories we generated started to build up a sense of community ownership. It was built on goodwill, but this goodwill wasn't ephemeral; it was ongoing, something real that everyone could engage with.'

The numbers of boys who attended the shed varied from weekend to weekend. Sometimes a dozen, sometimes fewer. However, there was a core group: 'The Magnificent Seven', the first ones to become involved in Ironman Welders. Andrew was one of them. So too, Michael, the deeply troubled youngster with whom Bernie felt a very strong connection. Gel Cutmore recalled how in the early days all the boys made her little gifts. One boy made her a name plaque surrounded with welded metal flowers and love-hearts; when he was a baby, he'd been cared for by Gel in a women's refuge that his mother had fled to because of domestic violence. At Ironman Welders every boy came with troubles.

'When Bernie first got in contact with me and said he had a shed, I think it was about the time I was living in a caravan,' said Andrew. 'My girlfriend had run away from home and moved in with me and Mum and my little brother, but then my mother kicked us out. I didn't know my dad at that time. I grew up without a dad. We had nowhere else to go, except a caravan; my older brother, his partner and their three kids were living there. They said we could have the top bunk if we wanted it. So, we moved in there for about a month. I was seventeen. My girlfriend was sixteen. We finally got our own caravan and were as happy as ever. No worries in the world. That's when we found out we were going to have a baby. I talked to Bernie about it; we both did because my girlfriend knew Bernie as well. He said he would back us whatever we did. And all that was going on while I was working at the shed. It took us about a month to clean it out. We couldn't see the cement floor when we first walked in. It was full of rubbish and dirt. Took a trailer load to the tip every Sunday. And then one Sunday, Bernie came and picked us up in his little yellow HiLux, and in the back he had his dogs, a little gasless welder, a grinder, a pair of earmuffs, an extension cord. And he said: "Right, what are we going to do?" So, we started working on scraps of steel, offcuts that the local welding businesses gave to us – there were times when they opened up on Sundays for us to go and raid their skip bins too – and we made all sorts of little things ... flowers, turtles, and before that long we were working on big projects and getting in the paper.'

In November 2007, Bernie received his first major formal recognition for his work at Ironman Welders when he was presented with a NSW Premier's Award at a civic reception in Armidale that coincided with the sitting of the State Cabinet in the town. To Bernie, the passing spotlight wasn't one to stand in as much as it was one to point in the direction of where BackTrack was heading.

'And that's when the dogs and their jumping started coming into their own with the boys,' he says. 'It was with The Magnificent Seven and a few extras here and there. We came up with the name PawsUp pretty quick, coz we were paws up a wall. And we had this mantra along with it: "Once the dog launches, it's a one-way ticket." Which meant, once the dog left the ground, we didn't want it coming back down, so there was a bit of a metaphor in there for the kids. But if the dog couldn't make it, we always made sure we had people there to catch it – another little metaphor. Give the dog another go, and if it still struggled, catch it again and push it up the wall, get it to the top with a helping hand, finish on a high. Good for the dogs and subtle lessons for the boys. On top of that, we got T-shirts printed. Black with white paws on them. One of the kids, Dave, drew a dog's head and we used it as a logo. We started winning. Got a bit of money here and there, some bags of dog biscuits, blue ribbons for the boys. So, we started to get a reputation. We Googled more shows and got invitations to some too. Like Singleton, where there were, ten, twenty, thirty, forty dogs, I dunno, even more. It was intense and there were dog-whisperer people there who were taking it properly seriously. But we still went well. It just kept growing. Wherever a show was on, we went there. The momentum just kept building and building.

'The further south we went into the bigger towns, the more we got seen, and word spread about us. We were a circus hillbilly mob. We took our own utes. We put trailers on and bales of hay and there were dogs tied everywhere. Bags and swags on roof-racks. It was all volunteer work, no-one was getting paid to help.

People like Flinty and Gel were part of it. We were paying out of our own pockets to do it. Putting fuel in the cars, feeding the kids on the road. We made packed lunches. And got juice without preservatives. No lollies, no red frogs and no Coke! We gave ourselves half a chance of managing them! And we just went.

'I think we did thirty-five shows that first year. It's a big hunk out of your life. We were always thinking ahead and crafty with our plans. Like, "Let's not stay at the showgrounds. Let's find somewhere else, maybe a cocky with a bit of land." We leant on all our bush networks. "Have you got a spare paddock where we can just pull in and drop the swags down and have a campfire?" If there was a shower there, well and good, and if there wasn't, too bad. We were still better off being away from the show. No distractions like sideshow alley where things could really go wrong, and the boys could go wild. So, we tried not to stay at the showgrounds whenever we could. Or we'd drive all the way, then get off and compete, and then load everything up and go back again. The dogs and boys both travelled well at night because they all slept. Through the day we'd have to stop every few hours to let the dogs out, and the boys were the same. But at night, you could punch through for six or seven hours.

'And it was all on the weekends, and we knew the cops, people like Matt Lynch, were watching us. So, we just started taking these troublemaking kids out. The crime rates started going down. And the kids loved what they were doing. They were pumped. Take the dogs back so they have a bit of a run-up, steady them, then let 'em go. Brilliant! These sensationally fit athletic dogs scaling these walls. We gave them stage names like "Leaping Leo", and "It's not a party without Artie", he was a barking bugger who drove us all mad. Could start a fight too. He couldn't finish them, but he liked to start them. He could throw the first one.

'We were lucky, coz we had these two outright superstars. Out of that litter of pups I put on the TAFE lawn. Zorro and Girl. Just extraordinary dogs. Zorro used to know his name. He'd hear it screamed out at every showground: "Zorro!" And he'd turn into this, I dunno what you'd call it, but he caught some sort of competition fever. He'd prick his ears and look around as though he was saying: "That's me, look at me, I'm here." You could start your dog at whatever height you chose, so we let our competitors start at five feet, and go six feet and seven, and all the while they were burning their dogs out. Then, we'd let Zorro and Girl take their first jumps at about eight feet. Zorro, he'd step up and do a bit of a scratch as though he was marking his territory, puffing out his chest. And then, bang up that wall. And everybody believed in him. That's why he rarely faltered. Girl was second in charge of the ship. When Zorro made a mistake, just one slip, Girl would win. Other dogs weren't making eight feet, but these two could scream over nine. If one didn't win, the other did. It was a real team effort. The dogs were brilliant, and the boys developed a strong ownership of what they were doing. But we couldn't have done it without Phill Evans. He reads dogs better than books.'

Phill Evans has been around dogs his whole life. In his childhood he was used to English setters and German shepherds being part of his family, and after joining the army at seventeen he was soon transferred to the Explosive Detector Dog Unit of the Royal Australian Engineers where he spent nine years as a trainer and handler. After that, he trained and handled dogs in many civilian capacities and he also worked for seven years at Fairfield City Council in Sydney where he was responsible for prosecuting the owners of aggressive dogs. He and his family moved to Armidale in 1991, and after providing consultancy advice to the local council, he ended up managing the New England Regional Companion Animals Shelter for twenty years before his retirement in 2018. Nowadays, in addition to training, he's an Australian National Kennel Council sports judge, and he breeds and shows Old English sheepdogs, 'the big hairy Dulux dogs'.

He first met Bernie through a mutual friend not long after the Evans family had moved to Armidale. At the time Bernie was on a break from his Parks and Wildlife job in Alice Springs. They spoke about training dogs to detect and chase feral cats in the Northern Territory, but despite some preliminary work nothing was put into practice. When Bernie contacted Phill many years later, Phill readily accepted the invitation to become involved with PawsUp, a program that was supported by the Armidale Regional Council.

'Bernie was looking for adaptable dogs,' said Phill in an interview in the smoko room at the BackTrack depot. 'He started the boys off with dogs that either he owned or that people donated. He would come and grab me occasionally to do some work with the boys if the dogs weren't performing at their optimum and we would look at some strategies to get the dogs performing better. Keeping in mind that some of the dogs in the program had different kids handling them quite a lot. That could affect the dogs; they had to learn to cope with different temperaments in the handlers and the different idiosyncrasies of each handler. And that's not an easy thing for a dog to do. The end result was that the dogs got very wise very quickly and they worked out where the boundaries were with the new handlers and what they could get away with. It's an interesting phenomenon to watch: a dog that's been handled by three or four different kids behaves differently for each of those kids.

'For me, it was about teaching these young fellas how to interact with the dogs and be responsible for them. It was about forming relationships. Dogs will naturally withdraw if they feel they cannot trust somebody, but the kids had all experienced that too, so they identified with that a bit. So, we worked on building this trust and a greater understanding of the dogs. For instance, having them take a dog that wasn't naturally obedient and be able to work with that dog and see tangible results within a relatively short period of time could create a fantastic sense of satisfaction and affinity with the animal. For them to realise they could influence a dog's behaviour and have the dog respond to them by merely giving the dog a command, and then finding out that the dog was enjoying it as much as they were. It could be as simple as a "sit" or a "stay", and when they got that positive response from their dogs, it was a really lovely thing to watch.

'Of course, we can all read more into the interactions than possibly exist. In the actual moment, it is all about the boy and the dog. But there are all sorts of underlying benefits out of that interaction. Just learning to have some patience with the dog, not losing your temper – the dog will quickly pull back if you lose your cool with it. Dog training is about finding what speed the dog is working at and what the idiosyncrasies are for the dog and adapting what you are doing to mesh with that dog, and then you can start to make progress. If you are moving at one speed and the dog is moving at another you don't make progress. So, sometimes it was about getting the kids to speed up what they were doing, and other times it was about getting them to slow down. For me as a dog trainer it's about working out where the dog is at, working out where the handler is at, and trying to get them to adapt to find out what works for the dog. The benefits of that can go right across the community. A person who understands how to adapt to all sorts of different situations can help many people. In the case of the boys, if they could adapt and work out what was going to get the best performance from the dog, they could work on strategies to make that happen. And then, maybe the principle behind those strategies could be used in other situations too.'

Phill believed he saw some 'really talented' boys among the very first group he helped at PawsUp. He said three in particular had the potential to pursue handling careers. Andrew was one of them.

'I think Guyra was the first show we went to,' Andrew told me. 'I had Girl for that one. She was just a chilled-out calm-and-collected dog. She might have been the same age as the others, but she was the older dog in the pack. She was the senior, dominant one. All the others respected her. And she chose me. Bernie's right. He says dogs always choose us. They work out our personalities. Girl and I did some good things together. Had some wins. At the early shows, there wasn't much talking. We weren't that serious. It was just having a bit of fun.

'Pretty early on we made one of the jumping walls at the welding shed. It was all part of it. Bernie made sure we were involved in everything. You know, picking the names of the programs, talking about logos. We had a big say in the direction we were going in. That's why it worked so well, like we had a voice.

'The camps were good for us, too. And it was good for the community. Kept Armidale a bit quieter. Bernie just gave us something simple to do. Camping under the trees. Fires and swags. It was a good group of people. Travelling around nearly every weekend with the dogs and the boys and Bernie and other volunteers, it was awesome. It saved some of us. The Circle Work we did. Bernie teaching us "If you fuck it you fix it" and "Own your own shit"; they are probably the biggest things I've still learnt. Everyone makes mistakes. It's what you do afterwards that's the most important thing. Ya gotta fix it. If it's an apology or giving something back or repairing something … whatever it is, ya just gotta fix it. Those dog trips were a lot more than just dog trips.'

It could be said the trips were in fact excursions. But there were no clipboards and stencilled questionnaires to hand out. The boys learnt through their experiences, watching and listening to others, including their dogs, and participating in conversations in which no topic was off-limit. Drugs, girls, cigarettes, pizzas, music, cars. 'Mate, how good was Zorro today?'

Sometimes, the excursions had lessons that no-one anticipated. At one show, a team of about twenty boys and volunteers arrived wearing their black-T-shirt-with-the-white-paw-print uniforms. As they walked towards the competition venue with their dogs they felt as though people were strangely making way for them, keeping their distance, and when the boys sat down as a group, they felt lots of eyes were on them. Some of the boys were Indigenous. Was this the reason? It was impossible to know, but many in the group had an uncomfortable feeling that they weren't welcome. And when the event began, the mood intensified. 'You could see it on faces,' recalled Gel Cutmore. 'People were thinking: "What do these boys know about jumping dogs?" I was really worried someone was going to say something, and things would go off.' But by the end, the PawsUp team had blitzed the field. Then, something else unexpected happened. 'All these people started coming up to us and saying: "That was the most brilliant thing we've ever seen." These people shaking the boys' hands and meeting the dogs. It was one of the most poignant moments of my life. Seeing all these kids being validated by these people,' said Gel. 'It was one of the coolest things I've ever seen.'

As the dog shows continued, the boys' confidence grew. They entered competitions believing in themselves and knowing they could win. On their return trips to Armidale, ribbons on dashboards told of successes, but the greater trophies were often left behind in the minds of the townspeople they had visited: Bernie's hillbilly circus mob was winning respect.

'The boys were proud of every little success they had,' says Bernie. 'Think about all the kids who get a buzz when they kick a goal in a soccer match, or they win a trophy at a dancing competition, or they get a good mark in a maths exam. They're happy, aren't they? Makes them feel good about themselves. Well, some of the boys at BackTrack hadn't experienced much of that in their lives, so to give them those opportunities was very important. Again, it goes back to what Paul Roots and Jimmy Matthews did for me: putting the opportunities out in front, giving the boys something to aim for. And then they win or do well, and they get their little trophies, but other people congratulate them too and tell them how well they're going. A simple pat on the back can go a long way. We all need to be told: "Good job. Keep it up." They're little gifts, little pieces of feel-good gold.'

And then there were those gifts that surpassed all others. In 2008, Andrew's girlfriend gave birth to a healthy girl. 'I was there for it,' said Andrew. 'It was magical, you know. When we got to meet her, I'll never ever forget that moment. Beautiful. I'll always cherish it.'

Parenting. It can be immeasurably rewarding, and immeasurably difficult. And being a child can be too. While devoting so much to BackTrack and the boys Bernie still had to find time for his family. They were renting a house and acreage a short drive from Armidale. 'Jayne found the place,' remembers

Bernie. 'She's a deeply intuitive person. When she took me out there, my first thought driving in was: "This is a place where young people should grow up."' Its name was Warrah, and from that moment on it became a special piece of dirt and bricks. However, there were cracks. Bernie and Jayne continued to have the 'up and down cycles' that affected their marriage. Jayne was running a health food store that she'd bought in Armidale, and Bernie was all too often out the door early and home late, or he was away for a few days at a time on dog-jumping duty. They were also worried about James, who had never truly settled after leaving the Northern Territory.

'Soccer was still his big thing,' remembers Bernie. 'That and Brazil, because Brazil was the big thing in soccer. He wasn't that fussed about school. Then he heard about this exchange program to Brazil. I don't know how he quite convinced us it was a good idea, but anyhow, Jayne and I agreed, and off he went. He was about sixteen, seventeen. I didn't think it was ever going to be like me going to India when I was that age, but we thought it was the right thing to let him go.

'It just never worked. He didn't make the full year of the exchange. He swapped families a few times. He closed down, put his headphones on in the classroom. He didn't even know the language. I remember him talking about this one little tree with a handful of leaves, and it was the only tree he could see. He was lost over there, but we tried to get him to stick it out; I thought that was important. We really didn't know what to do, you know. He came back, and it was move on, but I don't think he was the same.

'I look back and think, "Should I have been there for him more?" Not just during Brazil, but at other times? I always tried to help with his soccer. Managing, coaching. Bits and pieces with other stuff, too. But when you're working at night and then on weekends and … there must have been an absence. I never really asked him how it was.'

Listening to Bernie's soft and slowly delivered words, I feel the interview is again touching on sensitive territory, but a question must be asked. An obvious one: 'How do you feel about your relationship with James, considering what you were building with the BackTrack boys?'

'It's a split thing,' says Bernie, as wind whistles through the gum trees near the horse yard. 'It would have been easy for me to go: "I should do more for my son or my daughter," and they were certainly conversations we had in the family all the way through. And I'd tell them: "Not everyone gets the start that you guys have had. You've wanted for nothing."

'Look, I'm all right with it, you know. James and Maeve were two different kinds of kids, and they handled things differently. We often used to joke that Maeve was so low maintenance we didn't even know she was there. Nothing was too much trouble for her. School was okay, she was all right at sport, she loved animals, had good friends … everything was okay. Whereas James, things could melt him down. I was probably too hard calling shit out with him. We had some good arguments. I used to come home and he'd say: "Don't try that youth-worker stuff on me." That went on at different times, and that affected us. Jayne and I would talk about it. But looking back, I don't think he missed out on terribly much. Could I have done more? Of course, I guess, but it's all hindsight."'

Sitting in his verandah chair, Bernie continues talking about his family, then after drifting back to memories about soccer in Alice Springs, we take a break for a late lunch. He walks through a few dimly lit rooms and into the kitchen. 'Wanna steak?' he asks. 'No, I'm fine.' He slaps a T-bone on a frypan. Sizzling fills some silence. Then, suddenly Bernie begins talking again.

'You know, I've been thinking about what you asked me. It must have had some kind of impact, you know. I suppose in some ways I never had much of a relationship with my dad, growing up. I was probably pretty angry about that for a lot of years. He never really spoke much. I've got a great relationship with him now, but relationships can take time to work out. Maybe James has suffered from a bit of that as well. Yes and no. I think it's about who the people are. I'd talk about stuff and he wouldn't. We're all different. But then I look at really busted kids and what they have to come through. James was still lucky. But, yeah, a late starter. And if that was because I was absent too much, well, the ball was bowled and we all had to play it. James drifted a bit after finishing school. He's in Alice Springs at the moment. Working in hospitality and pursuing his love of music. A bit similar to me coming back to Armidale, I think. And it's healing country, central Australia. Maybe that's why I went there? Maybe that's why James is there now? It was the biggest growth time for me as a person. Oh well, that's food for thought.'

—

It took some time to chase James down for an interview; there were a few unanswered phone calls and text messages, and a bit of a hurry-up from Bernie before we finally spoke. James had left the Territory and was living 'up the coast' in a place that Jayne owns. 'I'll help her renovate it and see how we go,' he said. 'I'm focusing on my music at the moment. The last few years I've been working in a hip-hop duo Skank and Shake; we've released a couple of albums, but now we're taking a break and I'm just going to focus on my solo stuff for a bit.'

During the interview we primarily spoke about James's memories of childhood, and his relationship with Bernie.

'When the family left the Territory, I got a bit pissed off, I guess. It was my home, where all my original friends were. I kinda took it to heart against my parents, both of them. I didn't really understand why we had to pack up and move. I guess that fuelled a lot of anger towards my parents.

'Dad? Yeah, we had our moments. I do remember, I think it was my mum at one point asked me if I thought my old man was spending more time focusing on BackTrack and the other boys than he was on his own family, and it came as a shock to me. I've never thought that. He is no bloody angel. He's got a lot of flaws, as does every other human. Did we always get on? No. Did we always agree? Bloody oath we didn't. And we still don't. But especially in the later years of my life, I know my old man is probably the biggest role model I've got. I've got a lot of respect for him. I know what he does, I've seen what he does and how hard he has worked. It hasn't always been easy for him. I witnessed that when I was growing up, and I've seen him try to figure shit out, and since he started BackTrack I've seen a huge change in the way he thinks about life, and the way he holds himself. He is tapping into something where he is making stuff happen, making a difference, and he talks to me about that. To see how he has got so much drive and his work ethic, it is massive for me. If I was to be half the man he is, I would be pretty proud of myself.'

James's teenage years ran parallel to the formative stages of BackTrack. He went to school with some of the boys in the program, and that, according to Bernie, gave him 'some street cred'. He also spent time at the depot and became friends with the boys. In particular, he developed a close mateship with Michael from The Magnificent Seven. Two young men from very different sets of circumstances who were both trying to find their place in life. And who were both influenced tremendously by a father and a father-like figure. Their personal developments were just two of myriad narratives in an environment that gained increasingly greater recognition and support as time passed.

In 2009, another program was introduced. AgLads provided training and work experience on farms, while also giving the boys further opportunities to gain certificate qualifications at TAFE. It was a logical step for BackTrack to take. The outdoors was the classroom in which all the boys felt most comfortable.

'By then, we were under the auspices of Armidale Family Support Services,' says Bernie. 'We'd grown beyond opening only on the weekends, and we were operating on a couple of work days as well. I was on a part-time wage and still relying heavily on volunteers. AgLads started coz basically we had too many kids. More than a dozen boys in the welding shed can get dangerous quickly. It didn't take very long to grow to that point. That was before we had the smoko room and the classroom. Too many kids were coming in, drifting in without referrals from the schools or TAFE or anywhere else, and we had to find solutions. So, some local graziers volunteered to help, and we were off and running. Fencing work, carting hay, feeding stock ... all hands on.

'But there was so much other stuff we had to do too. Insurance for one. Jayne and others were writing business plans and doing a SWOT analysis. I had to be very respectful to everyone who was helping, but all this paperwork and formalities weren't very important things to me. I don't ever remember any bunch of countrymen sitting out in the bush going: "Right, let's sit down and get a strategic plan for how we're going to survive the next year." It just didn't make sense to me. I could see the value of it, but I couldn't do it myself coz I guarantee by the time we got all the plans nailed down I would look at them and say: "Nah, it's all changed; we're going this way now." I was always looking at how things would work for the kids. Nothing else mattered much. So, it was best left to other people. Like Kevin Dupe. Time and again he stepped up. I still don't know half the stuff he did for us. Somehow, he made everything work. Made me look like a lightweight. I know he covered a lot of stuff out of his own pocket. I'm grateful to so many people who went in to bat for me, but more importantly, the kids.'

The cricket analogy was apt. Bernie may have been the leader, but his success was only as good as the team he had around him. It was a team that was growing. Graziers, teachers, youth workers, tradespeople, miners, lawn bowlers, businesspeople. For the most part, the Armidale community believed in what was happening at the old Dumaresq Council depot. Bernie knew he was doing the right thing. There were enough headlines to tell him so. But the biggest were still to come.

16

Mid-afternoon. Sunny but cool. The troopy, driven by Warnie and laden with boys, comes in through the depot gates. It's hauling a trailer of cut wood and a couple of chainsaws. Warnie parks near the bottom shed, and the boys get out, some laughing and pushing others aside in the playful scramble to be first out. The very last who steps foot on the gravel is in no rush at all. He is lanky, the type of build that can see dust on the top of cupboards. He's wearing long shorts and a hoodie and is tossing something into the air. Bernie comes out of his office and sees the boy taking an effortless one-handed catch.

'I always say you should never go to work without a basketball,' says Bernie.

The boy grins and lopes towards his mates.

As Bernie and I sit on the verandah, the moments that need to be discussed for this book all find their place. Occasionally, they are punctuated by impromptu asides from Bernie: 'Remind me to tell you about so-and-so or such-and-such later.' Usually, I tell him to go with it while it's on his mind, but sometimes I scribble a note telling myself that I must steer Bernie back to his passing mention at some point. As the interview progresses, one word is fleetingly referred to time and again: Casterton. It's so obviously a top-shelf memory for Bernie that I know we must discuss it in detail, but then, in the midst of talking about dog jumping at Singleton (where in 2009 Girl set a Countryfest record of nine foot three) Bernie himself zips back to the topic, and this time he opens the gate.

'When we first started those shows, if you got a dog to seven feet you were among the prize money. If you could get seven-and-a-half feet you would come home with the number-one prize. But with Phill Evans teaching us, we're inching up that wall. He was just sensational with the boys, and the boys got it. Now we started looking like this professional outfit. So, it started stuffing up the sport, because by about 2009 people would see us pull up and they'd go: "Here come those professionals." They didn't really know the back stories to these kids. But they could work it out if they really wanted to. It's not that difficult to make a judgement on ratbag teenagers if you see them all in a group smoking or mucking about a bit. But we were on to that shit and we were always having conversations with the boys, like: "What do you think these people would think if we came into their town without the dogs? Would they be locking their cars and making sure their kids were at home?" Of course. So, we made the kids think about what they were doing and who they were representing. To be honest, and it's funny to say it now, some of the boys wouldn't even know that their dogs were collies, but they knew how to win.

'Anyway, we ended up going to Casterton. It's a small town in Victoria, not far from South Australia. And they held this annual kelpie muster. I don't think there'd ever been a collie there, but because of what we'd been doing, we got this invitation. It was great. There was so much hype about who's got the highest jumping dog. We were saying we could jump nine feet and these kelpie lovers were saying they could go an inch higher. So, it was on!

'We travel fifteen hundred kilometres, twenty-five to thirty hours. Five dogs: Zorro, Girl, Flash, Leo and Artie. Six boys. A bus that Jobs Australia Enterprises lent us, and an old box trailer that Rootsy and I'd made. We did some media interviews on the way down. National radio. The hype was extraordinary when you think about it. All for a dog jump. Against the Victorians.

'We get down there – it was the day before the competition – and the vibe … Oh dear, here we go. The organisers had been terrific on the phone, but we could sense there was something else going on with some other people. This was not about black and white dogs. This was about black and white people. We'd already talked to the boys about what could happen. We always did. We were really cagey about how we treated racism, so we made any potential divide into collie versus kelpie. But when we stopped and walked down the main street, I knew it was going to be hard work. We had some tough Indigenous kids with us, and they weren't going to put up with much shit. They would go the knuckle.

'We asked the organisers if we could have a go on their wall, coz it was a bit different from the ones we were used to. But no way. Fair enough. Their competition, their rules. I don't think we were even allowed to see the wall. This is where good old Dusty stepped in. He and I were still doing the odd "Left and Right", and he'd offered to be a wheelman for the trip. Or maybe I'd prodded him to come and help us. Either way, he loved the long drives, so it was a good fit. He was also brilliant with the psychology stuff.

Hadn't become a teacher. He was doing other things, but he is a great educator. He just got what people were about. Always has. He said: "Let's put the dogs away, and we'll go down to where they're setting up tents and we'll offer to give them a hand." So, there we are helping with the set-up. "Can we set those pins up for you?" "Can we help you with those tables and chairs?" We've got these boys running around doing all these jobs, and it turned some heads, coz I hate to say it, but we'd already heard some pretty ordinary stuff.

'The next day we were invited to walk in this parade down the main drag. Dogs and all. It's a big set-up. Hundreds of people, a thousand or more. And we get booed by some. Maybe it was meant to be fun. But then you start hearing things. "Who brought the coons to town?" "Take your fuckin' black and white dogs out of here." Some savage stuff. Embarrassing. Of course, not everyone was in on it, but enough that we couldn't avoid hearing them. You get them everywhere, you know. Other country towns, cities … stupid stuff. But Dusty, he made everything funny; he could really read a situation. "We'll do our talking with our dogs, boys. Nobody open your mouth." Dusty did, though. He was stopping and explaining to people: "Did you know kelpies were actually bred out of collies? So, mate, that makes that dog you've got there a half-breed." *Boom!* Dusty could stir it when he wanted to.

'We get to the high jump area, right in the middle of the street. Lots of people packed in around. It's deadly serious. We had to have vests on and a competitor number. We were used to the more laidback approach. You know, where we could help the boys handle the dogs, coz it's about looking after the dog, not the kid. Making sure they're safe, and there's always someone there to catch them if they fall from the wall. But this was all getting super-heavy. One person, one dog.

'We get to the competition, and we're looking really smart in our specially made black-and-white shirts. There was this one lady – I will never forget it – she yelled out: "Go border collies!" And she was in a sea of all these kelpie supporters. Brave. We were only allowed to have two dogs in the competition. So, it was Zorro and Girl. Dave and Joel were the boys in charge of them.

'Then the real business starts and it's a drizzly, rainy day. You know those For Sale signs that real-estate offices use? The material they use? It's fine when it's dry but when it's wet. Slippery as … And they used that material to screw all the sponsors' names onto the planks of the jump. We'd never jumped on anything like that. I thought that was gonna stuff us up a bit, but on we go. I can't remember all the ins-and-outs, but I know there was good prize money offered; enough to feed our dogs for a year. But it was tough. The dogs were hitting the wall and slipping on the signage and banging their chests into the wall. Zorro did it a couple of times. And there were people in the crowd laughing and carrying on coz the collies weren't any good. But hang on, guys, wait to see what happens to yours. Their dogs, they all did it as well. And I was thinking: "We're going to bust a dog here." So, I stopped the show and started arguing with the organisers. I said: "You're going to have to turn those boards around so the dogs can hit timber not ice." Well, didn't that start a shit fight! I'd thrown the hand grenade in. "But they're our sponsors!" There were news cameras and photographers, journalists, all these people who'd been talking up who could jump nine feet and be the Australian champion. But no way that was going to happen. I didn't care about the sponsors. Think of the dogs. Anyway, finally everyone agreed, and the organisers explained to the crowd what was going on. Then, the boards got turned around and we went to work. I knew we had them. From the moment they turned those boards around. Psychological warfare. It was a battle, and it was Zorro's finest hour. Better than Michael Jordan. Eight foot two. Girl jumped eight foot. First and second. Third was a few inches back. The place just erupted. We turned from villains to good guys. We went in other competitions too. Sprints – Zorro cleaned up again – hill-climbs, all good fun. Casterton have got their statue of a kelpie in town and before we left we made sure we got a photo with it. Of course, the collies were at the front.'

Bernie smirks after he says those final words.

The win was well worth celebrating, and media attention duly came. But to those who made the trip down south, what wasn't said in the news were stories that still needed telling. In the right place, at the right time.

'What are your memories of Casterton?'

Andrew laughed when I asked him the question. 'It was a long time ago,' he said. Andrew knew what it was like to win. He and Girl had carved a formidable reputation on the show circuit, but at the time of the kelpie muster he had got his own dog from outside PawsUp and had handed Girl on to other boys. He went to Casterton to help. Both the boys and dogs respected him.

'Some of the things that were said there shocked the Indigenous boys. And that hurt me because they were my brothers. After the parade Bernie got us into a circle and asked us how we felt. Shit, basically. But Bernie said to us: "Do you want to keep feeling like that, or do you want to feel like winners?" Bloody oath we wanted to feel like winners. And he said the only way we were going to do that is if we got the dogs to the top of the jump, and "kick arses".

Bernie then left us, and we said: "Right, we're going to do this!" And look what happened. We were all over the moon; we still stayed calm, but on the inside we were jumping and cheering. We had to show them we meant business. We weren't just some stupid kids from Armidale. But there was a bigger thing too. I think we left that town with our imprint on it. That's what we wanted. We wanted to leave an imprint for the right reason. That trip is always going to stick in BackTrack history. It was a legendary moment.'

Something else happened on that trip that also lives on in memories, and it's a moment that reveals another important element of BackTrack: putting the boys in unexpected situations to see how they respond.

'We were driving down there, and it would have been about three in the morning, I guess,' recalled Dusty. 'Only Bernie and I were awake, and Bernie said: "We're going to have a bit of a game here." We were actually running a bit late, and we only had two jerry cans of fuel with us. It was really foggy, and we pulled off the main highway and went down this dirt road and banged over some big bumps and then we swung around. Then Bernie and I got out and pretended to have an argument: "You bloody idiot, you told me to come down this friggin' road." And of course everyone wakes up, and they get a bit of a fright because we're in the middle of nowhere and it's foggy, it's three in the morning, zero degrees, and "you two idiots have got us lost again". Because on other trips I'd done with the boys from time to time, Bernie and I did a lot of what we called "shortcuts"; there was always a "shortcut" we'd take on any trip, but it didn't always turn out to be a shortcut. Never mind, it was always worth having a go. So, anyhow we were having this blue: "You took me down here, it's your fault, it's your shortcut." You could imagine the swearing going on. And the boys are starting to panic, and we're asking them what we should do. Turn around or keep going? We don't have much fuel. Things to make them think. Then a truck came past along the highway – we were only about sixty metres off it – and we had to give ourselves up then.'

To Bernie, it was all about getting the boys to 'react and make decisions under pressure'. He and Dusty would go on to do similar things on other trips. 'If you can keep your cool when you're bleary-eyed in the middle of the night, you don't know where you are, and there's a lot of tension in the air, you're doing all right.'

The success at Casterton further strengthened Bernie's belief in BackTrack. By then, there were dozens of boys in the program, and many more who either wanted to be in it, or could have been in it. At various times girls had come too. BackTrack, however, didn't have the financial strength or resources to accommodate them all. Despite the program's successes, there wasn't overwhelming confidence that the gates at the depot would swing open for as long as there was a demand for them to be pushed. Chasing dollars was a never-ending battle. Yet, Bernie and his supporters remained determined to keep going. Indeed for Bernie, BackTrack may as well have had the tag line: No dead ends.

'I know I annoyed people, frustrated them, probably made them angry too, but I've always had the view that if you want something to happen, make it happen. All the details, just work them out as you go.'

Bernie stands up from his verandah chair and walks out of sight into the living room. He returns with a photo album, and hands it to me. We flick through the pages. Boys playing baseball; doing Circle Work; cracking whips; sitting on the top rails of yards; riding horses; ... There's a common sight in nearly every photo: red dust.

'I forgot to tell you about this,' says Bernie, his knees cracking as he sits back in his chair. 'Took some of the boys up to the Territory. Pretty early on, it was. Flinty helped. Did a lot of work for us, Flinty. We went up to Santa Teresa, an old mission about an hour out of Alice Springs. It's home of the Eastern Arrernte people. They call the place *Ltyentye Apurte*, or pronounced "L-Ginger Porter". It's the start of the Simpson Desert. MacDonnell Ranges. Stunning country. Gibson, that dog we have, he was named after one of the fellas out there. He was a horseman like you've never seen. He was a drover as a kid; lived life in the saddle and is maybe half horse, this fellow. He and some of the other countrymen took the boys – about ten of them – out riding. They were part of a bigger group of about thirty that included some corporate funders too. It was all part of Will MacGregor's terrific Bush Mob program. You should have seen these horses. They had this program of catching brumbies and breaking them in. And some of our kids, they'd never ridden before. I'm watching Gibson and these boys saddling up the horses and I'm thinking: "Shit, anything could happen here!" We ended up riding for three days, fifteen to twenty k's a day, but we didn't have one buster. Gibson and his mates, they were as cool as cool could be. Just another experience for the boys. Again, put the opportunities out in front of them. I know some of the boys did it a bit tough. Poor Andrew got a bit miserable and homesick, but that helped make him a stronger person too. And the other boys, they were all learning. All works in progress. But, some slipped.'

Bernie leans over and points to one of the boys. 'He ended up getting locked up later on. One stupid fight with alcohol involved.

Into the big house. He was just one of those kids. Not violent. A beautiful kid. Raised by a single mum. Indigenous. All the same stuff. Kicked out of school, struggled to fit in. I got him multiple starts in multiple jobs. He was really skilful. Had a gift with welding, measuring ... He was always just, you know, be careful of the quiet kids. He was always the quiet kid. He was a guy I spent a lot of time with. But he got involved with someone who makes you realise: "That's why they build jails." A real bad egg. One night things got out of control. A racist comment from a white guy. Grog. It should have been, "Walk away, keep your hands in your pockets. Run away if you've got the speed." But nah. Stuff happened. A bloke was put in hospital. In a bad way. Our boy was too drunk to remember what had happened. That was a traumatic one for me. I believed in the kid, and I'd backed him but ... you've gotta own your own shit. The cops showed me where it happened. I was: "Oh fuck!" I saw the photos in court. It was distressing. Really distressed me deeply.'

Bernie sighs. His voice softens.

'So, he went to jail. Of course, the bad-egg guy blamed him for everything. He still got locked up as well, though. We ended up getting more legal help and proved that our boy hadn't done as much as first thought. Got him out in a shorter period of time. There were tears in the court. Jail would have eaten that kid up alive.

'Moments like that proved that we couldn't always help the boys as much as we wanted to. Sometimes we had kids come in who couldn't be helped. They didn't even want to help themselves. Or they'd already been looped through the system too much. But we had to try. Look at Andrew – could have gone the other way, but all the way through those early years, and even now, he's making progress. We're just there to help guide him. Michael, he had his ups and downs after leaving BackTrack. He got a labouring job up in the Territory and was up there with James. He did a bit of drifting, but he's still alive and not in jail. The Magnificent Seven, they all got into jobs. Welding, driving, manual skills. Easier for some than others, but most of the time I reckon they're looking forward.

'And that's one of the most important things all my work with troubled kids was teaching me. Go back to the lessons of being house parents to Scott and the boys at Tarago. Only using ten per cent of your energies looking into the past. By BackTrack I knew it was ten per cent past, ten per cent present, eighty per cent the future. Keep looking forward. And keep giving them experiences. Like Casterton. Like Santa Teresa. You know on that Territory trip Gibson and the others really took our boys under their wings. Took them hunting. One boy with a bit of Indigenous history, they got him to eat a bit of the 'roo, a bit of the heart, the guts, the real deal. They took him right in. That was massive for him personally.

'After that, the Santa Teresa crew came down to Armidale. Old women, men, a busload of them. It was great. Great for the boys to feel important and be hosts and introduce them to their territory. Geez, Gibson, here's proof he knew about horses. We camped them out at Warrah. I woke up that first morning and Gibson is in his swag over near the fence and all my horses, seven or eight of them, are almost in his swag with him. All lying down around him. I'd never seen it before ever; these horses wouldn't go near strangers. But here they are, sound asleep.

'That same time, I took him out with some of the boys for a ride. We went through some pretty rough ground, over gullies and in long grass. All's going well, then I saw Gibson looking round, and I said: "What's the matter?"

"'I lost my Winfields, eh."

"'Don't worry, have one of mine."

"'No, I gotta find 'em."

"'Where'd you lose 'em?'"

'We'd ridden quite a long way. They could've been anywhere. Anyhow, he turned his horse round and rode off. We get to this long grass, and I'm sure we're in the wrong spot. He just stepped off his pony, picked up his packet, took out a Winfield and lit it. No-one else in the world would have found those smokes.

'All those moments added up for me. By then, I definitely knew BackTrack was my future. It's what I liked doing. Kicking around with kids and dogs, horses, interesting people. I don't think I have ever called BackTrack work. It's not work. It's a way of being, really.'

But did that way come at a cost? Bernie still had to find time for his family. His daughter, Maeve, is an assistant nurse at an aged-care facility in Newcastle. In a phone interview she said she was too young to remember BackTrack's formative years in detail, and she accepted her father's absences as 'the way it was'. There were no judgements made, just 'the happiest of memories' of times spent together:

'A lot of my memories with Dad are with animals. Horse riding, and the dogs. Dad and I did pony camps together, and they were always funny. We'd go mostly to Bendemeer [a small town roughly seventy kilometres south-west of Armidale]. Lots of friends; quite a few people from Armidale went. It was more of a fun thing than competitive. Just mini holidays. Through the week we'd get sectioned into age groups or riding abilities, and we'd be trained and go on big trail rides. Then at the end we'd have a gymkhana. All sorts of events, like dressage, barrel racing and flag racing.

'There was one year where family members had to go in an event. Dad had been talking himself up all week and how he would come out with a blue ribbon, but when the day came, he was put in the bareback-rider class. Dad watched a few performances and started to lose hope. He probably worked out that he wouldn't be able to do what they wanted him to do. So, instead, he made a deal with the judges: if he could do a figure-of-eight on the horse and roll a smoke on the first circle and send a text message to the judge on the second circle he would get a blue ribbon for it. So, off he went. He rolled his cigarette, sent the text on his phone, and then ended up barrelling through the judges and knocking them off their chairs. But he got the blue ribbon!'

When I told Bernie that Maeve had mentioned that story – and that she had laughed loudly about it – Bernie replied straight-faced: 'And they're still talking about that buck-fest!'

The gymkhanas not only flourished on the joys of family bonding, but they frequently reminded Bernie of one of the most influential relationships in his life: the one with Paul and Annette Roots. Prior to Maeve's pony club days, Paul and Annette had a horse named Option. He was, according to Annette, 'brilliant', which surely wasn't the first time a horse bred from the esteemed Spinifex bloodline had been described in such a way. But he'd also been raised as a poddy foal, one that had lost its mother and been fed by hand; by the time he arrived at Paul and Annette's property, he was showing the signs of his upbringing: poddy animals often think they're as much human as they are animal. Although Option went on to have an incredible campdraft career, nowadays when dinner-table talk turns to his achievements, it's the moments that depict him as a Gary Larson *Far Side* character that are remembered most. Using his teeth, he could take head-collars off other horses and open gates – not a good combination when at campdraft events; he could also turn on taps and drop branches over electric fences to break the circuit. On one occasion he untied himself and pestered Paul who was trying to do some shoeing; in frustration Paul raised a rake and shook it at Option. The next day, Paul and Annette looked through their kitchen window to see their horse dragging a manure fork – the one he presumably thought was the offending rake – down to a dam and drop it in the water. Another time, he invited himself into the garage and walked up steps into the laundry only to discover he didn't have enough space to turn around, so he patiently waited until Annette returned from a shopping trip to laughingly rescue him. 'He really was too smart for his own good,' said Annette.

An injury cut his campdrafting career short, but eventually he was ridden in competition again. After Maeve showed an interest in joining the pony club, Bernie went looking for an appropriate horse. It was a 'tricky business trying to buy one for a kid', and Bernie struggled to find the right fit until Annette suggested Option might be worth a look.

'It turned out to be a match made in heaven,' says Bernie. 'He was still a smart-arse but, geez Maeve went out to her first pony camp and she cleaned up everything. Option had never seen pony camp, didn't know about barrel racing, or bending through flags or standing in line. Nailed it. An extraordinary horse.'

For a moment, Bernie stops talking.

That squint again. Then the grin.

'Rootsy. That bastard. There was this one gymkhana on up at Ebor. A big campdraft too. At this stage Maeve might've had Option for a couple of years, and there were kids up there who didn't have a horse, so we shared Option out. Maeve was just a generous soul, so she was saying: "You can do the flags, and you can do the barrels." And everyone who ended up winning rode that horse. I'd never ridden him; I might have sat on him bare back a few times, but never really ridden him.

'Anyway, we're there and it starts flogging down rain. It's freezing cold and the open campdraft gets going, and I hear the voice over the loudspeaker: "Bernie Shakeshaft on Option." I thought: "What!" I certainly hadn't put an entry in an open draft. I hadn't ridden the horse and I hadn't been in a campdraft for years! Now they were calling out the next six riders. I don't know how many riders there were in it altogether but it was a big campdraft. And the cut-out pen had been turned into a filthy mess coz of all the rain. I didn't know I was riding. I didn't even have a saddle. "Bernie Shakeshaft on Option. Contestant number blah blah. Bernie Shakeshaft on Option." Fuckin' Paul had stitched me up. And he's saying: "Get that saddle. Quick. You're on in three." So, I'm here on this horse in the floggin' rain. Ten different kids had ridden him in ten different events. I hadn't even looked at the cattle. All the ground was like quicksand and soup. No-one was getting a good score. I sat on that horse, and I'll never forget being in the camp. "Which one, boss?" I was asking Paul, see. "That one there." He nodded at a beast, and I'm still going: "What am I doing here?" So, I cut this beast out and it slammed up against the fence and moved away. I start thinking: "We need to get over there." But that horse is already over there. Nearly tore me out of the saddle. From then on, I just thought: "Whatever you do, don't get dusted here. Don't end up with your face in the mud looking like an idiot in the open campdraft." Well, that horse just chopped across, blocked the beast, my head is still ten seconds behind him, and he's already gone out underneath me again. I just held on with me legs. "Just stick it, be here at the end of the day." I couldn't walk for a week after that, but we had walked away with the second-highest cut-out score of all the horses. That was the sort of shit Paul did.

'It's funny, I reckon things happen for reasons. I wouldn't have met Paul and Annette if I hadn't been a run-amok as a kid. They helped steer me on my way, and it's because of those directions I met Jayne and all the rest of it, and then all those years later I was back with Paul and Annette with my own kids. They've always been there. And they've been there for the BackTrack kids too. All I have to do is ask them.'

Of course, Paul and Annette weren't alone in the good-deed network. People continued to drive through the gates of the depot and offer their services. Supervising; teaching; driving; cooking meals; giving tools, dogs, dollars, petrol … all and more. In his casual, let's get-onto-other-stuff kind of way, Bernie turns his head at a slight angle, and sometimes screws up his face when I quiz him on dates. He doesn't know when the depot opened for longer weekday hours, nor can he remember which staff were on the payroll at various times; there were just 'lots of different people making it happen'. Jobs Australia Enterprises was one of them. Under the direction of its CEO, Nigel Barlow, a staunch supporter of BackTrack, it was a community-based organisation that provided various employment solutions throughout the New England and north-west regions of New South Wales. 'They took us under their wing in 2010, and with all our ups and downs getting money, we would've fallen over if we didn't have them,' says Bernie. 'Nigel was a champion of our cause. So many people were.'

It wasn't, however, a one-way process. Bernie made sure the BackTrack boys all knew of the number and diversity of people who were helping them. In return, the boys became increasingly involved in community events. They worked on a restoration project of the Armidale Pine Forest after sections were destroyed by a hail storm; they picked up rubbish on the streets and in parks; they visited retirement homes with their dogs (on one trip to meet dementia sufferers, the forever popular Zorro was upstaged by his niece Pirate, a pup out of a litter from Girl); they staged jumping displays around the district and further away (where Zorro usually regained his status as top dog); they held public exhibitions of their welded artwork (flowers, nutcrackers, dogs, abstract pieces); they accompanied Bernie to speak at functions (some agreed that breaking-and-entering made them less nervous than addressing an audience). In all, they tried to 'give back'. And in doing so, they felt good about themselves, and made the community feel good about them – or at the very least, have a greater understanding of what those boys were doing at the old council shed out on the Grafton Road.

Helping. Understanding. Growing.

They were all integral parts of Bernie's vision.

17

He sits and swivels in Bernie's black office chair. Side to side, side to side, always moving. It's hard to tell if he's nervous or in complete control. He has soft whiskers on his chin and scars on his arms. But it's his eyes that catch my attention. They are hard and knowing. They've seen ...

When compared with many other BackTrack boys, the broad themes of his life are common: trouble at school, wrong crowd, suspensions, a spiral downwards.

A spiral, and then some.

'I was living in a car when I was thirteen until I was about fifteen. Nearly a year-and-a-half I lived in a car for. Just an old car that didn't run. I had all my clothes in the boot. That was when I was going downhill; that was when I was doing it my hardest. I was on a lot of heavy drugs. I was on ice, and I was selling a bit of drugs as well: ice and cocaine and weed. I started hanging out with older boys.

'Dad has been in jail most of my life, and Mum was ... I dunno, it's been pretty rough for me. I never really got to see Dad much. And Mum was never really at home. So, I just done my own thing. I used to steal food from Coles and take it over to public barbecues and cook it for dinner. Steal loaves of bread and sausages. It was just what I knew at the time.

'The rough guys I was with was pretty rough. I've seen someone get shot. I've seen people stabbed. I ended up going to juvey [juvenile detention]. When I was young, I wanted to be a police officer, and look what happened then.

'I done it pretty hard in there coz I'd just had my first son, my first kid, so I went in there when he was a few months old. I missed out on his first birthday. Yeah, I did it pretty rough in there, away from the family. You got no-one, you know. You're getting told what to do all day and locked in a room that you can't do anything about. You can't just walk down to the shop and buy an apple. It's hard to explain it to the [BackTrack] boys. I've told them about what it's like being inside and I try and put fear into them. I tell them it's not safe for anyone. If you want to be locked in a cell eighteen hours a day, what are you going to get out of that? You don't get any certificates for that.

'But now ... It's good when I take a few boys out to build a fence or something and I look at what they've done and it's all perfect and at the end of the day I can think: "I taught him that!" or "I helped them with that." It makes me feel pretty good, and it makes them feel good. I like work. I would go mad without it; it keeps my mind off things. I love working.

'I'm savin' up for a house deposit. Hopefully in a few years I'll have enough for a home loan, have enough for a deposit. That's my main goal at the moment, so I can get my own place.

'I've seen a lot of horrendous stuff. I suppose it has made me who I am today. When people say: "Would you take anything back in your life?" I say, "No, it has made me who I am. All of it made me who I am today."'

Our interview lasts for twenty minutes. Only after the boy has gone does the chair sit still.

Bernie and I should be closing in on our second full interview day, but despite the long hours in the verandah chair, Bernie keeps talking. He dismisses some subjects, such as awards, with the wave of a hand – 'Some of the big ones are in my office. Have a look when you go in there next.' – but other topics slow him, make him think and dig into his memories. Many are pre-empted by the customary 'uuuuum' or 'aaaargh', or are introduced in ways that intrigue me about what will follow.

'Generosity. Isn't that important?' he says. 'Dusty was big on it – he hadn't started working for us full-time yet, but he was always lending a hand – and he was always driving round designing 'generosity activities' where you find something that needs doing and you just go and do it. He used to go and find back streets where rubbish had been dumped, and he and the boys would pick up the rubbish and take it away. There was no need to tell anyone. They just did it. Also, there was this funny time they came across an elderly lady who was kneeling down in her garden trying to pull weeds out, and Dusty pulls up with these kids and explains who we are, and before you know it the garden is full of kids pulling out weeds. Another time, there was a broken steel fence and a gate at this place; Dusty went in there with one kid, didn't even knock on the door, took the gate off, then took it back to the shed where they welded it up, painted it, then went back with concrete and set a new post, and went about their business again. Dusty was always doing stuff like that. I'd say to him: 'Are we going to get in trouble for doing this stuff?' But we didn't. It was all about doing good things. We were really pushing that generosity angle with the kids.

'Then we hit the Mingoola Floods [January–February 2011]. I was away on holidays, and one of the boys rang me and said he'd lost friends up over the border in Toowoomba. Remember those floods? Devastating. This kid, Joel, said why don't we take some crew up? And I reckon part of that was coz Dusty had planted this generosity seed so well. I said: "No worries, great idea." I told a few people what we were going to do, then Richard Torbay, the local state member, got in touch, and said there were people in trouble closer to home on the border. Mingoola, Bonshaw. Floods don't differentiate. So, we went to a big farming community up there. Took about a dozen boys up there with Murray Lupton [Muz] – you'll have to talk with him, he's good for a yarn. Took up a lot of fencing stuff, barbed wire, three-star pickets that local stores donated.

'When we drove into the area, it was the quietest I'd ever heard a bunch of kids. Looking at these bridges washed away and dead animals everywhere and rainwater tanks washed into gum trees. It was a disaster zone. I had never seen anything like it. Concrete bridges, like a bomb had been dropped in the middle of them. So, we roll in there, and the local deputy mayor came and met us, and he was great. Someone had these shearing quarters we could use for our base, and next thing you know we were given this one spot to start at the next day. The deputy mayor said: "Make sure you start early in the morning if you can, then knock off in the middle of the day because it's hot as hell." And it was. Stinking, filthy hot. Like Darwin. And the stench of dead animals. Cows, kangaroos. The waters were still going down.

'So, we rolled up at this big fella's place. A big farm fella. Thank God I took Muz so he could go and talk to this bloke. You'll know what I mean when you meet Muz. It's probably about six am, and this fella is all bleary-eyed and Muz is trying to explain to him that we're here to help, and this fella is looking at our boys in the background and he must have been going "mmmmmmmmmm". Shirts and cowboy hats and jeans and boots. Pimples. Anyway, it all started from there. I dunno how much fencing there was that needed doing, but it was a fair bit. Boundary fences along the road.

'Well, Muz had those boys rippin' and tearin'. Those kids were bustin' keen. We had them strung out for hundreds of metres along the fence line standing in knee-deep filthy shit just pulling stuff out of the fences. And we've taken our welding man, Rocket, and he's already welding up new strainer assemblies. We've got fencing contractors and Muz has done fencing his whole life. I've got cement mixers and all the wire and star pickets. Resources were scarce on the ground, but we came with everything that was donated from Armidale. Truckloads of stuff; we were ferrying it up. Someone was just driving backwards and forwards with barbed wire, plain wire, strainer posts and steelies. It was about three hours one way, probably a little more in those conditions. Anyway, these boys were working like champions. Kids crawling up trees to pull gates out and tanks and pallets. And we'd run over the gates in a truck to straighten 'em out and weld 'em back together again. It was some time that day, I went and knocked on the big fella's door and said we'd done a bit. He drove down the road with us to have a look, he got out of his ute and just burst into tears. The big fella. Coz he had this beautiful brand-new fence.

'So, by that afternoon we had foolscap pages of names of people to help. Now we had to split our group up. That guy needs cattle yards done. This one's got fencing. Hectic.

'Two weeks we spent up at Mingoola. Generosity. The boys became stars. Farmers' wives would be dropping off food to us and asking if we were all right, telling us what a good job we were doing. You should've seen the boys' faces. Tough boys. A lot of Indigenous kids.'

Bernie reaches for his cigarette packet, and then follows his customary routine.

'It must have been towards the end of the second week and everyone is wrecked. Dusty has come up to help. That's the sort of stuff we've had all the way through BackTrack. People lending a hand when they can, giving their time. Look at Muz, walking off his farm for two weeks to help. Anyway, there were some other volunteer groups up there at the time. All doing good stuff, but you know, a bit of competition never goes astray. And that's where Dusty comes in. The motivator. These other volunteers were picking stuff off fences, but they weren't doing the real hard yards. But our boys were. And they were fried. Digging in some big strainer posts, some wooden ones. Hard work. And these volunteers were coming closer and closer to us, covering a lot more distance, and Dusty decides we should show them a thing or two. So, he eyes off a couple of the boys and starts an argument about whose turn it is to use the crowbar. He keeps at it and starts pumping these guys up so much that they're just about to go the knuckle: "Give it here, it's my turn now." "Fuck off, you can't have all the fuckin' turns on the crowbar!" And these other volunteers could see all this going on, and I could tell they were thinking: "Where do they get all that energy from?" Dusty was doing that sort of stuff all the time. It was one of the funnier afternoons I've had at BackTrack watching these other poor bewildered volunteers wondering what the hell was going on. What a ding-dong.'

Bernie chuckles, and a thread of smoke seems to wait for a moment before carrying away the laughter.

'I'll tell you what else happened up there. Rocket made a six-man steel post driver, the heaviest goddam post driver you've ever seen for driving strainer posts. There's no such thing; normally you use tractors. But not our crew. It had six handles on it for six guys, two hands on each handle. *Bang, bang, bang.* We were driving these strainer post assemblies, *bang*, and then on to the next one. Kilometres and kilometres of fencing in torrid conditions. And these boys were worn out and all their hands were bleeding and blistered but we weren't giving up. We were lying down, having a break for lunch from this job. Flaked out, Muz and me and everyone down near this riverbed. Before we'd stopped, we'd run out seventy steel posts, pickets. Just tapped them in and ran a wire out so they were all in line. Five metres in between each post; you can't see the end of the steels. And while we were all having lunch and sitting down, this little Aboriginal kid, he was only a pup at the time, can hardly read or write, has gone out with a postdriver. By the time we were coming back from lunch he was driving in the third-last post. We just walked out and went: "What the hell!" This kid had gone down there and driven in all those posts by himself. Each post needed about twenty hits. So, someone, I can't remember who, started calling him "Seventy". After that, all these old-school cockies would be coming along, and they'd just stop in the middle of the road and ask: "Where's this Seventy kid?" He had become a legend. And the nickname stuck. Muz and me, and all the older boys at BackTrack still know him as Seventy. And you know what was beautiful? We were doing Circle Work the other day and I asked everyone what was something that made them feel proud about being at BackTrack, and this boy said, "Seventy."'

Fittingly, I met one of the boys who went to Mingoola when he was welding on a strainer assembly on a property close to Armidale. Sam agreed to be interviewed on another day and we finally got together a few months later. We chatted in the BackTrack classroom, which wasn't there when Sam first walked into the depot as a young teenager. These were steps in a nomadic journey that had already seen him attend several schools in the region and live in a tent for about five years with his parents and two sisters. After dropping out of high school midway through Year Seven, he slipped into crime. Breaking into cars, and then breaking into stores and stealing money to buy cigarettes and 'smoke cones'. He went to court a few times, just 'in and out' earning a 'bit of street cred'. He wasn't nervous. It was just an accepted part of his life until: 'The magistrate, the old mate, the judge told me: "If I see you in here again mate, you're gone."' Sam was thirteen at the time. And he was 'scared'.

In his recount of his childhood, one word echoed with a poignancy that all too many troubled youth can relate to. 'I had a very hard time and never belonged anywhere, I guess,' reflected Sam, calmly. 'But once I came into BackTrack, straightaway off the bat the boys were coming up and shaking my hand and saying: "How are you going, brother?" And that's when I met Bern. He was cool as; actually meeting someone who wasn't a boss or a teacher. More just a bloody good role model.

'I'll tell you what, those first couple of days I always felt nervous, and I felt, "I'm gonna stuff up here in a second." I really didn't do any good with stuff-ups; like whenever I stuffed up in the past I thought, "I'm gone, I don't want to do it anymore." But I had some good mentors, Bern and others, because when I did stuff up they sat me down and said: "Mate, it's not the end of the world. You can do better. You can actually fix it." So, I thought: "Okay, I'll have a go at fixing it." That was one of the turning points for me: knowing that it's not always that hard.

'At that stage I didn't know how much I was growing as a young man. Not at all. Until I started to talk about it.'

Whether or not Sam realised it at the time, BackTrack had become a refuge for him. A safe place where he could grow and learn in ways with which he connected. After beginning in the welding shed, he soon shifted to the AgLads program, and the sense of belonging was immediate. 'It was awesome working on the land. I loved it. I just got a boost out of it. Especially at the end of the day when someone might say: "You've done a good job today." And I'd think: "Shit yeah!"'

The praise and constructive feedback began on the very first property he worked on. It was run by Murray Lupton, the 'no bullshit bloke' whom Bernie was very keen for me to chat to. When we had our interview, he walked into the smoko room at BackTrack as though he'd just dismounted from a horse after a month-long ride. He had whiskery eyebrows, gingery and grey, and his hands were fleshy; when he clenched his fists, there were no ridges for his knuckles, just plains of weathered existence that included marks from the occasional 'all-in'. 'We're not all saints,' joked the father of two teenagers.

'I was one of the original farming enterprises with BackTrack. Fencing, haymaking, lamb marking, cattle branding, all and varied jobs that could be used as a training program. The boys now call me Cranky Muz, but someone's gotta be the firm hand. If someone plays up, you take away the jobs they like and give them jobs they don't like, and you can see them think about it.

'I'm a big believer in direction. Telling the kids. Communicating.

At the end of the day: "Hey boys, you've done beautifully." You shake their hands, pat 'em on the back, give 'em a hug. Many of them have never ever had that. They've never had anyone talking them up, so it's building their esteem, and all it might take is a couple of good words at the end of the day. And vice versa, if they've stuffed up you need to tell them. "This is why you stuffed up." And it works. Some of these kids are coming from families that haven't worked in generations; it can be so frustrating. Getting them out of bed, getting them somewhere on time, but we're getting there … small steps, you know. It's going back to the basics: "Okay, this is work, this is play." Enhancing it, going back to the same old thing: "I'm proud of you for the day," or "I'm not so proud of you but what do we do to make it better?" It's going backwards to go forwards all the time.'

Sam is testament to the successes that can be achieved. While still in the BackTrack program, he earned a traineeship with an Armidale business. Confident in his growth, and understanding he also needed to broaden his horizons, he then left for a few years, and worked as a jackaroo on a Queensland sheep station, before being a farmhand in north-west New South Wales, and getting his hands dirty for that familiar couple Paul and Annette Roots. He has now returned to the Armidale district, and is an obvious role model for all coming through.

'I can't believe the journey I've had over the years with BackTrack,' he said. 'I wouldn't think I would be here today. BackTrack means a brand-new life compared to what I thought I was going to have. It's hard to say how unreal it is. Bernie has become a close friend. Somebody you can talk to, somebody you can go to. I really like Bern. I've got a lot of time for Bern and everyone who has helped me.'

There is another integral part to Sam's development. When he first arrived at BackTrack he had a blue heeler named Jumper, given to him by a cousin. Then, within a couple of years of him working with Bernie's and Paul Roots' dogs in the PawsUp program, Bernie offered him a black-and-white collie pup Reggie. Despite his father's protests, Sam kept him, and in the wake of Jumper's death a couple of years ago, Reggie has become a young man's 'best mate'.

'I remember tying him to a gate one day, and I came back and he was dragging the gate around. He sort of reminded me of myself because I had a lot of energy as a kid. We just done so much together. Everywhere I went through town there wouldn't be a day go past where you wouldn't see me and him walking somewhere. If he wasn't next to me, there was something wrong,' said Sam, laughing.

'I started doing cattle trials [competitions in which dogs have to work cattle around a course] with him. Had the very first one in Armidale, and everyone was coming up to me afterwards saying: "Good job, mate." So, I went to a few more of them, and ended up doing the Dorrigo trial, and there was me, Bernie, Paul Roots – and I ended up coming first. I couldn't believe it. I was thinking: "I beat Rootsy!" And he's the man.'

To listen to Sam is to listen to a young man who is thrilled about what he has achieved and what lies ahead. Among his dreams is one that creates no divides: 'To own me own house.' He also wants to have his own fencing contracting business. 'When you build a fence you can go, "That looks good." You get a boost off it, and that's why you keep doing it. You can see it.'

Other rewards of the BackTrack program can, as Bernie said, be seen at the BackTrack depot. One of them, a framed certificate, was presented in 2011. The Premier of NSW Community Service Award, in recognition of 'outstanding contribution to the community'. It's a permanent reminder that mending fences in a flood-ravaged district can be every bit as powerful as metaphorically building bridges. Further political accolades followed; and none was bigger than in 2012 when Sam and his 'brothers' were invited to a house bigger than any of them had ever seen.

18

He is known by many of the boys (and girls) as 'Uncle Steve'. He often drops into the depot to attend Circle Work or contribute in the classroom, or just to be there, sip on a tea and chat with anyone. And he listens. Listens very closely. Right now, he sits on the bench seat near Bernie's office and listens to the comings and goings around him. Soon, he'll get on a minibus or the troopy or in a LandCruiser and go with some of the boys and some visitors on a trip to Dangarsleigh Falls. Until then, though, he has time to be interviewed.

'I'm happy that BackTrack has worked,' he says. 'And that comes from the hard work and commitment here since day one. Bernie was so committed that he hasn't looked back. One thing is for sure: he has more vision than me.'

Uncle Steve laughs. It's likely he has used similarly themed jokes for many years.

Why?

Because twenty-eight years ago, to the very day of this interview, he was driving when he suddenly said to his brother in the passenger seat: 'I can't see. I can't focus. There is something ahead of me, but I don't know what it is.' Blindness quickly followed. The diagnosis from experts, including world-famous ophthalmologist Fred Hollows, told of a rare condition associated with the macular.

Uncle Steve now uses a cane, and at the BackTrack depot there's always someone, young or older, to take him by the arm and guide him. 'Are you okay, Uncle Steve?' 'This way, Uncle Steve.' 'Uncle Steve, would you like a cup of tea?' In return, he offers his presence. An elder from the Anaiwan people. A man whose wisdom has been shaped by his own experiences and by his cultural heritage. He talks about rivers: 'The old blackfellas, they saw the water as the blood of the country, and if the blood didn't run, the country died.' He also talks about resourcefulness: 'Aboriginal people were conservationists, they were environmentalists, ecologists, artists, storytellers. They were doctors. All their medical supplies, all their food came from the land. They were engineers; you know, they had a bigger hardware shop than Mitre 10 or Bunnings. They would go and get all their tools and implements out of the country. And they did that for thousands of years. People took what they needed not what they wanted.' So much of what he says relates to connection. Connection between people and country. Connection between one person and another. Connection between cultures. Connection between differences. Connection as a key to our future.

Chatter, footsteps and jostling around us tells he will soon be on his way to the falls. But before he goes, he says a little more.

'Being blind, I don't look at colour. I can't see whether these boys are black or white, and it doesn't matter to me. And it shouldn't matter to anyone else. If a person is down and out and needs some guidance and support, you don't discriminate. When Bernie first talked to me about BackTrack years ago, I didn't even know that he was a white bloke. I think we should all be like that. We shouldn't see colour.'

'Uncle Steve, are you coming?' asks someone.

'Yes, I'm coming.'

And soon he is going. A well-travelled man who can take you places just by sitting on a bench seat.

On the trips to and from Mingoola, the BackTrack boys rode in a white truck acquired cheaply by Jobs Australia Enterprises. By then, it had become a common sight throughout country New South Wales and Queensland. It had a driver's cabin that fitted three people; directly behind that was a ten-seater cabin; and then there was a tray on which sat two tiers of dog cages prominently marked with black paintings of a collie's face, and the words: PawsUp.

The truck had served BackTrack well, but it was prone to rattling and clunking, and in 2012, on a trip back from Cunnamulla, in south-west Queensland, those sounds signalled a warning. Dusty, who had recently begun working full-time at BackTrack, was driving.

'Not everything goes according to the script,' he said, laughing, in his phone interview. 'It was the middle of the night, and some of the boys had become pretty freaked out about the darkness because we'd actually seen a Min Min light on the way up there. It freaked me out too; it seemed to come right through the cabin and out the other side.

'Anyway, the truck had played up all the way to Cunnamulla in pouring rain, and on the way back it played up really badly and we could only do a top speed of about thirty k's an hour. Then one of the guys just got fed up with everything and lost it. He got off the truck and away he went into the night. When that sort of stuff happens, you do all you can to get them back; most of the time something works, but this time it didn't. He just walked off down the road. So, I came up with this cunning plan. I drove off with the other boys, and we went a few k's down the road, then I stopped and said: "Everyone get your dog out, get your leads out, and we'll start walking back. Let's stick together, and when we see so-and-so just keep walking past him. Don't stop." So, we did that. You can imagine what it was like for the lone fella. Walking by yourself in the night, no sound, just darkness, and all of a sudden eleven boys and eleven dogs go past you. He joined them and there you go, problem solved. We all got back to the truck and everyone was all right again.'

Everyone, but not everything. Later on, in the early hours of the morning, the truck broke down, and Dusty and the boys swagged it by the roadside until daybreak, and then had a long wait through the day for help to arrive. They passed the time playing football, fetching water for the dogs from a trough, and talking to passers-by who stopped to see what they could do. Back in Armidale news of the breakdown was cause for concern. Of course, the thoughts of tired, restless, hungry, bored BackTrack boys 'in the middle of nowhere' were reasons enough to turn plans into actions, but there was another factor that added to the urgency. Just weeks before the Cunnamulla trip, Australia's Treasurer Wayne Swan announced in the 2012 Federal Budget that BackTrack would receive an $800 000 grant to be spread equally over four years. The budget paper stated: 'The funding will be used to help run the Iron Man [sic] Welders Shed — a fully operational welding workshop; the PawsUp program, which helps teach self-discipline through boys training working dogs; and AgLads, which offers boys formal as well as on-the-job training on local farms.' (Budget Measures, Budget Paper Number 2, 2012–13.)

It was an extraordinary windfall for BackTrack. Independent Member for New England, Tony Windsor, had helped secure the funding at a time when independents held the balance of power in parliament, and Windsor supported the minority Labor government under Prime Minister Julia Gillard. At a time of political instability, BackTrack had found financial stability. Following the budget announcement, it was arranged for some BackTrack kids and dogs to visit Parliament House in Canberra and meet Prime Minister Gillard. The problem was, just days before the planned meeting, the truck and the boys and girls who were meant to go to the nation's capital were stranded in the back-blocks.

'That was an interesting turn-up,' says Bernie. 'What we had to deal with, you'd have no idea. A mechanic had been out and had a look at the truck, and he couldn't work out what was happening, so he thought they were going to have to tow the truck to the nearest town. But that wouldn't help us, because we were pushing the clock. How are we going to get the kids, the dogs, the truck full of gear, and get to Canberra? We had to ferry everything back. About three vehicles and trailers with some sort of dog boxes that we had to borrow. By the time we got on the road to Canberra everyone was already fried. And we still didn't have the truck. And that turned out to be a bit of a problem, coz when we got to Canberra, the truck was the registered vehicle we'd initially told security we'd be rocking up to Parliament House in. But then, these cars and roof-racks and dog jumps, and dogs and kids turn up, and it's like a circus. Took about fifteen dogs, by then we had kelpies as well. We rocked up to the front of Parliament House and stopped next to the grass there and said, 'All right, dogs out,' and then we were swamped by the Federal Police. We didn't have the truck they'd been expecting, and then you got some of the kids having meltdowns and they're nervous and edgy and … it was a debacle. No-one was sure what to do or how much we had to be checked, and remember we've got some kids who can go off like a stick of dynamite. I suppose it was hilarious, but bloody stressful at the time.

'Anyhow, we got through the day, as we always do. Meeting Julia Gillard was sensational. I don't care about politics. When you judge people, it's what you see and what they do. Actions not words. I have the same approach with the kids. Don't tell me what a great kid he is, or what a great dog he is – I want to see it. The way the prime minister treated those kids, I won't forget that. She had minders tapping her on the shoulder and looking at their watches, but she was telling them to back off. She gave those kids her time and interest, and we have no idea what that might have meant to some of those kids. We put on a jumping show for her, and on the top board of the jump we wrote $800 000. I think all the politicians there had a good time. Simon Crean, Rob Oakeshott, Malcolm Turnbull, I think.'

Obviously, Tony Windsor was also there. He'd first met Bernie soon after BackTrack was founded and was impressed with what was trying to be achieved. He remains a staunch supporter. In a phone interview he said to me: 'One of the fascinating things about that day, something that really struck me, was later on when I went to have a yarn and say thanks very much to the parliament's security people; they'd gone out of their way to help the kids. And one fellow said to me: "Look, if we had kids like that coming through all the time, we wouldn't need security." It was a good example of what BackTrack does. I've seen different kids develop over time. From the fourteen-year-old who won't even look at you to a year or so later, when he's a young adult; he still has his problems, but he's on the way up rather than going down. I think it's an extraordinary program. Bernie is not involved in BackTrack to make a living, but to make a difference. He really does care about every kid. He's saving lives.'

Without prompting, Bernie also tells me about Tony Windsor's recollection. It's just one tiny but telling piece in a kaleidoscopic story. Another is the moment Radar, the dutiful collie owned by 'Seventy', sneaked in a lick of the prime minister's hand. Regardless of how well – or badly – the dogs and kids may have behaved in Canberra, Bernie was relieved when they were back in their truckless convoy and heading for home.

'But gee, it can be ridiculous, you know. Absurd and all the rest of it,' says Bernie. 'Two hundred grand, eight hundred grand – a lot of money. We didn't have much at the time, so this was a real kick-along. Thanks very much, let's put it to good use. Around then, we had these really rough kids; it's sad, but they were too busted, too far gone. Kids that we couldn't help. They'd been on and off at BackTrack for a while, but they never quite made it. Disappointing for me and everyone in the program, but it can happen. That's the world that keeps turning. Anyhow, after the show in Canberra, I had to fly back for the Armidale Business Awards. And there'd been a bit of talk among some of the boys about how we were going to get all this money. And some of them also knew that we kept one little safe at BackTrack. It was bolted to the floor in the shed. Just the size of a tissue box. We used to throw the keys in there at night, and I had a busted camera and a few other old bits and pieces in there. Well, these rough boys broke into the shed, got a crow bar and stole the safe coz they thought that eight hundred grand was in there, and they were ready to take a trip overseas. Go to Bali or somewhere. They got a few hours away down the road. By then they've got an angle grinder coz they couldn't open the safe. Imagine their surprise when they finally looked inside. The overseas trip faded quickly! I have to admit, we've had a few laughs about that one over the years.

'But, back to that truck up there in woop-woop. We got it fixed, but … When the boys had camped at Cunnamulla it had been flooding down rain, and they couldn't light a fire coz everything was so wet. Dusty got some paper and dipped it in the fuel tank, soaked it in diesel, and they got their fire going. Now, the boys must have seen him do this, coz after Dusty had gone to bed, the fire was getting a bit dim, and someone decided to get a few flames again. And the truck had all these PawsUp brochures – we'd printed hundreds, thousands of them – all on this glossy paper. Proper flash things they were. And I dunno, someone must've got some of these brochures and tried to do the Dusty thing with the fuel tank. Move along the story a bit, and the truck breaks down and then it's fixed. Right, no worries. But then after that, the truck would go for a while and stop, go for a while and stop. Dusty never told me about all the tricks with the paper until we pulled the fuel tank out of the truck for the first time. Those brochures never fully broke down in that tank. We must've taken that tank, changed our injectors dozens of times in the next two years. Everywhere we'd go this truck would go along swimmingly and we'd be thinking, "Yeah, we've got it covered this time," but then it would break down. "Not again. Here we go. Another bloody brochure." They were just breaking down bit by bit and filtering in and getting stuck in the fuel line. The things we could've told Julia Gillard.'

The truck's start–stop history was symbolic of something else Bernie had to come to terms with: his marital relationship. By the end of 2012, it was clear it wasn't working, and Jayne moved with James, who had finished school, and Maeve, who was about to enter Year Ten, to Tamworth, about a hundred kilometres from Armidale.

'Things didn't work out,' says Bernie. 'But I will always have the greatest respect for Jayne. She's an incredibly smart person who loves and cares for her children. We still have an amicable relationship. I'm lucky she's part of my life.'

Maeve and James often visited Bernie on weekends, and when Maeve was old enough to legally drive she clocked up many hours going up and down the New England Highway. For Bernie, as always, life was primarily about the road ahead. Boosted by the federal injection of funds, all programs developed and the gates swung open at the depot every weekday. Then, on weekends, the boys and dogs continued to leap into hearts and consciences, including in Melbourne where the PawsUp team, wearing specially made NSW rugby league–style jumpers, won a state-of-origin contest against Victoria. And while Zorro and Girl had reached an age at which their bones were telling them to take walls a little easier, the next generation of dogs filled the voids with the joyful enthusiasm that only dogs have. Among them was the kelpie Bindi, who claimed a national record of nearly ten feet.

BackTrack also maintained its community involvement, and in early 2013 the boys packed their swags and fencing materials and headed three hundred kilometres south-west to the bush surrounds of Coonabarabran where fires had destroyed tens of thousands of hectares, more than fifty homes, and killed livestock. Hard work, high rewards. By helping others, the boys knew they were also helping themselves. By then, perhaps hundreds – don't ask Bernie about exact numbers – had participated in the various BackTrack programs. As the safe thieves confirmed, not everyone was a success story, but others who'd gone on to gain TAFE qualifications, secure jobs and stay out of trouble reaffirmed to Bernie that 'BackTrack really works'.

'But [you] don't ever think you've done enough,' says Bernie. 'Over the years there isn't a staff member who hasn't heard me say this: "I judge how well BackTrack is going when I drive through the front gate and look into the faces of the kids." Simple as that. And let me tell you, if there are no faces to look into, straightaway I'm going to say, "That's a problem, Houston." It'd be nice to think no-one would come through the gate because all the kids everywhere are all happy and floating along, but that's never gonna be the story. So, let's hope the ones who need help come in and keep coming, and we'll try our best to do all we can for them.

'By then, I suppose there were a few things that made us different from some of the other youth work programs around. The biggie was, there was no time limit on how long the kids could stay. Other programs might have kids for sixteen weeks, six months or whatever, and then they might be told: "See you, give life a crack, good luck." But we didn't and will never do that. If the kids have to stay for years, they stay for years. Look at The Magnificent Seven. They got their jobs and eventually moved on. No worries. But Andrew, he stayed with us. Not just for his benefit, but for the overall benefit of BackTrack. He was at a stage where he could be a role model to new kids coming through. He was a real-life example of someone who'd walked it, talked it and was coming out the other side. Then, you look at the other people the boys could learn from. Muz [Murray Lupton], Geraldine

Cutmore, Julia Gillard; Uncle Steve Widders – when he rolled up with his walking stick, the kids would line up to help him. More and more Indigenous kids were coming into BackTrack, and that changed dynamics as we went along.

'When we first set up, I wanted to follow the Indigenous lines-of-the-kinship system. Say you and I are brothers and we both have children. The theory is that your kids live under your roof with you, but I take a much deeper responsibility for things, as you do for my children. In modern-day terms it might mean I go to parent–teacher nights for your children, and you do the same for mine. Or I might take yours to football on the weekend. It's a system of shared responsibilities where many more adults become involved. It can be complex but it's powerful. It's about community. It's like that saying: "It takes a whole village to raise a child." All through those middle years of BackTrack it was a work in progress and it continues to evolve. One of the questions I've been asked all the way through is: "Why are there not more girls in the programs?" Well, we've always had them, but you have to have the right people to handle the kids. Gel Cutmore was great with that. She could handle the girls, so terrific, let them come in. But when Gel stepped back to do other things, we had to reassess. Always a work in progress.'

Bernie leans forward and scratches the back of his hands. The verandah is starting to get cold, and in the garden Girl and Lou can no longer find patches of sun. We keep talking, meandering a little. From laughing over Muz's public-speaking efforts in front of Julia Gillard and company – 'Hilarious. Great man, but Christ, there was no hiding he was from the bush, I can tell you.' – to more serious discussions about the establishment in mid-2013 of a two-day-a-week classroom in the depot shed where boys were taught literacy and numeracy skills: 'That was a winner in the community. Showed a lot of goodwill. We found a cracking teacher, businesses supplied bits and pieces, and Armidale Rotary got revved up about doing an upgrade.' We also spoke of more 'Left And Rights' with Dusty: 'Ended up at Cape Tribulation on one trip. In this old HG. Crocodile-infested waters. Crazy stuff.' And then we returned to politics. Julia Gillard had been ousted as Prime Minister after a Labor Party squabble, Kevin Rudd took over the leadership for a second stint only to lose to the Tony Abbott–led Liberal/National Coalition at the Federal Election in September 2013. Independent Member for New England, Tony Windsor, didn't contest his seat, which was won by former Queensland Nationals senator Barnaby Joyce. The politics meant nothing to Bernie until, towards the end of the year, it was announced that the remaining three years of the $800 000 federal grant to BackTrack was under review. Barnaby Joyce visited the depot and told local media that BackTrack had been moved to a different funding category, but he was 'getting a sense that we are going to try and line a few things up and we should be all right'. However, it wasn't, and although BackTrack was given a twelve-month reprieve, the end result was a loss of about $500 000.

Bernie takes a deep breath and shakes his head. 'So, talk about cat and pigeons. That was a knock for us. Just before that the Vincent Fairfax Family Foundation came on board with us. And they're still supporting us. Great people. Always looking to help communities, and their support has been a rock for us. Some of them came up and we did a Circle Work at the back of the shed. I remember tears. At some point we also took some kids and dogs down to Sydney and presented to their board. Trying to get the dogs into a lift, that was interesting. But that original support from

VFFF – I'll never be able to say how grateful I was. After we lost the federal money, some other organisations that had supported us hit the skids. It was the closest we came to falling over. Restless nights for sure, and for a while there I went to bed thinking how we'd keep the gate open. But, then I woke up one night and just went: "Right, I'm not worrying about money anymore. If our intentions are right and we're getting the right outcomes we'll get there. We started out as volunteers who gave kids another chance … if we have to we will start again." Looking back, there was a bit of blind faith going on.

'I don't want to get into the ins and outs of politics. Doesn't interest me. What happened, happened. Move on. But that whole federal funding thing taught me a lot about not relying too much on one source of income. It also started me thinking of business models that could work without government funding. We'd been lucky with Julia Gillard, and over the years we'd had support in different ways from the state government, but if we were gonna kick long-term goals, we had to change. I knew philanthropy was going to be so important to our future.'

Future. A sound word to finish our second interview day. Bernie stands up and stretches his arms above his head. He'll soon stretch his legs with a walk down to the horse yard. It's feeding time. Sunday afternoon. We agree our final intense chat will be 'sometime in the week'. In three days, or four. We'll hold it at the depot. Maybe in the shed, but more likely in Bernie's office. After the quiet of a country homestead verandah, a session in town will feel very different. The depot is on a relatively busy road that heads to the coast. We might hear the noise of passing trucks. Closer, there may be the sounds of laughter; feet scuffing in gravel; a tennis ball pinging off a tin wall; electric saws and drills; hip-hop;

'Fuck you!' 'Fuck you too.' Phones will ring. All sorts of messages will be announced by riffs and licks. Closer still, there may be knocks at the door, and, 'Excuse me, Bern,' or, 'Sorry to interrupt.' Who knows what will happen? At the BackTrack depot, there are too many pieces in motion to predict any one day, let alone a few hours when two blokes hope to have a quiet yarn.

19

The two boys are sitting on a pile of wooden planks at the back of the shed. They've just shared a lighter to fire up their rollies. Then they swap stories about how they've come to be here. Raw, real revelations. One prefers to talk more than the other. He has been to 'this place and that'. Out of school and into crime, drugs and alcohol. He says some of his friends and members of his family 'didn't have much of a really good rep with the police'. And, as a result, they lugged those reps wherever they went.

'Me and my friends, like, we would get stoned, just go for a walk downtown or to the river. Walking along with thongs, footy shorts and a towel, and the coppers would be: "All right, let's pull these kids over and search 'em." Were they serious? I've got thongs, a towel, and footy shorts on. What is there to conceal? So, they'd be patting us down in the middle of the street. Thirteen- and fourteen-year-old kids, and I'd be thinking: "What is going on here? You seriously have something against us." It didn't help that my friends had mouths at the time. I was like, "Boys, just do what you're told, and they'll leave us alone." But they were always like, "Fuck you, dog, you're a fuckin' copper." We didn't have much of a good relationship. But then there were these couple of coppers that had caught us a few nights when we were running away, and they'd say, "We thought you kids were better than that." And we'd say, "What do you mean?" And they'd say, "You should be able to outrun us because you've got no shoes and we're wearing these big boots and gear and shit." And out of that, one of these coppers built a relationship with us. Just by talking shit with us. And then he'd see us on the street at some other time and he'd be in a car and he'd point at us, and we'd give him the finger or something like that, and quickly on the sly he would give one back.'

The boy grins. It's the full stop to a happy memory. A memory built from the flaws of a reputation.

The grey wooden cabin wouldn't be out of place near an English beach, lining up eave to eave with the rainbow coloured change sheds that have posed for many a traveller's photo. The only thing missing is the flock of scattered seagulls. There are, however, a few old chips sprinkled with dust and mashed by boots, near the cabin's steps. The structure is new, and a conversation piece for Matt Pett, a recent addition to the BackTrack staff. He has been here only a few months and has told just snippets of his story to the boys. He left school when he was fourteen and worked on the family farm in the Tweed region. But by the time he was eighteen, he knew he should have stayed at school longer. He went looking for work as a carpenter, only to be told by an apprenticeship company that he wasn't smart enough, although he could be a painter. So, he picked up the brush for four years, but one day he woke up and thought, 'I'm sick of this, I'm going to be a builder.' He contacted a company and asked for an apprenticeship. No go. But he was told to keep in touch. He rang the company every day for about three months until the manager yielded after Matt said to him: 'Put me on as a labourer and I'll prove I can be an apprentice.' They did, and Matt did too. That alone is a good, solid story. But there is more to it. Domestic problems, a family torn; a story all too common. Then, the bull riding: trophies, two broken tail bones, a busted arm with a plate and six screws, and a leg that was very nearly amputated.

Matt is thirty-two, married and a father of two young girls. He said to me in the depot shed:

'We own a house, I've got my nice truck, my partner – she is a huge part of what we've created; she's got a nice car. We've got great kids. We've worked hard for a good life, and I'm really proud of it and I'm – you know, some people – even my missus says: "You don't have to tell everyone all the time." I say: "Well, I'm proud of it, I'm proud of what I've achieved throughout my life."'

That pride has infected others. The grey cabin is proof. The boys helped Matt build and paint it.

'I reckon it's a pretty good job,' said one boy.

The screeches of a circular saw announce the construction of two more cabins. One for Jannelle, the operations manager, and the other for social worker, Haley. As for the first? It's where Bernie and I are sitting on black office chairs either side of a desk upon which there are a few pieces of paper and a laptop. The office includes a hat-stand, a small fridge and some shelves topped with photos, trophies, awards and ribbons. There are also two artworks by Matt Pilkington, the youth worker/artist in residence. The first is of a stockman on a horse working sheep with a collie; the second shows another black-and-white dog scrambling over the top of a high jump wall while a boy wearing a red shirt watches from the ground.

'Right,' says Bernie, looking at my shirt rather than me. 'We didn't get our wardrobes sorted out today, did we?'

We are both wearing blue-and-white checks.

Soon we are back into another familiar pattern: Bernie talking, and me steering the conversation when necessary. We move on from the funding dramas of 2013 to an additional disappointment during the same period: the struggle and eventual folding of a BackTrack venture on a property at Somerton between Tamworth and Gunnedah. It involved TAFE, the Department of Education, the Tamworth Local Aboriginal Land Council and four local high schools, who, following the same model as in Armidale, provided access to hands-on programs for troubled students. There were many reasons the operation 'died a bit of a death': funding issues, the hardship of aligning all the different parties, and Bernie's distinct way of looking after kids first before turning to the formalities of paperwork and details. It was also a challenge for Bernie to spread himself between overseeing Armidale and Somerton, and according to some people familiar with the project, there was tension over what a white fella would know about looking after Indigenous kids. Bernie's response to this question has always been the same: 'Well, we're having a crack.' Importantly, he has also stressed throughout the history of BackTrack that the program is not solely for Indigenous kids; it works with kids who are 'having a hard time', but it 'just seems to suit many Indigenous kids'.

Despite the disappointments of the time, there was a notable development: the refurbishment of the two-day-a-week classroom. Sizeable contributions – and further in-kind donations – from the Rotary Club of Armidale, Regional Australia Bank, and the NSW State government led to a new-look area in the shed where classes took place. It was opened in September 2014 by state education minister Adrian Piccoli.

'We must have been doing something right for a minister to turn up,' jokes Bernie. 'It was a big moment, and a long journey to get there. Before that, I remember this distinct moment when I knew we needed a teacher. The boys liked playing "I Spy" on long road trips – I can't stomach the game coz it just goes around and around and around, but the boys loved it – and I didn't get involved in any of the games unless they were turning to shit. On this one trip, there was this one fella, Flip – and reading and writing weren't his strengths – and he had something beginning with "E". And this game had been going for a long time, and Flip had been giving clues: "It's in the car. It's near this, near that." Finally I thought it was going to go to scrap so I said: "Right, stop! Tell us what it is, and we'll move on." Coz they had all these rules that no-one could give up. And Flip, he'd been getting really frustrated coz no-one could get it, said: "You dumb fucks, it's the thing you put your foot on to make the car go faster." Oh dear! I looked at Flip and said, "Ah, that's *Accelerator*, not *Eccelerator*.' And that was the defining moment where I knew we had to get a teacher. We couldn't even play "I Spy".

'But that leads to the never-ending question: how do you best teach kids that the "system" says are unteachable? I remember seeing something with Rocket, our welding teacher in the early days. Go back a long way before that and I remember trying to do Pythagoras' theorem at school. It was such a foreign, weird concept; why would you teach anybody that stuff? Then I walked into a lesson and saw Rocket kneeling on the ground with chalk. And here were these five or six kids so focused on what he was doing, truly they were in the zone. And I was going: "What is he up to?" He was showing them how to get a gate square, and he was doing Pythagoras' theorem. He had it all written down on the floor. And he had the calculator out, saying to the boys: "Here, you have a go." Of course, the boys would have done the theorem at school too, but if you were considered in the "dumb" group, you'd probably be going: "I don't get this shit." But Rocket? He was tapping into the boys in a way they would understand: "Let's get this gate square, boys." Rocket got it. He got what we were doing.

'Then, when all this new classroom stuff starts happening, we get this new teacher. Sarah Mills. Crikey, she could hold her own with the boys. Just extraordinary to watch. What's education all about? Look at Sarah. Took us ahead, *all of us*, in leaps and bounds.'

Appropriately, I interviewed Sarah in the classroom at the depot. We sat at an island of three wood-laminate tables around which the kids generally, although not always, sit during lessons. Sarah had initially become involved with BackTrack when a friend suggested she could help Bernie behind the scenes. At the time she was battling through a horrendous divorce and custody dispute, and she'd resigned from an eleven-year teaching post at a school in the district. Sarah accepted her friend's suggestion and was soon writing letters with suitable 'education speak' that BackTrack sent to schools. In short, she was a knowledgeable communications link who could 'smooth out processes'. Later, after she'd decided to return to her home city, Sydney, she received a phone call from Bernie. Recalling that moment, Sarah laughed.

'He said to me, in typical Bernie style: "Listen, word on the street is you're a pretty gun teacher. You want to come and work for us?" I told him: "Oh geez, I don't know, Bern. Can I have some time to think about it?" "Yeah, but you need to be here by Term

Four." And that phone call was at the end of Term Three! Next thing you know, I'm in this classroom.

'What I've always liked about Bernie is that he has given me the freedom to do what I know works. I always say I don't take myself seriously, but I take my profession seriously. What worked in this classroom – and you have to remember I'm a female who often had fifteen stinky teenage boys – what worked in this classroom was very simple. The first thing some of them would say to me was: "I fucking hate teachers, fucking hate females, and I don't want to be here." And I'd say: "Well, you've lucked out, mate, because one, I'm a teacher, and two, I'm a female, but I can tell you what, I am going to give you love in this classroom. Love and friendship." And by the end of the day, I'd have them wrapped round my little finger, just through kindness and friendship. I never forced them to have a go, but it was absolutely rewarding if they did have a go. I had kids who would never read out loud, ever, and then we had a mini punch-up one day over who was going to read next. And we had an argument in a lunch room over synonyms. Some of the boys were: "That's not a fuckin' homophone, you dickhead." That day I said to Bernie: "I bet you never thought they'd be fighting over grammar."

'When we were reading, I'd always have a focus book. I'd choose stories and subjects that I knew the boys – and girls – would get right into. This one time I chose a local author, John Heffernan. He's from Walcha, a fantastic writer who writes a lot about dogs and the country, so the themes totally fitted in with BackTrack. So, we were reading this book in class. Generally, I'd read it out to them; often they hadn't been read to, or even sung to as little kids, so this was something quite special. But I'd have the text in front of them so they could access it if they wanted to, or if someone put their hand up and asked to read, that was great. Anyway, this day, I finished a chapter and said: "Righto, we've got to go to lunch now." But the kids were: "No, we want to find out what happens."

'There was this one guy who was: "Oh, fuck you, Sarah." He went off, rode to the town library, borrowed the book, read it, and came back and told everyone what had happened. I asked him: "That your first time to the library?"

'"Yeah."

'"So, who wins there, mate?"

'It was wonderful.

'Another time, we had a massive fake gambling racket going on with Monopoly money in our maths sessions. I used to do things like: "If we all put fifty dollars in and there are twelve of us, and there are two winners, how much does each winner get?" Maths fundamentals. One day Bernie came running in because he'd heard all this cheering and thought there was a big blue happening. And all he saw was a boy standing on the table, going: "Woo-hoo!" because he'd won the three hundred dollar jackpot.'

Education is full of discussions about techniques, theories and practices. But, in a constantly evolving field, the word at the hub doesn't change: pedagogy, or in basic terms, how students are taught. When interviewing Sarah, I was gathered up and swept along on a wave of extraordinary enthusiasm; listening to her was a lesson in itself.

'Teachers can get principals who want to walk past and see heads down, everyone quiet and traditional learning happening,' she told me. 'I always said to Bernie – and he'd let me do it – I had the upside-down classroom. Someone could walk in and see a kid hanging upside down here, there'd be one on a cushion over there, another might be lying down somewhere. We used to have a lounge, but we had to get rid of it because everyone was slouchy! But you could ask any single one of them, "What are we doing?" and they'd say: "Oh, we're working on this." They weren't disengaged, they were just engaged in another way.

'What they did – there were just so many moments. We were studying *Percy Jackson and the Lightning Thief*, a fantasy novel with a Greek mythology theme, and I asked the kids to make up their own gods and philosophies. One of our gorgeous boys came up with *Rum and Coke-us*, the god of camping, and I think the symbol was a can, a fire and a fishing rod; and there was another boy who came up with *Mischievous*, the god who could put mischievous thoughts into anyone else's mind, and get people to do things without the god getting the blame for it.

'It was a very special time. One of my nicest memories, a sad memory, but – my marriage problems – there were times when things just got to me. I came into the classroom one day and I was crying, and the boys were: "Shit, are you okay, Sarah? What's happened? Do you want to go home?" I told them I'd rather stay – all airs and graces had gone – and they were saying: "It's all right, it's all right." Which made me cry even more because they were being so nice to me. Next minute, one of the boys just goes: "Right, so-and-so go over there and make Sarah a cup of tea. Everyone else, sit down. What literacy game are we playing?" They ran the whole show by themselves. It was amazing. I was: "It's all right, I'm okay." But no, they did it all themselves. "You just look after yourself, Sarah."

'It was all built on relationships. God help any new boy who came in and disrespected me; they'd get eaten alive by the others: "Don't you talk to Sarah like that, she cares about you, whether you know it or not." Just beautiful relationships. And they made me feel safe again, which might sound really silly because I was with some of the toughest boys. I'd have kids in the class coming down off ice, but I never felt unsafe in this classroom. Ever. It actually taught me a lot about how to talk to my own kids: "Yeah okay, we know there's a problem, what's the solution?" And that's an ethic and a value that Bernie taught me.'

Bernie, or more precisely his actions, influenced Sarah in another way as well. As the interview continued, she told me that when she returned to Armidale to take up the teaching position, Bernie gave her one of the old collie ladies, Lou (Girl's sister), to look after. 'I still can't believe that she likes *Antiques Roadshow* and red wine, the same as me. Who would have thought?'

Sarah became known to various school kids around Armidale as 'the dog lady'. The nickname, however, had nothing to do with cosy nights in front of the television. In 2014, BackTrack introduced two new programs: Running Strong, which formally recognised the inclusion of girls; and School Outreach, which involved a youth worker taking dogs into primary and secondary schools to spend time with disengaged students. The latter quickly became popular, and it was this program that would put Sarah and the brown-and-white woolly Gibson, a perpetual classroom favourite, at the centre of one of BackTrack's most poignant moments. I'd heard the story from several people. It was about a boy having a meltdown: naked, urinating, smashing pots, hurling chairs in a fenced section of a school. Had the years perhaps encouraged embellishment? It was best to ask Sarah.

'I'd just arrived, and usually I'd get to a school about half an hour early, quieten the dogs down and get myself ready. But this day, I got there to hear the carry-on and see the boy. He was in a troubled way, and the police were about to be called. I thought: "Do I get involved or not?" I didn't want to step on anyone's toes. But I asked if I could have a minute. All the other kids were in lockdown. It was a massive situation. As soon as I was given approval, I knew I needed Gibson. "Okay, Gibbo, come here." I let him off the lead and he ran down to the fenced area where the boy was, and the boy started saying: "Gibson's off the lead, Gibson's off the lead." And I said to him: "Oh, no, what am I going to do?" Straightaway his pattern of thought was changed; I wasn't someone talking about him or his behaviour. And the boy goes: "I'll get him."

'"Well, you put your pants on, mate, put your shirt on and then I'll give you a lead, and can you come and help me?"

'"Okay, I'll come and help."

'Then I walked to the teachers and told them, so the boy could hear too: "He's going to come and help me find Gibson. Gibson's off the lead and I can't get him back and I really need his help." And they said: "Righto."

'So, the boy put his clothes on, walked out, and put Gibson on a lead. I said: "Good boy, do you want to come for a walk, darling?"

'"Yeah.'

'We went and sat on a chair and I asked him what had happened. Basically, he didn't want to do an activity that the other kids were doing. It was amazing to see. I couldn't have calmed the boy down. It was Gibson, and everyone loves Gibson. Here was this boy going: "Gibson, Gibson, come here."'

Sarah spent more than three years as the BackTrack teacher before she knew she needed a break. She hadn't yet burnt out, but she was tired and felt it was time for a change. She now runs the Intensive English Centre at the Armidale Secondary College, a new school that is the result of a merger between Armidale and Duval high schools. Carolyn Lasker is the principal. Sarah primarily works with refugees, 'starting from scratch with their education in English'. Again, she is building relationships with children from highly traumatised backgrounds.

Our interview was over too soon. I wish it could have lasted longer. One of my final questions to her was: 'What is education?'

At first, she wasn't sure what to say. I prompted her with one line of thought: the Latin word *'educere'* means to 'draw out', and thus education 'draws out' of students, a somewhat appropriate description of what can happen in the BackTrack classroom. Sarah nodded thoughtfully, then said: 'Education is a gift. If you get the right person to give it to you it can last a lifetime.'

—

In 2014 Bernie was presented with a gift that certainly enhanced his educational journey. He was awarded a Vincent Fairfax Family Foundation sponsored Churchill Fellowship. Organised by the Winston Churchill Memorial Trust of Australia, the fellowship enabled successful applicants to travel overseas to study their chosen fields of interest and gain knowledge of practices and philosophies that could be beneficial to Australian communities. When it was first suggested Bernie apply for one, his response was: 'What's this all about?' Carolyn Lasker and Myf Maple helped him write a proposal, and local magistrate Karen Stafford provided a reference. After a few rounds of intense pitching and interviews in front of judging panels that had a mix of social and professional backgrounds, he received the good news. Officially, he would go abroad to 'study alternative organisational and funding models for programs supporting youth at risk'.

Sitting back in his office chair, just metres from where a framed certificate of the fellowship hangs on a wall, Bernie states rather than asks: 'I've had some luck, haven't I? I thought the Churchill Fellowship was for academics and big smart people, so I had to get over that hurdle. But Carolyn and Myf walked me through it. As it turned out it came just at the right time. I knew I had to learn more about funding, and how to make the business side of things work.

'But geez, there was a little bit of fear when I left coz I hadn't travelled overseas since my trip to India. Thirty years ago, when I was just a kid. Wow. Six weeks, I was away for. It's hard to wrap everything into my head right now, but yeah, some memories there. I went to Amarillo, Texas, first. Big boots, big monster vehicles racing down the main street, this whole let's-get-cowboyed-up type of business. And you know what feed lots smell like? That acidic, pissy smell. Big feed lots out of town. Huge ones. Texas style. I didn't know at first what the smell was until I asked someone, and he said: "That's the smell of money."

'That someone was Dan Adams, the CEO of Cal Farley's. Cal was this bloke who set up a ranch for boys during the Depression, and it's been going ever since. It supports at-risk kids. Young ones, teenagers, just kids, boys and girls, that need help for all the reasons you could imagine. Just while I think of it, I saw my first squirrel there. I was over the moon with excitement about that. And I bumped into someone with a blue heeler dog; they were calling it something else and I told 'em: "No, mate, that's a blue heeler!" On my first evening there I went for a walk on this dry riverbed, I came across these fresh tracks – fresh as – and the hackles started coming up on me neck coz I knew whatever this thing was must have been really close. I had no idea what animals lived anywhere, except in Australia, but I was looking at this track thinking: "That's a cat track, a big one!" It was bigger than my hand. And that got me a bit worried, so I hiked back and told everyone about my great discovery, and they were: "It's a cougar, you idiot! What are you doing walking down there by yourself?"

'Anyway, back to big Dan. He took me under his wing. I looked at the residential and farm programs and the funding models; I even met the two ladies whose job it was to open the donation cheques. I really learnt a lot about raising money. In a perfect world you wouldn't have to bother with that stuff, but this is reality; dollars keep the kids afloat. That part of the trip reinforced the need not to rely on any single funding source. Of course, you maintain good relationships with government, but you also have to have great community engagement and get that positive feeling among a wide cross-section. It's a community "buy-in" that's so important. I'd like to think BackTrack is doing that pretty well.

'Dan also rang me up one morning and said: "Do you want to go for a drive?" "Yeah, no worries." But I didn't realise it was going to be a six hundred–kilometre round trip in one day. He took me down near the border with Mexico. We visited a refuge for women fleeing domestic violence [Genie Farley Harriman Center for Women and Children]. At various times Dan asked his staff to go out into the community and work out what the needs were. And that's how they set up this refuge. A big-time valuable lesson for me there: look for gaps in the system. If someone is already doing it, and there's no need, don't do it. Where's the gap? Find it and work out how you can fill it. That's still bang in the middle of my thinking.

'After that, I went to a number of places in Canada where I looked at a lot of programs for the First Nations people who were facing similar issues to Australia's Indigenous communities: education, health, job training, suicide prevention, pathways for kids coming out of custody. One of the big things that struck me was a lecture at the Winnipeg University with Kevin Lamoureux, a First Nations man and academic. He spoke about the Circle of Courage, a traditional First Nations healing model that we were already using at BackTrack. It's all about belonging, mastery of yourself, generosity, and the sort of independence that allows you to make your own decisions, set your own goals, and own your successes and failures. Very human, holistic.

'I visited a lot of places. Even Médecins Sans Frontières [MSF – Doctors without Borders] in New York, where Rosemary Mort's daughter, Kate, was working. There was just so much to take in. And then over to Italy, and San Patrignano [La Comunità di San Patrignano]. It's a privately funded place that helps recovering drug addicts. An extraordinary set-up. About thirteen hundred or so residents with peer-to-peer mentoring rather than professional counselling. It's its own little thriving community. Farm, bakery, furniture making, leatherwork factory, blacksmith ... all these little industries.

'We had this kid who took us round for the whole day. Stinking hot, it was. He was from Canada. Had just about lost his life and had tried to get into a whole lot of rehab places before getting into this place. I vividly remember asking him: "How long can you stay here?" He stopped, had a think for a minute then turned around and said: "This place will never leave you while you've got nowhere else to go." What a powerful moment. They had men, I dunno, in their sixties, who'd built cabins there and were helping out doing bits and pieces. In some ways you could say it was a bizarre set-up, but it was successful. "This place will never leave you while you've got nowhere else to go." That's pretty wonderful human goodwill. And it told me we were doing the right thing back home. You can't get kicked out of BackTrack. Help a kid for as long as the need is there.

'That place, geez … they were running their own vineyard and making wine. Prestige wine. With recovering drug and alcohol guys! Their metal working shed is like walking into the BackTrack shed, only their shed is on steroids. With a big eagle sculpture made out of scraps just like we've got a crocodile at the front of our shed. If you come in with a trade in welding, guess what? You're working in the wallpaper factory. Nothing to do with welding. They shift things up. Everywhere I went I was thinking: "How clever are these guys?" Seriously so. Because they've got the winery, of course they've got barrels – always looking for something to do with them – so, they get the top designers in Europe to design a piece of furniture out of a wine barrel. Then they make these pieces in the factory. Just one-off pieces. And they sell them at auction and get extraordinary prices for them. Some of the ladies we met were putting together designer leather handbags, and in another section, there were these graphic designers working on signs for various companies. Everywhere things were happening. Self-generated work for thirteen hundred people. So many of them feeling that sense of community, that sense of belonging. And not one psychologist. I saw a photo there that summed everything up. It showed some graffiti written in Italian from years ago. Translated it was: "We're already doing what's possible. We're trying to do the impossible. We're setting up for a miracle."

'Everywhere I went on the whole trip I kept collecting information and knowledge. It was definitely a key period for me in the development of BackTrack. Coz, by that time, I'd run out of steam. I needed something to get me back going, and that trip flipped me upside-down. I thought I'd been thinking big and left field, and then I met all these people doing remarkable things. Highly committed people with smashing track records.'

Meanwhile, when Bernie was overseas, something happened back home. In isolation it was just one of those things that occurs in life, but when you ask the man it happened to, there is no ignoring its significance. Scott, the once-boy now-father who had been under Bernie's and Jayne's care at Tarago, was driving through the Armidale area when he pulled over by the side of the road to have a cigarette.

'Then me car died,' said Scott. 'Flat battery, no jumper leads. It would've been nine o'clock at night. What am I gonna do? I got onto Facebook and contacted Bernie.

'"Are you in Armidale?"

'"No, I'm in Canada."

'But he ended up ringing a few blokes from BackTrack and they drove out and got me going again. One was a big wood-chopping fella, a big tall fella with a beard [Matt Pilkington], and a younger fella. Great blokes. I let Bernie know, and he said: "Just do a day's work for me down the track." I still owe him that day. I'd love to go up there and pay him back.'

When Bernie returned to Australia, with his own batteries re-charged, he 'clipped all the pieces of knowledge together' from his trip and started working them into BackTrack. He paid special attention to funding and strengthening ties in the Armidale community. In his executive report to the Winston Churchill

Memorial Trust he noted: 'Long-term survival and growth has to involve direct marketing, investments, and adapting to local opportunities in order to capitalise on the unique characteristics of any one particular community, environment or context.' He also quoted Churchill: 'What is the use of living, if it be not to strive for noble causes and to make this muddled world a better place for those who will live in it after we are gone?' In Bernie-speak, this simply meant: 'I got back from the trip and knew there was a lot of good stuff we could do.'

20

He sits on a bed, a shaft of sunlight warming his grey-stubbled face. A few metres away, a cabinet mirror reflects his profile. He has travelled many, many miles in his life. A truck driver, a tourist, and a reformed alcoholic who hasn't touched a drop in thirty-eight years.

'My wife says I talk too long, and I use too many big words,' he says.

Sometimes he does.

'The only thing that gives me the strength to talk like this is the reciprocation and understanding of the fact that we are all connected in a certain way and, if we reciprocate on that, then I talk.'

He talked too, one day in court. But there were no big words at all. Just lots of discussion about discharging the defendant into the care of a responsible person.

'The magistrate said to me: "Will you report him [the defendant] if he steps sideways? One step sideways and you cop it. No second chances." I knew what I was taking on and I stood up and said: "My f-ing oath I will. Because if we don't stop this now, we never will. You have to stop this now. If that is what it takes, that is what it takes." So, I reached down into the system and got him. The family had broken down, which a lot of them do. The first thing you have got to stop is the blame game, and instead look at where we are at.

'I said to him: "All right, mate, don't get too over-confident. We have to stick to the plan. One wrong step and you are going to a place where you already have experience [juvenile detention] that you do not want to go back to. Also, I have to stand beside you, so from now on, you have to look after that. Because, if you step sideways, I am in a position now where I will go down with you. You will lose me, and you will lose yourself." And he has stayed, to this day, exactly on that plan. And he knows that he is looking after me, who is looking after him.'

So many miles.

A grandfather in charge of his teenage grandson. A teenage grandson who 'is very mindful of me. If I am laying there and I cough or even if I stop breathing or just sometimes, when I am eating bread and I can't ... He will sense that straightaway and he will say: "Are you right, Pop?" But he does have problems. Like, sometimes his moods and emotions go up and down. He's a teenage kid. He will work at BackTrack, but then I can't get him to mow the lawn at home. He's typical.'

Since mixing BackTrack with his formal education the boy has received one school report: 'It was absolutely impeccable,' says Pop. 'His father said, "It's the best report I have ever seen, and I wish I could have had one half like it myself."'

Early steps on a long, long road. One on which well-travelled Pop has already promised to his grandson: 'I will go to the end of the earth for you.'

In 2015, BackTrack began its residential program. Half a dozen boys staying full-time with Bernie at Warrah, the house surrounded by enough land for anyone to walk out the back door and find some space to themselves. Sitting in shade under the eucalypts. Skimming stones at the dam. Taking the dogs for a walk. Leaning against a fence post.

Space.

Having his first cigarette during today's interview, Bernie stands in the doorway of his office. Half-in, half-out.

'We didn't have any specific funding for Warrah,' he says. 'But once those kids were in there, who was going to kick them out? Just before that there was a steady trickle of break-ins at the depot. You know that little hidey hole up above the classroom? [An annexe in the shed.] Kids from within the program were sleeping there. They'd spend the day at BackTrack then come back at night. At some stage or other they must've got a key because we could tell they'd been in the smoko room. But they weren't doing anything other than eating, sleeping and then rackin' off at seven o'clock in the morning, and coming back an hour-and-a-half later to start another day at BackTrack. Of course we knew what was happening, but these kids didn't have a good alternative. They were safe there and it was better there than sleeping in a rough place somewhere. I suppose we had about a year of that.

'Then we got Warrah happening. I'd stayed there after Jayne, Maeve and James had gone. It was a pretty rough period because I was living with the boys full-time as well as working full-time. Sometimes you've just gotta do what you gotta do. Try it for yourself. Fuckin' difficult. Two to a room. Testosterone. Different personalities. All the rest of it.

'And that was our starting point. Build on that. Start developing the simple stuff from there: clean your room, pick up your shoes, don't touch someone else's property. The need was immense, and the inexperience these kids had ... There was one boy – I told him to put his clothes in front of the washing machine, and I'd show him how to use it. So, he went and put his clothes in front of the dishwasher. I said to him: "No, have another go. This is the kitchen. You need to find the machine in the laundry." So, he had another go, and he eventually got there. I showed him what he had to do. "You put your clothes in, throw in a scoop of that powder, turn this knob to high and push the start button." I came back a little later and the laundry was a bubble bath. I stopped the machine, opened it up, and the kid had put the whole box of powder in. And here's the thing: he put the whole box in – my favourite part – plastic shopping bag to boot.

'There were always issues. A new kid comes in and the older ones say to me: "You don't care about us anymore." Mind games. Lots of them. High-energy stuff, and you stretch that elastic band and see how far it keeps going. Then it snaps, you tie a knot in it, and go again.'

By this time, Bernie was in a developing relationship with Francesca; she was university-educated, a musician, a horse and bush girl and an Italian–Australian who had lived in Armidale 'on and off' over the years, between spending time in Italy where family roots stretched back generations. After her close friend Gel Cutmore, Bernie's Street Beat colleague, first suggested she meet Bernie, she thought against a clichéd get-together in a cafe. After all, she didn't even drink tea or coffee. Instead, she offered what she thought would be a more comfortable date.

'Of course, I vaguely knew of him because of all he was doing in town, but the first time I really met him was when he came to my front gate, got out of his ute, took a stock saddle out of the back, and we went for a ride,' Francesca told me as she sat on the same verandah from which Bernie had talked away the hours. 'I guess the first impressions matched the sense I'd been given by Gel. For me it was all about the energy of the person. And I found this touch of humour, and a very thoughtful way of being in the world wrapped in this fabulous sweary, drinky, smoky, rough, tough tall iconic Aussie silhouette. A very authentic human being who had his flaws.'

Francesca, an accomplished dressage rider, had spent most of her professional life working in strategic planning and policy in various sectors of conservation and natural-resource management. But it was one of her other interests that was, quite literally, instrumental in the formative days of Warrah's residential program. As a child she'd 'latched on early' to music, and she can play the double bass, some wind instruments, and can 'scratch around on the guitar a bit'. It was the latter that contributed to a powerful moment during the trial period at Warrah.

'I remember one beautiful night after dinner,' said Francesca. 'We got on to talking about the Paul Kelly [and Kev Carmody] song "From Little Things Big Things Grow". I said to someone, "Google the lyrics." And they said, "What the fuck are lyrics?"

'"It's the words, man. Let's find out the words."

'So, we found the words and I said, "Righto, so-and-so, read them out."

'"I can't read those."

'"You'll be okay. Have a crack."

'So, suddenly, this night became a bit of a literacy exercise as well. And then we asked what the song was about. And this is where Gel helped out. She said: "Do you know any of this shit? This is important. Especially for you blackfellas." So, we talked about who Vincent Lingiari was, and his role in land rights and reconciliation, and what Gough Whitlam had to do with it all. That was a kind of acknowledgement and a bit of a history lesson. After that it was: "Okay, what are the chords, boys?" Because we had a couple of guitars in the house. So, the boys start learning a few chords, and it's now a music lesson. It was all very organic; we could go where we needed it to go, and this amazing moment happened, and we played and sang the song. To me, it was a beautiful example of the holistic, untimed flexibility of BackTrack, and what, when given the opportunity, the boys could do. And it was all born out of someone being half curious about a song at nine o'clock at night. It was also another little lesson for me. If I wanted to go hang out with Bernie, and if he was at Warrah with these boys, I had to be there too. And that's how I became involved.'

Others did too. Familiar faces. After his retirement from the police force, Matt Lynch, along with his wife, Lynda, helped in whatever ways they could. Some afternoons, the Lynches would pick up a few Warrah boys from the depot and take them grocery shopping. This, at times, was revealing. 'A few of the boys didn't know how to use the self-service scanners,' recalled Matt. Then, they'd go to Warrah and under the direction of the Lynches, or other volunteers, the boys would prepare and cook meals. Initially, most could do little more than put a sausage or two in the microwave, but as time passed, they had international theme nights: Italian, Mexican, Chinese, Indian. However, no matter how unique any cuisine may have seemed, by the time the boys sat down together at the dinner table, they left behind a familiar scene in the kitchen: an area that looked like a 'dog's breakfast'. So, finally it was agreed that anyone who prepared and cooked didn't have to clean. 'That backfired a bit,' said Matt. 'You should have seen everyone scrambling at the start for the knives and other bits and pieces. There was standing room only in the kitchen; we couldn't all fit.'

Those nights brought everyone together, and in the Circle Work that inevitably happened, differences between people could become the bridges that brought them together.

'When we first started,' Matt told me, 'we worked on developing a good rapport because this whole residential idea was new to everyone and we all had to feel comfortable with it. One night, Bernie said to me: "Tell the boys what you did for a job, Matt."

'"I was in the cops for twenty-eight years."

'Their eyes lit up and you could see them thinking, "Oh shit!" By then, we'd already broken the ice, but moments like those showed the kids I wasn't an enemy, and the cops were real people. At subsequent cooking nights, some of the kids would pull me aside and say, "Can I get a bit of advice?"'

The goodwill of the Lynches went far beyond Warrah. When one boy with an infamous reputation was about to enter the BackTrack program Bernie said to Matt: 'I've got this kid, and he's a bit squeaky. I just want to get him settled down into a family situation while he's trying to fit in, before we put him at Warrah.' The Lynches accepted despite the challenges they were facing in their own lives.

'We were in the middle of our young daughter going through chemotherapy, and we'd had nearly a year down in Sydney at Ronald McDonald House but we were back home. Lynda just wanted to keep giving back, doing stuff for the community. So, we took this boy in. He was full of chat and Lynda said to him: "Listen there are a few rules here, mate. There's no smoking because our daughter is still doing chemo. And there'll be no swearing and carrying on. We'll do some fun stuff, but you have to toe the line and be part of our family." And he was great. Funny to have around. We took him to Lynda's mum's farm, we took him out with our horses, and we went swimming in dams. He'd have a go at everything. That went on for a few weekends, and at one point Lynda asked him: "What's the best part of coming here?" And he said, "I can be a kid again." He'd been in survival mode that long, trying to get a pecking order among the people he hung around with, that he hadn't been a child. Hearing him say that was one of the best things I've ever heard.

'I remember Lynda took him clothes shopping. And she said, "What do you want?"

'"What do you mean?"

'"Well, you can get whatever you want."

'"No-one has ever said that to me before."

'They went around and got some hats and shirts and shoes, and he was loving it. When he came back home, he said to Lynda: "I just want to leave all the new clothes here coz I don't want them to get wrecked." They were such a treasure to him.

'We did the same with another boy. A good little kid. He'd had a pretty savage upbringing. His mum was on ice and he wished she'd go to jail. We wanted to take him to the farm, but he chucked a wobbly and refused to go. Eventually he got in the car, had a great time at the farm, and when he got back to Armidale, he asked Bernie: "When can I go with the Lynches again?" Moments like that make you realise just how many kids need them. It feels good to be able to help.'

Not at all surprisingly, Paul and Annette Roots were others Bernie turned to when home environments were desperately needed. On one occasion, the drovers-turned-graziers were returning from a trip to Adelong when they popped into the BackTrack depot to say hello to Bernie, and found him 'pulling his hair out'. He was trying to find accommodation for a boy who was coming to the end of an allotted period in a refuge. His father was in jail, and he had nowhere to go.

'So, we picked up the boy,' said Annette. 'We didn't know him, but it was no different from what we did for Bernie when he was young. We had to go through a lot of red tape, and all we wanted to do was give him somewhere to stay. But we got him, and he stayed with us for four or five months. It was just what happens. If Bernie needs us, we are there. Actually, I only got a message from that boy the other day. He has grown up now. Working and getting on with things.'

Still standing half-in, half-out of his office, Bernie takes a moment to survey part of the depot. The cabins that Matt Pett and the boys are building. The woodwork shed that's behind the welding shed. There's fencing wire, some old road signs and shiny new welded dog cages. A few four-wheel drives and dual-cabs. A squashed can of energy drink under a tyre. Cigarette butts in the dust.

'It's not rocket science, is it?' says Bernie. 'Whether it's at Warrah or through the goodwill of the Lynches and Rootses and everyone who opens their doors. Provide safety, shelter, love, belonging and learning. All those words. Maslow's Hierarchy. It's interesting, though. A lot of people who don't know much about these kids box 'em up all the same way. Not school smart, troublemakers. And here's the interesting bit: so many people put the blame on broken homes. All the time. Yeah, we've got some real busted ones with parents and family, but not always. Sometimes it just happens. Happens in ways that take everyone by surprise. Shocks 'em. Mum and Dad don't know what to do. It just happens.'

—

It *just happened* in the suburbs a long way from Armidale. After speaking over the phone with Jenny, the mother of one BackTrack boy, I arranged to go and meet her and her husband, Nick, at their middle-class home. Both are white-collar professionals. After I arrived, Jenny took me past a recently plastered hole in a living-room wall.

'That's an example of one of my son's outbursts,' she said, with a sad, soft laugh. 'We had to patch it up after he put a fist through it.'

We sat down on opposite couches.

'There were times where I felt so isolated as a mum,' said Jenny. 'If someone else is in that space and can pick up a page of this book you're writing and they read it and go: "I'm not the only person that's been through this," then, to me it's worth sharing our story.' Nick agreed: 'I felt extremely isolated as well. Like, I'm trying to be a good father and just do my best.'

They then painstakingly and at times painfully went through an unimaginable timeline. They said Lachlan's speech hadn't developed as quickly as most other children. When he was about four he went to a speech pathologist, the starting point for 'years and years of work'. He was also a 'very sensitive child'. As a young boy he once saw a magpie attack a sparrow. He cradled the sparrow in his hands until it died, and then laid it on the ground because he thought other sparrows would want to come and say their goodbyes. The family also had a rainbow lorikeet they had hand-raised; one day it flew away, but several weeks later it returned, lice-riddled and very sick. It soon passed away, and Lachlan was so upset that he wrote letters to the dead pet. Amid this, he suffered bouts of extreme fears: of bees in the backyard, and of going to the beach and dipping his toes in the ocean. He received his first psychological help when he was six and was diagnosed with General Anxiety Disorder. At that time he was in Year One, and such was his fear of separation from Jenny that he screamed and had to be 'peeled off' by Nick. As a coping mechanism Jenny taught him to shoot the 'worry monsters' off his shoulder, with a cocked finger: 'Sounds like they're there, honey. Shoot them off. Pffww, pffww, pffww ...'

Regardless of his own challenges, he was thoughtful of others, and as the eldest brother in a sizeable family he was 'very protective' of his siblings. 'One of the most loving, attentive big brothers I've ever seen,' said Jenny. He was also very athletic, a regular ribbon winner at various sports carnivals. However, relative to a younger sibling, he was a little behind in his academic learning, and went through a stage of labelling himself as 'dumb'. He did, though, love drawing, and was good at it. Throughout this, his emotional battles continued, and by the time he was in late primary school, his parents noticed he was losing motivation 'to get up, go for a ride, go out and play'. He had a lot of friends and acquaintances, but noticeably, no 'rock solid mateships'. Then, remembered Jenny, came the day 'he sat down on the couch and said, "I just don't know if I want to be alive."'

Although they were initially reluctant to see their son on medication, Jenny and Nick heeded a psychiatrist's advice. A period of trial-and-error followed. Different drugs, different doses, different reactions. Eventually they found a 'really good one' only for it to be taken off the market, and another medication had to be used.

'It really stuffed him up,' said Jenny. 'One day we'd just gotten back from holidays – he was about twelve or thirteen – and I was busy unpacking, and Lachlan goes: "Mum, I've got to talk to you."

'"Okay, but just not right now."

'"Mum, I feel really shit."

'"I know you do. You've been feeling that way for a while."

'"No Mum, I got Dad's air rifle last night and I was going to pull the trigger."

'Obviously, he had my attention, and I asked him what stopped him from doing it. He said he couldn't because he kept thinking about the baby we'd just had. "Thank God for that," I said.

'But then we went on suicide watch. We had to lock away all the alcohol, all the meds, every single knife in the house because at the same time he was going through this, he had a fixation with knives and weapons and fire. I had to unpadlock a knife every time I wanted to chop a potato."'

Jenny and Nick took Lachlan to a new psychiatrist and after 'six to twelve months' a correct medication plan reduced the suicidal thoughts and behaviour. The diagnosis remained as anxiety and severe depression. And the worries continued. When he was in Year Seven, Lachlan refused to go to school, and the toll on his parents and the stress on their marriage was showing.

'He took up so much of our energy, so many resources,' said Nick. 'Everything. Money, time, energy. It just sucks you up. As parents, as human beings, we just … everything we had went into that. And yet we had other kids who needed our attention. There was this constant battle, and we were completely exhausted. One day I got up and just couldn't do anything. Just couldn't go to work. I'd just had it. Absolutely had it. I know there were no guns or bombs going off, but there might as well have been a form of that inside our home, just with the fighting. If Lachlan was having a moment – for example, if he wasn't going to school – then everything had to stop. How many times were we late for work? It was extreme emotional distress.'

In desperation, they went to a new psychologist, who gave them a book.

'We read it,' said Nick. 'And we both went, "Holy shit, this is ..."'

'"This is what we've been dealing with,"' continued Jenny.

The book was about autism.

The challenges continued. A suspension from school. Off to a new school. The relief of not wearing a tie because a tie made Lachlan feel 'strangled'. There was another bout of refusing to go to school; it became so much of an issue that Jenny and Nick rang the police and a liaison officer spoke to Lachlan.

'He hated us for that,' said Nick.

'Oh, he did,' agreed Jenny.

Lachlan's self-esteem declined, and he began to self-sabotage positive situations. He didn't engage at all with school and edged into a group of other disengaged students. He hung around a skate park; there was marijuana. Sometime later, he also confessed to his mother he had done ecstasy and cocaine but would never take heroin or ice.

'How did you get the stuff?' asked Jenny.

'At parties.'

'But you've never been allowed to go to parties.'

'I would just wait until you were asleep, and then I'd sneak out at twelve or one and then come back in at three or four in the morning.'

It was a revelation that made Jenny question how Lachlan was still alive. As she and Nick tried to fathom all that was happening, Lachlan continued to alarm them with his fixations. And when these were mixed with the increasing physicality of a strong pubescent youth, the worries heightened.

'If Nick wasn't home, there was always more risk that Lachlan would be aggressive. One time I had the baby strapped to my back, and Lachlan was in bed with a lighter, and I was trying to get it off him, but he was refusing to give it to me. He pushed me, and I almost fell backwards. I was, like, "I can't do this." I was so worried he was going to set fire to something. I screamed for one of my other boys to come and help. And all I could do was sit on Lachlan, because that was the only way I could stop him from pushing me, while my other son prised the lighter out of his hand.

'There were times when Lachlan melted down and was so destructive that we needed to get the other kids out of the house … We also wanted to protect them from seeing anything that might be damaging to them. Lachlan had such a strong bond with his siblings that we didn't want his meltdowns to destroy those relationships, or for his siblings to be scared of him.'

'We asked the police as well,' added Nick. 'I needed to know where I stood. I didn't want to hurt Lachlan, I *never* want to hurt Lachlan, but the police said if he was hurting other people, I could escort him out of the house. It happened once. But no dad wants to do that. And that type of stuff never leaves you. It's always there.'

There were 'a hundred other' incidents that contributed to the family's exasperation. There were the random admissions by Lachlan to Jenny: 'I've jumped trains on that track;' 'See that graffiti over there? That was me.' Lachlan also went missing for hours on end, unable to be contacted on his phone. Jenny would drive around looking for him. As their list of options thinned, Jenny and Nick spoke about some form of separation; one parent would live with Lachlan in another residence, and everyone else would remain in the family home. 'It had become toxic,' acknowledged Nick.

Then, they heard about BackTrack. Jenny spoke with Haley, the program's social worker who liaised with families and was all too familiar with distressed calls for help. After that, Jenny drove her son the many hours to Armidale for a visit.

'And that's when we met Bernie for the first time,' said Jenny. 'Lachlan shook Bernie's hand, made eye contact and said, "Nice to meet you," and Bernie's response was, "Wow, you've got manners, and everything." Bernie was funny, down to earth, and he struck me as being very pensive – he thought before he spoke. I could see he was deeply thinking about the situation and was really skilful in the way he spoke to Lachlan. He seemed to have this really great balance of knowing the right questions to ask, knowing how to ask them, and knowing how to correct things without it seeming like a criticism or a put-down.'

Lachlan felt comfortable in the depot environment, but Jenny and Nick were uncertain.

'Then one night back at home,' recalled Jenny, 'I was really tossing and turning. I knew we were in desperate need of help. I knew we needed respite. Lachlan is a beautiful kid with a really good heart. And we love him deeply. But our family was in crisis. While we needed help, I was also really concerned if I was doing the right thing as a mum. Lachlan wanted to go to BackTrack. Was it right? What happened if he was led further astray? Because these were rough kids at Backtrack, and I know it was wrong of me to make judgements, but … maybe he didn't belong there? Maybe we should try to put him in another school? Or should I leave work and do it all myself? All these things went through my head.

'And then, on this night, he broke into our room while we were sleeping. He'd army-crawled in and was trying to steal money out of our wallet, and we woke up and caught him. He stormed out of the room and I followed him. He totally went off, called me names I've never heard any man call me in my life. So much went through my mind. And one of them was the realisation that the only reason Lachlan had never been arrested was because he lived in a suburb where the police didn't drive around looking for kids making trouble. If you saw him walking down the street you might think: "Oh, he's going for a nice healthy walk, isn't that nice?" Whereas if he was in a lower socioeconomic suburb … It dawned on me that night. In many ways, he was actually no different from some of the BackTrack boys who'd had upbringings without love and privilege.'

Lachlan joined BackTrack. The first notable change that Jenny and Nick witnessed was when their son returned home for a visit and spoke of all the lessons he'd learnt in his new environment. Among them was: 'When you say sorry, it doesn't really mean anything unless you change your behaviour.' It was something Jenny and Nick had been trying to work on with their eldest child for years, but somehow, for whatever reason, the message didn't sink in until he was at BackTrack. As with so many of the boys, Lachlan may remain a work in progress for years to come, but at the time of the interview with Jenny and Nick, there was relief. And hope.

'I honestly think the BackTrack people are amazing,' said Jenny. 'I don't know how Bernie, Haley, all of them, do what they do every day. If I had a spare million dollars in my back pocket, I'd happily throw it their way because of the work they're doing.

'As for my family, I look at the children and think: "Oh my gosh, how did we get to this place where we needed somewhere like BackTrack?" Nick and I just look at our kids, all of them, and go: "You know what? We've raised them and loved them all the same way."'

—

'It's all walks of life,' says Bernie, half-in, half-out of his office.

And all those walks – and every walk within those walks – leave tracks. Before the Warrah residential program began, there was an afternoon when Bernie and Maeve did as they so often did: they saddled up two horses, Pete and Whinny, and went for a ride. It was late, after school, and they knew they had to be quick if they were to make it all the way around the dam before it became too dark. In the previous months the area had seen substantial rain, but neither Dad nor his teenage daughter had thought much about that as they headed off. But by the time they reached the back of the block, there was a problem.

'We just started to sink,' remembered Maeve. 'The horses were down to their bellies, their entire legs were in the ground before we knew it. I just panicked and had no idea what to do. The horses were panicking too, trying to get out of this mud. It was starting to get dark and we couldn't turn back. To watch Dad in that situation was incredible. I definitely think that's where his tracking skills came in. The first thing he did was look for kangaroo tracks. The kangaroos had obviously hit the solid ground and we needed to follow their tracks if we could. And then Dad looked for the nearest big trees. If they were still standing, it meant that there was hard ground around them. So, we had to get as close to them as we could. He just totally kicked into gear. He just thought it out practically. "Right, how do we get out of here? What do we do?" Finally, we found some hard ground and got out of trouble. The poor horses were completely lame, but we nursed them home in the dark.'

Bernie's memories of that incident are dominated by one thought: 'I had to look after Maeve.

'Coz, when those horses tried to come up out of the mud their front legs were striking, and if you were anywhere near them it was terrifying. Panic-stricken horses can do enormous damage. These ones were absolutely desperate to get out, and our job was to slow them down but still keep them moving. It was like quicksand. Shit, I went down to my knees. And Maeve kept getting in front of the horses, and I was thinking: "If they come out of there, you're dead." Those sorts of moments you take for granted in hindsight, but when you're in the middle of them, they can rattle you badly.'

The greatest tracks Bernie left that evening were in Maeve's mind. They tell the story of a man's ability to calmly read and react to a serious situation. That ability was one of the reasons the Warrah residential quickly became an integral part of BackTrack. Eventually, Bernie sought staff to run and supervise the facility, and he moved to Francesca's rural block, where he still lives with her, his dogs and his horses. In theory it offers a retreat away from the depot, but in line with the early years of BackTrack the latter years, 2016 to 2018, showed that Bernie could never truly leave his work behind.

21

It's early evening, cold and clear, and Sydney's CBD is in a rush. High heels ... green man flashing ... swipe left, swipe right ... a buck for the busker ... where's the Opal card? ... then squeeze in among elbows and armpits for the trip home.

Meanwhile, in the inner hall of a turreted stone building, two young men wearing red shirts, jeans and sneakers are moving at a more genteel pace. They shake hands with people wearing suits and smart frocks. They engage in conversation, notably looking everyone in the eye. Then, when the formal meets-and-greets have lulled, they go for a walk, and look around them, especially at the grand oil paintings of people, from centuries past, posing with authority. Who are these well-cloaked people? Obviously they are important. But tonight, the answers don't matter. Tonight, the paintings merely hold solemn faces that stare from the walls in a room where the boys are the ones in the middle of the frame. They, together with Bernie and Dawso, are here as special guests for the screening of a documentary. How many of us can say we've rubbed shoulders with the NSW Governor and his wife at Government House, in the Botanic Gardens?

The documentary is shown. In one of its scenes, a boy named Tyson is led handcuffed into a cell at a juvenile-detention centre.

Silence overwhelms the audience as sixty people are collectively transfixed by a moment they have never known.

The documentary continues. It evokes many reactions: laughter, tears, shaking of heads, grimaces, raised eyebrows, fidgeting hands, feet shifting on the floor.

Afterwards, Bernie addresses the gathering. He wears a suit that hangs off, rather than sits on, his shoulders. There is no tie. He walks from side to side, comfortable with his movements, his manner, his ad-lib speech. Then he invites one of the two boys in the red shirts to come forward to speak. The young man is slightly built. Put a rugby-league jumper on him, and you could see him darting from dummy-half and leaving tired forwards grabbing at air. He appears nervous. He stitches his fingers together, then pulls them apart. He does it again. Then he speaks: 'Hands up if you remember where you were on your eighteenth birthday?' Some hands are raised, others stay down, and murmurs fill the room. Seeing the reaction, knowing that everyone is really listening to him, he gains confidence.

'On my eighteenth birthday, I was in that same cell you saw Tyson in.'

There is silence.

'But thanks to BackTrack I've now got a job. I've got two kids, a partner, we live in a house, I'm about to get my driver's licence, and life is looking up.'

The audience claps.

And the young man lets slip a tiny smile.

Bernie is sitting back in his office chair. We've been talking about individual BackTrack kids. Those with 'their shit together', and those who 'will get there, but aren't there yet'. Then, we change topics and Bernie is about to answer a question when there's a knock, the door opens and a face shaded by a cap pokes into the gap.

'G'day Ricky,' says Bernie. 'How are you, buddy?'

'Good, how are you?'

Bernie looks at me: 'When you see a kid that comes into BackTrack and says: "I'm gonna fuckin' stab you. I'm not fuckin' stayin' here. You're not my parents; you don't tell me what to do."'

Ricky shakes his head.

'Who did that?' I ask.

'Not me,' says Ricky, grinning.

'Really?' replies Bernie, grinning too.

Ricky takes one step into the office: 'Yeah, not joking. That was me.'

Bernie says nothing for a moment. A pause that allows Ricky to absorb his own answer.

After several seconds Bernie continues: 'So, James has just asked me why I do what I do and what keeps me going.'

'Because he loves me so much,' says Ricky. 'And I would never stab him.'

Bernie smiles and looks again at me, knowing Ricky is listening intently to every word.

'Looking from where that kid that came in and how he was gonna stab me, and he was telling all the boys, "I'll fuckin' stab that cunt." ... Look where he is now, look at that. Does he still have a few slips backwards? Absolutely. But do I still have slip-ups? Absolutely. We all fuck up from time to time, but it's what you do with that. Then, when I see Ricky smile and go home and half get it right, and almost not bring drugs back. When I see those improvements, and the development of young men, I go, "That's what I do it for – there's a bloody inch."'

'That's a good rap for you,' I say to Ricky.

'Thanks for that, Bern.'

'I haven't done anything, mate. It's all to do with you.'

Ricky smirks. 'All right then,' he says. And he walks out, shuts the door and returns to working with Matt Pett on the new cabins.

Bernie continues as though the interruption were all part of a carefully scripted stage production.

'But it can take years before you can get some of those sorts of wins. Then you see the kid, the young man, and he's out of the program and he's a tradie or he's driving a truck, or he's putting up fences, or he's got an apprenticeship. The boys and girls that come through here … the people out there on the street have no idea who they are. Or where they've come from. Look at Pedro out there helping Matt Pett. He should just not be alive. How he does it! The last three weeks he's been turning up every single day. He'd been in care when we met him. Two or three different places. He knows how to hang in. I think they're the kids that touch me the most. The ones that you look at when they're in here and you're going …'

Throughout our interviews, this is as emotional as I've seen Bernie become. His eyes soften. His pause tells as much as his words.

'Um … a kid like Ricky, I know we're going to win. It will just take time. But with a kid like …'

Bernie shares some of the details of Pedro's past. He sighs. A long, deep sigh.

'There's just that collection of kids where you think: "We're never going to stop trying." The prospects of the flower blooming might be slim, but then you get those little moments, just glimpses, and … You know, if I ever whinge about what I'm doing, I watch that kid Pedro doing what he's doing. And then I go, "That's why I do this job." That kid out there, and what he represents. That's why I do it.'

It was this extraordinary compassion that was evident on a particular day in January 2016 when two strangers came through the depot's gates. The kids had been told they were coming, but that meant little or nothing to some of them. Indeed, there were those who were more interested in the strangers' car. 'Is that real gold on the number plate?' one of them asked. Bernie thought that their reactions were 'hilarious', but there was no use adding spit and polish to them; they were who they were. And that was all they needed to be to win the hearts of His Excellency General, The Honourable David Hurley, [the then] Governor of New South Wales [and Governor-General of Australia from June 2019], and his wife, Linda, who were on one of their official monthly trips into the bush. The kids and dogs put on a jumping display for their guests, and they invited them into the classroom for a lesson with Sarah Mills.

'There were so many good points that lined up to say: "Well, you've got something special happening here,"' said Governor Hurley in an interview with me at Government House. 'We could see it was really making a difference in these kids' lives.'

Mrs Hurley, a former primary school teacher and mother of three grown-up children, was enthused by the 'level of engagement' and 'upbeat atmosphere'. She was also intrigued by the metalwork art she'd seen, and at one point in the shed she asked Matt Pilkington: 'Do you think you could make a waratah flower?' It was a question prompted by interest rather than any sort of request, and the governor's wife thought nothing more about it.

However, for Matt the challenge had been laid. A long-term employee of BackTrack, he had seen kids come and go; staff too at a place where the workers either 'got it' or went 'wow, this is full-on', and moved on. Matt felt at least part of his connection with the kids was due to his own upbringing. He'd been kicked out of school in Year Eleven. But well before that, another experience had helped found his attitudes in an invaluable way. When he was ten, he moved with his family to Palm Island, on the Great Barrier Reef, where his father had accepted a teaching position. Matt, the eldest of four siblings, was the only white kid in his class, and he 'used to get beaten up every afternoon' by other students. Then, one day, some elders came to his home and …

'I'll never forget it,' said Matt, in an interview at BackTrack. 'We lived in a house on stilts, and I was watching my favourite cartoon and Dad said: "Come on outside and have a chat with these guys." And they said, "Right, this is it, we're sick of this, we're going to have to teach you how to box. You're going to have to learn to defend yourself; you've given shame to your family." And I was like, "Whoa, can I do this?" So, they taught me how to box in the backyard. They got a big sack and filled it full of sand, and they trained me with that. Then I started punching on after school and everyone went: "Oh, you *can* throw a punch!" A lot of those guys who used to beat me up became my best mates and we used to wag school, go fishing and head up into the rainforest and eat bush tucker all day. From that time on, I've always had things to do with Indigenous people.'

Matt, a self-taught welder, launched into the waratah project with the boys. 'We're doing what? We're making a flower!' some said. It was no easy task. At one stage, Matt got some engineer chalk and drew up everything the would-be floral fabricators needed to do. There were jigs and wires and rods and plasma cutters and sparks and cursing and, 'What the fuck are we doing?' But slowly, the detailed work began to take shape, and so did the boys' recognition of what was happening.

'It's the confidence thing,' said Matt. 'Just telling the boys: "That's bloody awesome. Well done." Just keep telling them how they're going.'

The end result was impressive: a metre-high grey metal waratah with a long stem, leaves and dozens of intricate florets. A work of art.

Six months after the vice-regal visit to Armidale, about twenty-five BackTrack kids – boys and girls – and a handful of dogs were guests at Government House. It was part of a trip that also included a visit to Parliament House, on the invitation of the Member for Northern Tablelands, Adam Marshall. Jumping exhibitions had been planned but were cancelled due to rain. Nevertheless, other activities went ahead, including a presentation that brought Mrs Hurley to tears when we spoke about it.

'I will never forget that day for as long as I live,' said Mrs Hurley. 'I walked into the ballroom and I saw the waratah and I just thought: "Oh, that will be for the Governor." But then it was given to me. It was just so, so special. Having the boys there, most of them who'd made it. I gave them hugs, and I felt just so happy, and ...'

'And you sang,' said Governor Hurley.

'Yes, I just wanted to sing that song, "You Are My Sunshine". I love that. And others joined in. I guess in a job like this it's often the Governor who everyone wants to meet, and the wife is there.

But that day the kids made me feel so special. I just love BackTrack and I love the kids and they're so respectful; they're, "Hello, it's good to see you." For us, to share this house with people that perhaps might normally never have had the opportunity to come here or to meet the Governor, that's just such a treat. To take them up into the turrets and share that world with them, and they just embrace it and appreciate it and ... it does more for us, really.'

In February 2017, the Governor and his wife returned to Armidale to formally announce they were to be the Patrons of BackTrack. When I asked Bernie how such a relationship was cemented, he smiled and simply said, 'We just asked the big fella.' In the lead-up to the day, Bernie's partner, Francesca, worked on a surprise element.

'I'd be in the car with six boys and we were off somewhere to collect wood and I'd break into this song that had become like an unofficial anthem of BackTrack. The boys would join in, and that would be like a little rehearsal. Then I'd do it with three others here and three others somewhere else. None of them knew they were in fact practising, but that's what we were doing. Then we got to the day ... and there was no turning back; we were going to pump out this song, whether it was only us or all the kids. But they turned up in their red and blue BackTrack shirts, the sun beating down, and ... it was just one of those moments. They sang really nicely. It was beautiful.'

The song was 'One Call Away' by American pop artist Charlie Puth. In the context of BackTrack the theme was poignant: someone always being there to give love and support. Backed by Francesca on an electric bass and youth worker Luke on guitar, twenty or more kids 'opened their chests' for the new patrons. A barbecue shelter at the Dumaresq Dam recreation area may have been a long way from turrets and portraits of kings, but on that day, it brought a Governor and his wife to the very centre of belonging.

'We didn't know Bernie before our first visit to BackTrack,' said Governor Hurley, who served in the Australian army for forty-two years, including as Chief of the Defence Force. 'Once we saw him with the kids, we knew he had their respect. He and everyone else there are doing tremendous work. I just go back to my military days of recruit training and we'd get youngsters coming in, and they'd hop off the bus with a pair of thongs and jeans and a plastic bag with all their possessions, and their fathers had told them they'd never make a soldier's rear end. Now, you've got to turn that around, and get them to the point where they can see they're actually achieving. It's about building them up. And each of those little steps you take you reinforce with some kind words and say, "Let's have a think about what just happened here; you didn't think you could do that but look at this! So, next time you don't think you can do something, why is that going to be a limit?" And that's what BackTrack does so well. The kids grow and grow and grow. I often say for many of these organisations it's not about creating opportunity, but you're opening doors for kids to go through. It's showing them how many doors there are, where they can say, "Oh, you mean I could choose from any of these?" "Yeah. But you're going to have to work. We're not just going to do things for you.'''

On that second trip to Armidale, the Hurleys met one particular boy who had endured too many doors in his face. A cheeky, funny boy with a quick tongue and a temper to match. While walking across a paddock with him, the Governor asked: 'Why did you come here?'

'Well, if I didn't, I'd be dead.'

That boy was Rusty.

At the time of meeting the Hurleys, he was one of three BackTrack boys whose journeys were being closely followed by Catherine Scott, an Australian filmmaker. Catherine had lived in the United States for thirteen years, during which time her work focused strongly on criminal justice and incarceration. Back home, she first heard about Bernie and BackTrack after she mentioned at a party that she was thinking about getting a border collie to be an assistance dog for one of her sons, who has Type 1 diabetes.

'A friend heard me, and he put dogs and jails together, and he said, "Oh my God, you have to meet this amazing man up in Armidale,"' recalled Catherine in a phone interview. 'So, I contacted Bernie, and the story completely captured my imagination.'

As with so many people drawn to BackTrack, Catherine felt she had some sort of personal connection. She too had been a 'pretty wild kid', a dyslexic who didn't do well at school and was eventually expelled. Then, after filming began and Catherine was drawn deeper into BackTrack, she realised her connection not only embraced her childhood, but her adulthood too.

'I also related to Bernie and the parents and the teachers, because I have two pretty wild boys of my own. And sometimes as a mother I really struggle with the way to bring them up; it's really important that I bring up boys who are not going to repeat the behaviour that I've been surrounded by as a woman my entire life. A lot of the stuff I filmed with Bernie was actually stuff that I applied to my own life. I would go home and try out his techniques on my own kids. I've always said to Bernie that *Backtrack Boys* is not just for youth workers. Everybody is going to see themselves in these kids' stories in some way, and everyone will want to know how you do what you do. For me, besides wanting to tell a beautiful story, there was a lot of personal learning in making this documentary. There was a lot of learning about how to be a better mum.'

Sitting in his office chair, Bernie shakes his head. *Backtrack Boys*, which was released a few months before our interviews, has won critical and popular acclaim across Australia. From metropolitan cinemas to country town halls with tired, yellowing screens, the images of troubled kids with their dogs in the bush are both seeping and slamming into the public conscience. The documentary is nothing short of brilliant.

'Who'd a thought it?' says Bernie. 'But I get it. Beautiful pictures of kids and dogs in the bush. Catherine has done an extraordinary job. We've done Q-and-As after screenings in all sorts of places, and you know what? At every single one of them, you can bet your life on it, that people will come up and say, "I know a kid like that," or, "Crickey we need BackTrack in our town." The documentary hits on a national problem. An international one. How do we look after the kids forgotten by so much of society? One documentary isn't going to answer the question, but as they say, it can get people talking. And we can only hope that some of those people then start doing.'

In *Backtrack Boys* the fortunes of Rusty, Zac and Tyson carry viewers into a world of vulnerabilities that tear at every possible emotion. Now, sitting in the office with Bernie, with a blaring radio and boys' laughter outside, I'm only starting to understand what these vulnerabilities have done to Bernie. Every day his emotions are like boxers in a ring. They duck, they weave, they cop a blow. Step forward, take two back, on the ropes, get off the canvas, duck again, land a blow. It's a hell of a fight, and above all, it's a fight in which there's no final bell, because there will always be some kid somewhere who is metaphorically swinging hard to survive. I'm thinking this because of something Francesca had said to me in our interview. It concerned one of the lowest points in Bernie's time at BackTrack: the first-time incarceration of a boy with whom Bernie had developed a very close relationship.

'That night, the night the boy was locked up, Bernie said to me, "I'm going for a ride." It was about midnight by the time that happened. Then at about two in the morning we got up and went out. It was a no-moon night, and the ride he was asking about was one he had not done before, and I thought I should go with him. But I was trying to read: "Is space more important for you right now? Or is support more important? And what type of support?" So, it ended up with him and me on two horses, and with Billy one of the pups alongside us. We just rode out in the pitch black. So, we were tracking along, then at one point, Bernie stops, gets off and just weeps. Absolutely weeps. And he is surrounded by two horses leaning in with their heads, and I am just holding him from behind, and the dog is there. And this is his circle under the sky about five k's from home. So, what do you do? You just hold that circle. Clearly this is something that just works for him. You gotta let it out somewhere, because if you don't, it will crush you.'

Bernie was lucky that night. He had support. But anyone involved with BackTrack knows how absent that support can be. Zac, who has gained a considerable profile from the documentary, understands what pain that absence can cause. When we yarned on a log at the depot, he spoke for all too many.

'Like Dawso says, one of the hardest things in society is growing up and being told: "You're a man, you're a male, you have to be tough, you can't show your emotions, you have to work and eat cement, and be fuckin' aaaaarrgh!" So, you grow up and sometimes you feel yourself welling up in tears and you think: "What the fuck are you doing? You are fuckin' weak." But at BackTrack, the boys and Bernie, Dawso, everyone, they've showed me you should never be afraid to cry. They showed me that. I bottled it up for years. Just bottled it all up. But when you do that, you build up all these other feelings. And then you snap. And whoever is around you, well, they're a victim coz you're in a shitty headspace.'

I want to push Bernie more about this topic, but then the office door opens again and Dawso comes in with a few beers. He is lean, a rugby captain in his school years, and a born-and-bred Armidale farm boy who's now approaching his fortieth birthday. On a roundabout life journey, he ran pubs for a long time, including in Singapore. He has been at BackTrack for four-and-a-half years and he leads others brilliantly. A day earlier we'd sat and talked at the table bench near Bernie's office. It was there that Dawso told me about a very strong bond he had with one of the boys who has moved on from BackTrack. With a name that appeared metronomically on police charge sheets, the boy had been in and out of juvenile detention but is now working as an apprentice in another country town.

'I was coming back from a long trip and I rang him up and said I'd be going through his town and I'd pop in and see him,' said Dawso. 'I was running late because I had to be out at Warrah for work, so I wouldn't be able to stay for long. But when I got there, he had a roast pork in the oven. I said I couldn't stay for lunch, so he then proceeded to go into the kitchen; pulled the roast out, carved it up, and made me up a plate with the pork, crackling and veggies. He put some foil over it and said I had to take it with me. And that's something my mum does. It makes me really proud, really emotional. I drove away with tears in my eyes, and I rang Bernie and said, "Mate, this is why we do it."'

Dawso puts the beers in the fridge, but before he goes, Bernie asks him: 'Can you remember that dog we used in court? Was it Girl or Lou?'

The question relates to a story Bernie told me earlier. He had been asked by police to provide a dog that could be used as a companion for a child who had to give evidence in a 'really dramatic' case. The child wasn't in the BackTrack program, nor had a BackTrack dog ever been used for such a purpose. In the lead-up to the court case, Dawso and Bernie took the dog to the child's home so the dog and the child could become familiar with each other. They played ball games, and on some nights, the dog slept at the child's home. They also went to court and became familiar with what would happen. The child and dog sat next to each other in a video conference room. The child could put a hand on the dog, but there was to be no playing or exuberance. Just touch that led to silent reassurance. The child became used to the dog, and the dog became used to the child. And then it was time for the real court case to happen.

As they throw the names of Girl and Lou back and forth, Bernie and Dawso can't say for certain which dog it was, but Dawso reckons it was probably Lou because Girl had diabetes at the time. After Dawso leaves, Bernie takes one of his long pauses full of thought before he says, 'I think Dawso's right. It must have been Lou.'

It's late afternoon. The interview is nearly over.

'We're almost there,' I say.

An abrupt, repetitive bark interrupts us. It's the ring tone on Bernie's phone. The call turns out to be a simple work inquiry. Nothing to worry about. Considering the nature of BackTrack and the job and life of the man sitting opposite me, that call is reason enough for relief.

22

A dark grey Holden Colorado dual-cab heads back towards town. Its driver wears a black-sleeved puffer jacket, a blue woollen jumper, blue shirt, blue thermal vest and dusty, grease-stained blue jeans. His eyes are also blue. So is his language.

'Every day. One step forward, two back, twenty to the fuckin' side. But we're always movin'. Gotta keep movin'. Goin' where we wanna go – bit like mustering cattle in the bush.'

The dual-cab passes a road sign. It says: ARMIDALE – UNLEASH THE OPPORTUNITIES.

The driver stares through his windscreen. Who knows what the day will bring him? But for the moment, the sun is just starting to break through the clouds.

During the period in which Catherine Scott filmed her documentary, BackTrack was undergoing significant change. In 2016 it moved away from being a subsidiary of Jobs Australia Enterprises and gained independent status as a charitable organisation. A familiar face helped implement the operational change. Mel Phillips, Bernie's close friend from their Gore Hill

TAFE days, was the project manager. She has remained with BackTrack and is now general manager. At the time of transition, a board was established under the chairmanship of Greg Paramor AO, a father of three and a businessman with more than forty years' experience in real estate and funds management. Living in Sydney, he first became aware of BackTrack after reading a magazine article about Bernie and the boys by journalist Greg Bearup in 2014. He contacted Bernie, and after meeting a 'straight-up, nothing negative, no-bullshit bloke', he offered to help.

In the 2016–17 financial year BackTrack had a revenue of just over a million dollars. A year later, it was about two-and-a-quarter million. More than half came from philanthropy, and nearly another twenty per cent from individual donations. Little came from government support. Without context, the numbers might look impressive, but BackTrack is expensive to operate, and during our interviews Bernie makes several references to the pressure of holding a cap in his hands.

In 2017, that cap had a strong element of baggy green when the Chappell Foundation provided its financial support. Established by Australia's famous cricketing brothers Greg, Ian and Trevor Chappell, the foundation raises funds and awareness for Australia's homeless youth.

'I look back on my own life and realise how lucky I was,' said Greg Chappell in a phone interview. 'We were born into a sporting family, and we were born into a loving family with great support. Our parents never sat us down and said, "You have a responsibility," but I think through our sporting careers we saw the impact that we could have on people, and particularly young people; and the realisation is there that you do, because of your profile, have an opportunity to make a difference. I just feel we all have a responsibility to reach out and help other people who haven't been as fortunate.

'What adds power to the BackTrack story is that it isn't only impacting on the lives of young boys and girls. It's impacting on the community in a positive way.'

To think Bernie, as a boy, dreamed of being Greg Chappell.

BackTrack is now spreading to other communities, including Dubbo, Condobolin, and Lake Cargelligo, but this growth will take time.

'Building businesses it is really important to get your roots down as deep as you can or in the construction game make sure you spend a lot of time making sure your foundations can withstand the tremors that will impact the building over many years – the same applies to BackTrack – and that is the job of the Board – so Bernie and his team can do their work with confidence and know the structure is safe and sound,' said Greg Paramor at his office. 'We're not there yet. We've got to get the roots right deep. We've got to have an operation that's fully funded, and one that really operates in Armidale without a peer anywhere. If other people see what we're doing, the roots go down from there.'

The meaning of 'success' is open to interpretation. In terms of BackTrack, these interpretations can be influenced by attitudes, perspectives and interests. What weight do you put on prizes as prestigious as the Australian Crime and Violence Prevention Gold Award (2017, Community-led category)? Or the NSW Youth Service of the Year Award (2015 and again in 2018)? Perhaps statistics tell you more? They say eighty-seven per cent of BackTrack youth progress to employment or back into some form of training, and since BackTrack began, juvenile crime rates in Armidale have decreased. But in isolation, numbers and framed pieces of paper can't define the narrative of BackTrack's success. They need dispatches from the frontline, the observations of those people who intricately understand the issues that confront disengaged youth. Commander of New England Police District, Scott Tanner, said in his office at the Armidale Station: 'This is the stuff that I lose sleep over at night. There are just bad people in life, and unfortunately jail is the only solution for them, but for the ones who you can turn you've got to get them into things like what Bernie has made. It's not death by a thousand cuts; instead it is success by a thousand cuts. Just little wins, little wins, little wins. If you can just change that trajectory. We have kids who will go and commit five or six break-and-enters in a night. Change their trajectory, and there are five or six less victims, five or six less reports, the community is safer, insurance premiums go down … it is all interrelated. So, change that trajectory. We might have a kid who we think: "It might be good for Bernie to look after him for a while." Or Bernie might ring me and say, "Scott, one of the boys has got in a bit of trouble, what can we do? What is the situation?" We've got a real fluid relationship now. It is gold. Absolute gold. We would be lost without BackTrack. If I could wave my magic wand it needs to be rolled out Australia-wide, but the only problem with that is there is only one Bernie.'

Karen Stafford first met Bernie in 2013 when she was appointed as the Local Court and Children's Court Magistrate to the Armidale Circuit. Towards the end of that year, Bernie rang her, and asked: 'Do magistrates like to drink coffee or beer?' A meeting over a gin-and-tonic eventually led to Karen visiting the BackTrack depot.

'I went down after court one day,' said Karen in an email to me. 'It was initially quite confronting to be face to face with the boys, including one I had just dealt with in court. But, as Bernie knows, to fully understand his work at BackTrack it is essential to see firsthand the boys at the shed. Of course, once the dogs were let out to say "hello", I was sold. To sit around chatting with the boys while patting the dogs broke down the inevitable barriers between me and the boys, in terms of age, gender and authority.

'I visited the shed and the classroom a number of times. I was particularly interested to see the classroom when the girls started. I had previously seen a couple of girls in court and was glad to watch their progress as their confidence grew.

'Bernie came to court with many of the boys to offer them support, whether through writing references, answering my questions about their progress, or offering them a position at BackTrack as part of their bail or bond conditions. I started to realise the level of commitment that took when he told me that he'd already been at the police station with one boy all night before court, being a support person and just making sure that the boy knew that he wasn't alone.

'One boy who came in front of me just after I'd started in Armidale could barely see over the dock when the police brought him in. As the years rolled on, he grew a little taller but unfortunately he had other stints in juvenile detention. Bernie could see his potential and spent time with him showing that there was always hope. When I sent that boy back to detention almost three years after I had first seen him, he spent his time mentoring some of the other boys inside, using the skills that Bernie had taught him. He was released and has now become a young man with a future, thanks really to Bernie.

'Magistrates on other circuits wish they had a BackTrack in their area. In a perfect world, every Children's Court Circuit would have access to a BackTrack.'

As a further statement of her belief in the program Karen was a director on the BackTrack board until February 2018. She is now magistrate on another country circuit.

Education is also on the frontline. From her role as head teacher of wellbeing at Duval High to her current position as principal of Armidale Secondary College, Carolyn Lasker has witnessed the entire development of BackTrack.

'People think about Armidale as a pretty progressive place, but there are a lot of kids here that are pretty disadvantaged and just don't feel part of anything. The beauty of the BackTrack program is that these kids can feel connected to something. Bernie has always talked about: "They all get the opportunity to experience success." And that's something that, sadly, doesn't happen in the school structure. These are not the kids who are getting up to get an award at a school assembly. A beautiful thing has been some of the kids going back into the schools with their dogs and showing their peers in that school setting: "Look at me. Look what I can do. I'm the centre of attention now." It would be awesome if some day BackTrack had accreditation through the Board of Studies (NSW) to be an education provider and stand on its own two feet as an independent school. But there would be a lot of box-ticking to go through, and I think that would be a process that would just blow Bernie's mind and he would go, "No way!" Whatever happens, there is a lot that still needs to be done for these kids, and Bernie and everyone at BackTrack won't give up on them.'

But not giving up comes at a cost. Inevitably, working at the front line leads to hard yards for workers. 'They either last for days or years,' says Bernie. Those I have interviewed are a diverse mix of people who come together because of a common yet complex motivation. It is one that in BackTrack vernacular can be stated in a matter of words: 'The need to give a shit.'

There is Matt Pilkington. Matt Pett is there too. And Ike, who 'had me first job when I was twelve, cartin' wood for the pub'. There is Dawso. And Jannelle, a mother of four boys, who can have such a strong presence in Circle Work. There's Mel, who takes Striker, Robin, Gibbo and others into the schools; on literacy days, some kids might confess to her: 'I can't read,' but Mel tells them: 'That's okay, neither can the dogs.' There's also Warnie. He loves the outdoors. One Boxing Day a mate dropped him off in Mungindi on the border of New South Wales and Queensland, and forty-three days later he arrived at Wentworth on the New South Wales–Victoria border. He'd paddled all the way, along the Barwon-Darling River. There is Marcus Watson, a bloke who has a background in the building trade, and he wields a powerful metaphor: 'A lot of these kids come here with only big hammers in their tool kits. They take a big hammer to every problem. We need to give them specific tools for specific situations.' And then there's Haley, the conduit between families and BackTrack. She's a mum of two little boys and she is also a sister who has seen a sibling come through the program. 'There is just so much love here,' she said to me. 'Just so much.'

All of these people acknowledge how their jobs can seem relentless and draining but then come the moments that, as Dawso said, 'keep your skin in the game'. Daz, a youth work veteran (and a Harley-riding grandad) is the team leader at Warrah residential. Wind back the years to his own childhood and there was 'a broken home, and a violent father who was in prison a lot'. Daz knows full well the walk and talk of the BackTrack boys. But after beginning his job in February 2018, a few months later he was wondering if he was 'getting through'. Then, one night …

'They asked me if I'd drive them up to the local lookout,' recalled Daz. 'That was usually code for: "Can we have a cigarette?" So, I took them up there, and sure enough they got their lighters out, but this time it was to light the candles of two cakes. Then the boys sang happy birthday to me. I didn't know they'd planned it. It was so genuine. With real heart. They'd got their coins together and spent fourteen dollars. A chocolate cake and a vanilla one. Wow. An absolute highlight.'

Success. Interpret it as you like.

In 2017, the Armidale Regional Council signed a Memorandum of Understanding to further its support for BackTrack. The council helps with work placements, and currently some kids have general maintenance jobs at the Dumaresq Dam Recreation area. 'I believe what Bernie and his staff are doing is just so special,' said administrator Ian Tiley in a phone interview.

Elsewhere in the district, sticks are picked, fences are built, lambs are marked – and youths who have so often been told they can't, are showing they can. You need not go far in Armidale to find someone full of praise for what continues to happen at the old depot out on the Grafton Road. Indeed, when I first started my research, a barista in a cafe overheard a conversation I was having with two customers about BackTrack. Afterwards, she said to me: 'Are you doing a book on Bernie? He's a legend.'

Peter Slattery, whose career spans nearly forty years, has worked in Australia and overseas as a youth worker. He is well credentialled, widely respected. Since first meeting Bernie before the BackTrack days he has witnessed the development of a 'pretty unique character' whose skills will never be learnt from a textbook.

'He is charismatic, and he is aware of that. He uses his personality and charisma to invite the person in front of him into a process which is irresistible and intriguing. And I think that's inseparable from who Bernie is. He's a superb orator. And he's also a smooth talker, so he can sell you things, and he can do that with absolute genuine authenticity, and he uses that when he works with young people. He helps them believe and feel that they are in charge.'

Of course, there are failures too, but if there remains any doubt about the positive change that Bernie and BackTrack have brought to both the Armidale community and specific lives further away, it is best to ask the people who have suffered more than anyone at the frontline: the kids and their families.

One evening I spoke with Gail and her husband, Alan, in their home. From the earliest days they have seen a few relatives, both boys and girls, attend BackTrack. Many were introduced to it for the same reason: they hated school.

'School is not for everybody,' said Alan. 'If they don't fit in there it doesn't mean they're going to be a bad person. Doesn't mean they're not going to survive or do good things. It's just that the system … if someone is a little bit different, there's nowhere to go.'

Gail added: 'We had one boy who used to complain about doing language and home economics. He used to say: "Why have I got to do it? I'm not going to do that when I grow up." He just didn't want to be there. "Can't I leave?" "Can't I get a job?" "Can't I move?" Just didn't like it, and then he'd muck up a bit and was the clown of the classroom. Wagged a bit too. He'd wait for me to go to work and then he'd sneak back home. He just needed something more than school could offer. When we heard about what Bernie was doing, we got him a start welding. There was lots of relief. For him to come home in a good mood and say, "This is what I've made. This is what we did today." Bernie arranged for him to do an apprenticeship, and he's now got his own business. If it wasn't for BackTrack I don't know what would have happened.'

'If it wasn't for BackTrack …'

I've heard it said by many people.

For another of Gail and Alan's relatives, it is too early to complete the incomplete. At the moment, the aim of his family is a simple statement wrapped in uncertainty: 'We want to keep him out of juvey.' A kid who has smashed a television with a shovel, put holes in walls and doors, been suspended from school many times. Can the cycle be broken?

'He goes to BackTrack every day. Gives him something to get out of bed for,' said Gail. 'He knows that he goes over there, does a bit of school work, mucks around with the dogs, does a bit of welding, then he comes home and he works for members of the family. Since BackTrack, he has changed dramatically. He has respect for other people.'

'But they've had a few dramas with him,' continued Alan. 'A couple of times it was pretty big goings on, but Bernie, the others, they say: "Feet forward [in the stirrups]. Tomorrow's a new day. He is welcome back tomorrow." We trust Bernie. Trust him with everything, basically, because what you see is what you get. He'll do his best and that's all you ask for in anybody. Bernie, the team over there at BackTrack, they're good people doing good things.'

During my time as an observer at BackTrack I have asked dozens of boys what Bernie, his staff and the program mean to them. Their answers are generally short and precise: 'I'd be in jail.' 'I'd be runnin' from the cops.' 'I wouldn't have a job.' 'I wouldn't have no-one I could talk to.' One answer, though, rings loudest in my thoughts.

'Do you reckon, you owe anything to Bernie and the guys here?' I asked a boy, while he was lighting a rollie. Immediately, he pulled his cupped hands away from his face, looked me in the eyes and said, 'I owe them my life.'

Every single day at BackTrack has a palpable edge to it. It is difficult, if not impossible, for an outsider to feel it. After spending time with Bernie, his team and the kids, the best way I can express it is with another question: How would *you* feel if there was a chance that every single phone call you receive, no matter where you are, might wrench your heart? Standing outside the gates of the Sydney Cricket Ground after a fundraiser for the Chappell Foundation, BackTrack director Philip Jarvis said to me: 'Whenever I get a call from Bernie at night, I get ready to ask: "Is the kid still alive?"'

Yet at BackTrack there is an overwhelming counter to such gravity. It is hilarity. And this, unquestionably, is another sign of success. Many of the people I have interviewed have laughed at the stories they've told. Stories that hold deep, sometimes fragile layers, but that can be shed with the knowledge that lives can be turned around.

'We had a kid one time,' said grazier Murray Lupton, 'and we were taking in a load of hay, and he said to me: "Before you got us to come out and help, who put all those bales in?"'

'I said to him: "I do it myself. I cut two hundred or three hundred bales. I cut them, make them, bring them in every afternoon. I put those two thousand in on my own."'

'Well, that kid looked at me and he said, "You're one mad white fucker!"'

Then there was Matt Lynch's story of escorting a boy to give evidence in a court case. They flew via Sydney to connect with another flight, and when in the terminal ...

'We got to an escalator,' recalled Matt, 'and this boy started stumbling.

'"What the hell are you doing?" I asked him.

'"I've never been on one of these things before."'

Of all the stories, few have as many layers as the one told to me by Balie. No matter which way success is interpreted, she is riding its wave. A troublemaker at school, she started at BackTrack when she was in Year Seven. Just one day a week in the classroom when the girls' program first began operating. She went for five years. Through BackTrack she secured a work traineeship. Now she is a university student. Among her greatest memories of her 'journey', she told me, is of going to the Sydney Film Festival to watch *Backtrack Boys*.

'I went to the bathroom with the Governor's wife,' she said. 'We were walking round the cinema, and you don't really expect things like that to happen. She said: "Do you want to come to the bathroom with me? I don't know where it is." I was: "I don't know where it is either, but I guess we can find it together." So, there we were, walking round. Then I sent Mum a message: "I'm just walking round with the Governor's wife." And my mum texted back: "Oh my goodness, make sure you look after her." But I think she knew how to look after herself.'

Laughter. On a journey that is paving the future.

'I was thinking the other day, the only dream that I have is to grow up to be someone I needed when I was younger. That someone [who] doesn't judge you,' said Balie.

The epitome of 'that someone' is sitting opposite me in his office chair. He is fifty-one years old. The brother of a professor (Anthony), a cinematographer (Paul), a speech pathologist (Maree) and a renewable-energy consultant (Mark). 'We are proud of them all,' said mother, Denise Shakeshaft. 'Different people who've followed their interests. As for Bernard, we feel humbled when we see the accolades he receives, and the obvious difference he is making.'

Bernie's family is now so much larger. It is made up of hundreds and hundreds of people. There's a tin shed. A house with turrets. Swags, a troopy, campfires under the stars. As is usually the case with 'success', it is hard to define Bernie Shakeshaft and all he has done. But maybe, this story from his daughter, Maeve, comes close.

'I went up with him to Fraser Island. I was about fourteen, fifteen. Dad was going to do some dingo work with the rangers up there. One time we were right up the top of this beach and Dad was showing the rangers how to catch the dingoes; the way the rangers did it was to catch them in a trap, then tranquillise them, put a tracking collar on and let them go. Hearing a dog when it comes out of the tranquilliser can be awful. It's a howling type of sound. I remember being woken by it one night. But Dad was showing them that you don't actually have to put the dogs to sleep. So, we were on this beach, and a dingo was in a trap, and Dad said: "I'm not going to tranquillise it. I'm just going to walk up to it in a calm way and we'll just put the collar on it and let it go." I went up with him, but the rangers stood on the back of a ute a fair way away. We just walked up to this dog very calmly. Dad went first. Then me. Pressure on, pressure off. Before you knew it, I was sitting there with this wild dingo in my lap with a piece of electrical tape that Dad had put around its mouth. Then he undid the trap, put the collar on, took the tape off, and let the dog go. It took a few steps, turned back, had a look at us, then walked away so calmly.'

Bernie has done much the same with wild kids.

'There's so much more that needs doing,' he says. 'Gotta keep working on awareness. We've all been kids. And we're pretty sad human beings if we don't help them when we become adults.

You've gotta look for the gold in them. In each and every one of them. Sometimes you lose, but geez you've gotta try.

'Yeah, the job knocks me around. I don't go into detention centres much anymore. I don't like them. I don't like going to visit the kids. I don't like seeing them in overalls. So, I talk to them on the phone.

'I still do court stuff. Crikey, some things have happened there. Copped a grilling on the stand once. Didn't see it coming one little bit. Barristers that flew in from Sydney wearing wigs. Grown men playing dress-ups. All I can remember thinking was: "I hope they're itchy!" But they nailed me. It was all about: "You don't have an education. You've got no formal qualifications." It was horrendous. I took it personally. Grappled with it for months afterwards.'

The pause is long.

'People might think I'm thick-skinned. But if I didn't care what people thought about me, I'd probably be in politics by now. I'm pretty thin-skinned. It's hard to see it from the outside, but yeah, I have a soft centre.

'You asked before about what keeps me going. Just a bit more on that. It's watching the kids of Andrew (from The Magnificent Seven) go to school and know that this next generation will finish school and they will have jobs and be solid citizens. And Andrew will be so proud of them. And look at "Seventy". I can still see him banging in those star pickets at Mingoola. Just a kid. Now a man. A working man. A good man. We've had kids go from here to become the butcher, the baker ... I don't think we've got the candlestick maker yet but if we had one that would be a mad old yarn to tell. If I'm banging on about this, I don't care coz it's just so important. It's seeing those kids that society says can't fuckin' make it, make it. It's seeing Scott from Tarago walk through the gate, and he says: "I haven't seen you for a while, but I just wanted you to know that you changed my life." When BackTrack started some people said: "That can't possibly work. That's ridiculous." Well, that just puts some fight into your gut, doesn't it? But here's the secret: I'm not going to do a job that I'm not bursting to get to. And I'm still bursting to get through that depot gate.'

'Mate, that's great,' I say to Bernie. 'I reckon we've got enough, but just one final question: You find that bottle, you rub it and the genie comes out. What are your three wishes?'

Bernie twists a pen in his hands, leans forward in his chair, and says, 'That we get a smashingly big donation that's just going to take all the pressure off. I know it's coming. I believe it in my heart. Then, we can really start helping other communities, including internationally; we can have exchange programs, we will learn from each other. And the final wish …'

Bernie leans back. Outside, a buzz saw whines.

'To have one of those kids sitting in this chair as the CEO.'

AFTERWORD

Six weeks after Bernie and I finished our major interviews for this book, the Golden Collar Cattle Dog Trial was held at Geurie Racecourse, near Dubbo, New South Wales. For Bernie and the BackTrack contingent, there was much excitement; only three days earlier some of them (Bernie included) had met Prince Harry and Duchess Meghan during their tour of Dubbo. They had performed some dog jumping, and Harry helped by releasing a dog. Just another extraordinary moment in BackTrack's history. The energy flowed onto Geurie where, for the first time, the Golden Collar would host a junior competition, a rarity in the sport. Armidale stock and station agent Victor Moar was one of a small group who had pushed for the new category. He had already introduced a junior section at the Armidale Show, and not surprisingly it had been dominated by BackTrack boys.

Fifty-three-year-old Victor, a grandfather, had long been a staunch supporter of BackTrack. He was with the BackTrack boys at Geurie where he spoke with Bernie about buying the sheep for a council block that BackTrack had acquired use of near Warrah.

Several hours later, a fierce storm hit Geurie. Bernie gathered the BackTrack boys under a large open-sided shed. 'Stay away from the sides,' he said to everyone.

The trial was halted. As competitors and officials hurried for safety, Victor Moar was struck by lightning.

The funeral service was held at the Armidale Exhibition Centre. About two-and-a-half thousand people attended, including some well-known kids in red shirts, and their dogs. In lieu of flowers, it was requested that donations be made to BackTrack.

'We are nothing without a strong community,' Bernie said to me over the phone afterwards. 'And Victor, he was as strong as they come.'

———

Bernie Shakeshaft is right. Community can change lives. But often it takes one person to galvanise a community and make change. And Bernie is one of those people. Just prior to us finishing this book he sent me a message that he had received on Facebook. It (with some editing) is worth repeating here, a statement that undoubtedly represents the thoughts of so many who have passed through the gates of the BackTrack depot:

12yrs ago you picked a bloke outta Armidale high school who was struggling with addiction, sense of belonging and overall complete lack of respect for all authority! To this day I'm still talking about those magical Fridays spent at TAFE with you mate. I'm now in ( ) got 4 kids, just bought (a business) and am building (another one) as well ...

You and your program gave me responsibility, taught me consequence of one's actions, gave me skills, taught me acceptance of others no matter what the social or economical background of a person, and your overall attitude Bernie made me believe enough to never give up! Mate I can't personally thank you enough for the opportunity you offered me way back then but this is something I've been wanting to say for a long time and if there is anything I can ever do to offer assistance to you or the Backtrack boys and girls please let me know ... Congratulations on all the success with BackTrack and I hope it only continues to grow! Kind regards mate and best of luck with all that you do!!

If you would like to support Bernie and the team at BackTrack and make an investment in the future of Australian kids who others have given up on, you can donate at backtrack.org.au/donate

RESOURCES

If you or your kids are having trouble, or just need someone to talk to urgently, there are people who can help.

Kids Helpline Australia
kidshelpline.com.au or 1800 55 1800

Kidsline New Zealand
kidsline.org.nz or 0800 54 37 54

Lifeline Australia
lifeline.org.au or 13 11 14

Lifeline Aotearoa
lifeline.org.nz or 0800 543 354

beyondblue
beyondblue.org.au or 1300 22 4636

National Depression Initiative New Zealand
depression.org.nz or 0800 111 757

ACKNOWLEDGEMENTS

BERNIE SHAKESHAFT

Thank you to my Shakeshaft family, especially Mum and Dad, my brothers and sister, my children, my partner and the Andreoni family for all the support and understanding you have shown me over the years.

Heartfelt thanks to many individuals, community groups, schools, organisations and local businesses that have supported BackTrack and made what we do possible. In the words of Rosemary Mort:

> *One of the keys to the success of BackTrack has been the incredible support from the local community, particularly in the early days when we were struggling to keep going. Our local MPs, Council, the Armidale Bowling Club, Rotary, the University of New England, the Chamber of Commerce, schools, Regional Australia Bank (previously the New England Credit Union and Community Mutual), Jobs Australia Enterprises, magistrates, the police and many individuals and other businesses that stepped in with either in kind or financial help and advice. In time our support base has expanded but we are so very grateful to those who saw BackTrack's potential at the beginning and have continued to support us. They will always be part of our family.*

To those who have been there from the start of the BackTrack journey, I'm forever grateful. It was our dogged persistence and belief that enabled us to offer young people in desperate need of a hand a chance for a new life journey. To the NT crew who taught me so much – thank you. To the staff, volunteers and board of BackTrack both past and present I thank you for all you have given and continue to give to our community and vulnerable young people. To all the donors and funders both past and present who have made it possible – from small contributions to major funding – without you BackTrack couldn't reach out and help the way it does. Without the efforts of funders, donors, partners, supporters, staff and volunteers we wouldn't be able to do what we do and help young people turn their lives around and chase their hopes and dreams.

Big paws up and gratitude to the many dogs who have been part of my life and taught me so much, and who continue to give so much to young people needing a hand.

To the team at Hachette, and Vanessa, thanks for inviting me into your world and walking me through that foreign world – have we finished yet?

To James Knight. Thank you. You have the patience of a saint. Having to pull someone's life story together in next to no time must be something like trying to catch a feral cat with a sack. Organising interviews at the shed alone looked a bit like letting twenty dogs out at once to greet a new day! Thank you to all those who agreed to be interviewed for the book.

For me personally, the young people who have entered and graduated from our programs have been the most inspiring of all. Many people make the mistake of writing off young people, who through no fault of their own, have had a really tough start to life. I have seen them struggle through their issues, take on challenges, persevere and then turn around and give the others a helping hand. I want them to know that everyone associated with BackTrack is so very proud of them and their mighty achievements.

JAMES KNIGHT

Back on Track was researched and written under an incredibly demanding deadline. Such projects are never easy, and if it wasn't for the great support of so many people, this book would never have made it to publication. Firstly, thank you to my wife, Clare, and our son, Iggy. Clare, I wish I had your level of patience and understanding; as we know all too well, writing a book can place enormous strain on relationships, but at no point did you complain. (Or not too much, anyway!) I couldn't have done this without you. And to Iggy: mate, I reckon we need to make up for a lot of lost time. Let's start by taking a ball out the back and giving it a good whack! Thanks for all your patience and love, mate. I love you and Mum much more than you'll ever know. Time for a family hug. Squeeze tight!

Okay, now to the work side of things. Bernie Shakeshaft, what can I say? You took me into a world I knew existed but knew so little about. Thank you for allowing this book to be written about you and BackTrack. You may still shrug your shoulders and ask: 'Why the bloody hell would my life be interesting enough for a book?' but it is, and it should serve as an inspiration to others from all walks of life. I appreciate your honesty and commitment at all stages of the process, but most of all I appreciate your friendship; I hope, as time goes on, we'll be able to do more things together, and become better friends. I will certainly put my hand up to help BackTrack in any way I can. On a broader note, I too am a country boy (and no matter where I go, I always will be at heart), and on behalf of country people everywhere, I thank you, Bernie, and all the people associated with BackTrack for helping the bush; it is, as we know, the meat and bones of Australia that is, sadly, all too often overlooked or not given appropriate time and thought by Australia's suburban population. BackTrack shouldn't only be a vital service in Armidale, but it would, *and will*, work in many other communities around Australia, and undoubtedly overseas too. In good ol' fashioned Australian vernacular, the mould was broken when you were made, Bernie.

To everyone interviewed for *Back on Track*, thank you. Firstly, to the boys and girls, both current and former members of the program. You guys are awesome. You inspire me, and when he is old enough to understand more about the ways of the world, Iggy will be inspired by you as well. I say regularly to people who know little or nothing about BackTrack that walking through the gates of the depot always takes my breath away in both good and bad ways. As much as BackTrack helps you guys, it has also helped me. Thank you all for offering your time in interviews and sharing your everyday lives and thoughts with me in so many casual situations. Throughout the interviews, time and again, I kept telling myself how privileged I was to be listening. Obviously, some of your real names aren't mentioned in the book, but rest assured, I won't forget any of you. To all others – workers, volunteers, community members, the many people who have come into Bernie's forever growing circle of friends and colleagues – thank you too for giving me your time and thoughts. In many different ways, you all reflected the very best values of humanity. For now, both misnomers and authentic names are in my thoughts: Murray Lupton, Matt Lynch, Sam Long, Matt Pilkington, Phill Evans, Haley Booth, Francesca Andreoni, Gel

Cutmore, Karen Stafford, Mel Phillips, James Warne, Kevin Dupe, Marcus Watson, Greg Paramor, Zac, Jannelle Brandley, Steve Widders, Carolyn Lasker, Matthew Pett, Ike Roberts, Andrew, Sam, Melissa Vella, Scott Tanner, Darren Harrison, Balie, Justin Flint, Philip Jarvis, Paul Dawson, Paul Roots, Annette Roots, Gail and Alan, Scott, Rosemary Mort, Tony Windsor, Nathan, Ricky, Greg Chappell, Antoinette Carroll, Dusty, Puppa Wati, Jenny and Nick, His Excellency General the Honourable David Hurley, Linda Hurley, Catherine Scott, Ian Tiley, Peter Slattery, Jack Singleton, Ray Matthews and Sarah Mills.

A special note to Bernie's family. Joe and Denise Shakeshaft were the very first people interviewed. It's amazing where a good cup of tea, some chocolate biscuits and a cinnamon loaf can lead! You have a great family; all of your children have gone on to do some extraordinary things, and the pride you have in each and every one of them is obvious. To Maree, Anthony, Paul and Mark: I appreciate your insights and look forward to chewing over more stories in the years ahead. And to James and Maeve: thank you for offering unique insights into your dad. Warts and all. Parents can be peculiar creatures, can't they?

I owe my gratitude to everyone else interviewed, who may not, for various reasons, be listed above. I have distinct memories about you all.

I also owe my deep gratitude to Jemma. The logistics needed to make this book work were considerable. Jemma, thank you for organising Bernie and keeping me posted with all his movements. It was always reassuring to get your emails or hear your voice on the phone. I look forward to meeting in person! I must also thank Alahna Fiveash, who also provided invaluable support with logistics.

To all at Hachette, what do I say to you? This project began after a conversation I had with publisher Vanessa Radnidge, who remains my biggest supporter in the publishing industry. Vanessa, *Back on Track* was completely your idea. I can never thank you enough for steering it my way. You have remained loyal and supportive every step of the way; if it wasn't for you, I doubt I'd still be writing books because, as you know, they can be (*insert a Bernie adjective here!*) hard to do.

To all the staff at Hachette, thank you. Publishing is a team game, and *Back on Track* only happened because each of you stepped up to play a grand final. I treasure the ongoing support and feel like I'm a member of a tight family, rather than an author with a book to get on the shelves. A very big thank you to editors Sophie Mayfield and Claire de Medici, whose job it was to sift through the minefield of a manuscript. Sophie and Claire, you're both terrific! Thank you as well to my production controller, Jenny Topham; my publicist, Lydia Tasker; and Group Publishing Director, Fiona Hazard.

At various times while writing, I sent the manuscript to people to get their feedback. My editorial rock was my mum, Anne, a much better writer than I will ever be. Mum, thank you for being the ear at the other end of the phone and the eye at the other end of the email. As with every book I've written, I couldn't have done this without you. Thank you for inspiring me. Now, get back to writing your own book! I also need to thank Peter Overton, Bill Woods, Susanne Gervay and Anne-Marie Newham.

Finally, a note to my dear mate Richard Tombs. I began working on *Back on Track* just before Tombsy suffered a life-changing accident in an Over 35s soccer game in Sydney. He is now an incomplete quadriplegic but is determined to get permanently back on his feet. Tombsy, you *will* do it. From the day we first met in kindergarten, you have been a one-in-a-million bloke to me. I thought of you and your crazy, beautiful family every day while I was working on this book. And nothing will change now that I've finished. I love ya, mate.

James Knight has worked in the media for thirty years. At various times he has been a journalist, presenter, commentator, producer, documentary maker and copywriter. He has worked for all main commercial television networks in Australia and has written for a variety of organisations including *The Sydney Morning Herald* and *CNN Online*. He has also worked in India as a television consultant. He is a popular guest speaker, and regularly visits schools and businesses to conduct workshops and presentations about the power of storytelling. He is currently studying a Master of Education.

Raised in the New South Wales country town Gunnedah, James now lives in Bathurst with his wife, Clare, son, Iggy, and their vizsla dog, Tango. This is his thirteenth book.

www.storyconnect.com.au